# Key Ideas in Psychology

*Ian Stuart-Hamilton*

Jessica Kingsley Publishers
London and Philadelphia

First published in the United Kingdom in 1999 by
Jessica Kingsley Publishers Ltd,
116 Pentonville Road, London
N1 9JB, England
and
325 Chestnut Street,
Philadelphia PA 19106, USA.

*www.jkp.com*

**Library of Congress Cataloging in Publication Data**
A CIP catalog record for this book is available from the Library of Congress

**British Library Cataloguing in Publication Data**
Stuart-Hamilton, Ian
Introduction to psychology
1.Psychology
I. Title
150

ISBN 1 85302 359 0

Printed and Bound in Great Britain by
Athenaeum Press, Gateshead, Tyne and Wear

To Kate

For dainties are all cates

# Acknowledgements

I would like to thank University College Worcester for continuing to support me; Jessica Kingsley for politely ignoring the fact that my manuscript was two years late; and last but not least, Ruth, Mark and Kate for continuing to tolerate my many foibles.

# Contents

# Introduction

This book is written with a simple aim – to tell people what Psychology is about. It presents a review of the key areas of the subject as it is traditionally taught, and provides the reader with an introduction to important concepts and findings within each of these. Armed with the information in this book, the reader should be able at least to make sense of most psychological topics. At the end of each chapter is a set of suggested further readings which will enable a more detailed exploration of the particular topic under discussion to be made.

The book is aimed at two groups of readers. The first comprises people who are new to the subject and simply want to know what Psychology *is*. Most standard textbooks are too long and unwieldy to make a comfortable read. They attempt (often creditably) to introduce as many topics as possible, with the result that the poor reader trying to read a whole book (rather than dip into it for a single piece of information) is left reeling from information overload after just a few pages. A telephone directory is informative, but nobody would read it for enjoyment.

The second group of people comprises those who want a general guide to an area but who wish to make up their minds on the details for themselves. In this book, I have attempted to give people just enough information and arguments for them to get a good idea about what an area of psychology is about, but then I have left it to them to explore further and decide on what topics they will explore in greater detail. Speaking as both a tutor and an examiner, a poor student is typically one who has simply taken what is written in a general textbook as the Gospel truth, and failed to examine any issues for him- or herself. Over the years, I have probably read each of the major textbooks several times by proxy.

These two aims are of course perfectly compatible. Essentially, anyone who has read this book should be able to hold a general conversation with a psychologist on their area of interest without too much difficulty.

Inevitably, this approach has meant some compromises in terms of what is included and what is left out. In planning this book, I deliberately wanted to create a physically small(ish) item which could be comfortably read in a few hours. One sacrifice I was not sorry to make was to exclude any 'humorous' cartoons, photos, etc. These are funny – *once*. Thereafter they just take up space. With slightly greater reluctance, I have also avoided use of figures such as graphs, barring two examples (both in Chapter 13). Figures and tables should only in any case be an illustration of the text: they are rarely essential.

Other 'sacrifices' have been more subjective. My choice of which topics to include and which to leave out has been to some extent guided by the frequency with which topics are dealt with in syllabi, and (if I dare say it) other textbooks. Thus, the book covers most of the topics found in degree courses and the UK A level syllabus; and also in general introductory courses for non-psychologists. Within topics, I have tended to take the experiments and arguments which everybody has heard of (e.g. Pavlov's dogs, Skinner's rats, the Burt Scandal, Milgram's obedience experiments), and others which are less well-known but which are of great theoretical and/or historical importance (e.g. Tolman's mental maps). To some extent, I have also tended to dwell on topics which will be important in helping the reader with further study. Hence, issues such as the nature–nurture debate are dealt with in some depth, because they underlie a lot of other work readers will encounter. However, some subjects are too large to encompass comfortably within a single chapter. Thus, in social psychology, I have deliberately not mentioned some topics at all, such as the increasingly popular discourse analysis. I could have attempted a catalogue of everything covered by social psychology, perhaps giving a paragraph to each topic. This would have read like a dictionary (not the intent of this text at all). In situations such as this, I have tended to concentrate upon the best known or most influential experiments. To a certain extent this is subjective, but then so ultimately are the choices made by any other writer of an introductory text. Even a large text is not a necessary guarantee of comprehensiveness. For example, it would be quite possible (though needlessly sadistic) to catalogue everything omitted from the 'big name' general texts. To take one (anonymised) instance – I have on my shelves a recent four volume encyclopaedia of psychology, which manages, inter alia, to omit any mention of dyslexia. Thus, I will admit that such topics as sex differences and cultural differences have been avoided (though they are mentioned as a group in discussion of the nature–nurture debate in Chapter 2). This is not out of vested interest – many of my own areas of research (principally, ageing and education) have likewise received short shrift. No slight is intended on any researchers or topics I have left out.

I have likewise tried not to give offence when dealing with potentially contentious issues, such as the nature–nurture debate or evolutionary theory.

On an unrelated topic, references are made to supporting literature for two reasons. First, specific studies are usually given their original reference or a useful summary of work by the author(s) responsible for the experiments. Where more general references are given, I have tried to make these to 'basic' rather than 'advanced' textbooks, to help readers who wish to pursue a particular argument further. The further reading sections at the end of each chapter are typically to basic general books, which should be easily obtained from a bookshop or library.

*Ian Stuart-Hamilton*
*Worcester, 1999*

# CHAPTER I

# What is Psychology?

## Definitions

The term 'psychology' is derived from the Greek words *psyche* ('mind') and *logos* (loosely, 'the nature of'). The first recorded use of the term was in the 1520s by a Serbo-Croatian philosopher called Marulic, and it has been used in a variety of meanings ever since. For a time, it described the study of souls (and by extension, the study of ghostly spirits), but entered general use as a loose term for the study of mental activity and behaviour in the 19th century (the first university department of Psychology was established in 1879 at Leipzig). 'Psychology' has now entered everyday language to denote anything to do with mental as opposed to physical activity, even to the extent of such curious phrases as 'psychological thriller', which seems to denote a film with too small a budget for expensive action sequences. Today, there is no single 'industry standard' definition of the subject, but within the field of introductory textbooks at least, there is general agreement about the essence of the subject. Consider the following quotations, taken from a random sample of best-sellers:

> 'The scientific study of behavior' (Huffman *et al.*, 1994, p.6)

> 'The scientific study of behavior and mental processes' (Crider *et al.*, 1989, p.6)

> 'The science of behavior and mental processes' (Dworetsky 1994, p.4)

> 'The scientific study of human and animal behavior' (Coon 1995, p.3)

> 'The science that studies behavior and mental processes' (Atkinson *et al.*, 1990, A-20)

All of the above closely resemble a much older definition by William James, one of the founders of the subject. In his majestic two volume *Principles of Psychology*, published in 1890, he stated in the first sentence that Psychology is 'the science of mental life' (James, 1890). What is less well documented is that two years later, he produced a slimmed-down edition of the book for classroom use, in which the famous definition is replaced by the following:

> 'The definition of psychology may be best given in the words of Professor Ladd, as the description and explanation of states of consciousness as such'. (James, 1892)

Which perhaps shows that some things are best left untouched. James's original definition has the virtue of being brief and memorable, and covers as much ground as five words can have any right to expect. As a general definition it is unmatched, and it will be adopted here without further discussion.

## Academic psychology

Within school syllabuses and undergraduate degree courses, the study of Psychology is largely of theoretical issues rather than instruction in how to apply practical solutions – what is often termed *academic psychology*. However, it would be wrong to say that the work has no practical relevance. Some of it is directly adopted for use in the treatment and analysis of mental states. In other cases, the work describes how we behave in everyday life (e.g. a theoretical analysis of why children's behaviour towards other children changes as they develop). 'Academic psychology' also of course refers to Psychology as it is taught and researched within academic institutions, and in particular to universities and college of higher education. The syllabuses offered by individual institutions vary according to the teaching and research interests of the members of staff. However, by general consensus, a 'core curriculum' would include the following topics:

*Individual Differences* The study of how and why individuals differ psychologically. This principally addresses two skills – intelligence and personality – and these are separately considered in Chapters 2 and 3.

*Social Psychology* The study of the psychology of social life, and in particular, how individuals behave in social situations. For example, how people behave in groups, how beliefs about people and events are formed, how people become attracted to each other, etc. This is considered in Chapter 4.

*Language* Not surprisingly, the study of psychological aspects of language: how it is acquired, some of the problems which can be encountered in its acquisition, and the relationship between thought and language are studied in Chapter 5.

*Developmental Psychology* The study of the development of psychological skills and behaviours across the lifespan (with particular emphasis on psychological development in infancy and childhood). This is considered in Chapter 6.

*Learning Theory* This is essentially the study of how learning of information when successful is rewarded. In Chapter 7, this will be examined, with especial consideration of *Behaviourism*, a method of enquiry into learning which has exerted an enormous influence on Psychology (arguably not always to the good).

*Memory* Related to learning (though nearly always studied separately), the study of memory occupies Chapter 8, and examines the various methods available for memorising information, and the limits of these methods.

*Perception* The interpretation of the environment through the senses. Most research has concentrated on vision, although not exclusively. In Chapter 9, perception will be examined with a strong emphasis on how our mental interpretation of sensory information manipulates our experience of 'reality'.

*Biopsychology* The study of how the mind controls the workings of the body and how the physical functioning of the brain (and the rest of the body) is reflected in the workings of the mind. This is examined in Chapter 10, and following Perception, demonstrates further evidence of the close links between the brain and the rest of the body.

*Comparative Psychology* The comparison of psychological life across different species and how evolutionary pressure can shape behaviour. Examination of this issue, and its limitations, are explored in Chapter 11.

*Mental Illness* The study of mental illness, its classification and treatment, is an issue of interest to many students attracted to Psychology. Chapter 12 examines the concept of mental illness, its classification and treatment, with examples drawn from the major illnesses which form everyday conceptions of 'madness'.

*Statistics* At the risk of deterring people from the subject, Psychology also involves learning something about statistics. Some people are deterred from studying the subject because they are afraid that their mathematical skills will be too weak, but in reality the topic is not terribly onerous. In Chapter 13 (entirely optional!) there is a gentle introduction to the world of statistical measurement.

As can be seen, Psychology covers quite a wide range of interests. The above topic headings have been arranged because they give perhaps the most accessible sequence of topics. However, other methods might have been equally valid. For example, the chapters on memory, language and perception might have been grouped together under a larger heading of *cognition*. This is the understanding, acquisition and processing of knowledge, or, more loosely, of thought processes; and by extension, their study. Cognition is perhaps the single largest study area in Psychology, but it is usually sub-divided into smaller topic areas, as has been done here. If one adds to Cognition the chapters on biopsychology and learning theory, then one has in essence all the topics primarily concerned with the internal mental state of the person. These might then be contrasted with the remaining chapters which have as their main interest the mental state of the person relative to others (e.g. mental illness, personality and intelligence are largely concerned with how one person compares with another, social psychology with how an individual interacts with others, etc). A reader who is so minded could choose to read Chapters 2, 3, 4, 6, 11, and 12 as one group and the remainder as another. Since each chapter can stand alone with minimal cross-referencing to other chapters, this is a feasible practice.

Whichever method the reader chooses, each of the above topics will be introduced in greater depth in the succeeding chapters. However, it must not be supposed that this is a complete list of subjects. Other topics, however, tend to be more marginal. For example, subjects such as the history of psychology, agricultural psychology (anything psychological connected with farming), parapsychology (the study of extrasensory perception, ghosts, etc) and the psychology of art are offered by a few, but not all institutions.

This is not because such topics are unimportant, but simply because: (a) they are not as 'central' to everyday existence as the mainstream topics listed above; or (b) because they have not attracted sufficiently large numbers of researchers and/or lecturers to specialise in them.

Having considered what Psychology is and how it is related to similar subject areas, the topic needs to be placed in context by considering how it is related to other disciplines.

## Applied psychology

*Applied psychology* refers to any branch of psychology in which psychological methods are applied to practical problems. These include *clinical psychology*, *occupational psychology* and *educational psychology* (note there are other branches as well, such as working as a psychologist within the prison service, or assisting the police in working on the psychological profiles of criminals). Occupational psychology (also called organisational or industrial psychology) is concerned with psychological aspects of the workplace. For example, some of the issues an occupational psychologist might be concerned with are: how to design machinery operating panels so that they are easily viewed and operated; how to devise tests to select the best people for particular jobs; and how to avoid stress in the workplace. Educational psychology is, at its broadest, the study of psychological aspects of education. The work can be theoretical in nature, but the daily life of an educational psychologist is often concerned with testing children with educational problems (or problems associated with education, such as poor school attendance) and administering or recommending forms of treatment.

The branch of psychology concerned with the treatment of mental illness is called clinical psychology. Psychology deals with all aspects of mental life. A lot of other occupations with 'psych' in their title deal with mental illness or more mildly, problems with one's lifestyle. For example, *Psychiatry* is the treatment of mental illness by qualified medical doctors, with appropriate specialist training. Treatment is often on the same lines as for a physical illness – i.e. drugs, or in some extreme cases, surgery. It would be inaccurate to say that *all* psychiatrists do is dispense drugs. Many may also provide non-drug therapies as well, such as counselling people on how to cope with their problems. Another method of treatment of mental problems is *Psychoanalysis*. This began with the work of the famous Sigmund Freud, who argued that many forms of mental illness lie in inappropriate ideas being created during childhood. These burrow themselves into the unconscious mind where the patient cannot directly deal with them, although their effects are felt in many unfortunate ways. Treatment involves sessions of discussions and mental exercises designed to prise out these maladaptive thoughts and deal with them. Psychoanalysis is usually confined to the treatment of relatively mild (though still unpleasant) complaints, where the patient is still in contact with reality (e.g. someone who suffers high levels of anxiety, though in mental discomfort, is still aware of the world around them). More 'severe' illnesses, such as schizophrenia, where the patient has to a large extent lost contact with reality, are not usually amenable to psychoanalytic treatment (see Chapters 3 and 12 for a more detailed discussion).

Clinical psychology is a separate discipline from psychiatry (because it is not done from a medical background) and psychoanalysis (because clinical psychology is based upon psychological theories, many of which explicitly reject the ideas of psychoanalysis). Notwithstanding these distinctions, some clinical psychologists work in conjunction with psychiatrists and psychoanalysts. It largely depends upon the working practices of the health care centre in question. Just to complicate matters, another term in common usage is *psychotherapy* which generally refers to *any* therapeutic method of treating illness by psychological means (as opposed to by purely drug treatments, surgery, etc). This may mean 'clinical psychology', but not always – it could refer to psychoanalysis or a psychiatrist avoiding using drug treatments. It can also refer to *counselling*. This is a term which broadly refers to any method of offering advice which has a systematic rationale to justify its existence (i.e. it is not just advice offered 'off the top of the head'). Often these methods have a basis in psychological theory. However, practitioners need not be formally trained as psychologists.

Most applied psychologists must have an undergraduate degree in Psychology plus further specialist postgraduate training (e.g. in the case of educational psychology in the UK, students must also obtain a teaching qualification and experience of teaching in a classroom).

The prevalence of the applied psychologies can lead to the impression that Psychology as a whole is about 'helping people'. Certainly the applied psychologies can largely be seen in this role, but it would be wrong to assume that the subject is all about being nice to others. The majority of psychological research is typically concerned with 'dissecting' one aspect of thought or behaviour and seeing how it works. Typically, psychologists tend to treat behaviours and thoughts very much as specimens to be prodded and examined. This at times can appear rather unfeeling (e.g. analysing the stages of bereavement in a dispassionate manner) but of course analysis has usually to be done dispassionately if an objective viewpoint is to be found (this explains why the psychological analysis of humour tends to be sobering). Even within the applied psychologies, work often involves taking one aspect of an illness and analysing it divorced from its emotional content. This in part is also a useful emotional defence for psychologists. If practitioners had to think fully about the emotional nature of some their work, then it would be a very distressing business. Some psychologists have argued that the researcher's own emotional response is an important aspect of the research process, but this is so far a minority view.

## Psychology's relationship with Philosophy

Precisely when Psychology became an 'official' academic discipline in its own right is open to debate. Many commentators select 1879, when, as mentioned above, the first department of Psychology was established at the University of Leipzig, by Professor Wilhelm Wundt. However, in the same manner that the French Revolution did not 'begin' on 14th July, 1789, so Psychology had its adherents and practitioners before Professor Wundt opened up shop. At a very broad level, the study of mental life and processes is amongst the earliest of all phenomena studied, as shown by the work of the philosophers of Ancient Greece and other early civilisations. However, it is important to note that Philosophy of mind and Psychology, although interrelated, are not synonymous (aside from anything else, Psychology also has historical roots in other disciplines, such as medicine). It is difficult to give a concise definition of the distinction, but perhaps the key feature is that generally, Psychology creates models of how the mind works based upon observations derived from experimentation, while Philosophy attempts to create models of how thought occurs based upon logical inference of what must be there. Hence Psychology tends to study specific aspects of mental life, such as how we remember things, how we form friendships, and how reading skills develop, whilst Philosophy addresses the larger scale issues of whether the mind and the brain are synonymous. This is because it is impossible satisfactorily to address questions such as 'how does the brain recognise colours?' without conducting experiments. Conversely, addressing issues such as 'how do we know we exist?' is beyond the scope of experimentation – answers to such questions can only be derived by appealing to pure logical analysis. Philosophy and Psychology are not antagonists, however. There is an active, if relatively small, discipline of the Philosophy of Psychology which examines the links between the two, and the two disciplines borrow ideas from each other relatively freely.

## Psychology's relationship within the Sciences

One of the jibes which psychologists endure are the remarks of members of the 'difficult' sciences such as Physics, Chemistry *et al.* that Psychology does not use conventional scientific equipment and research methods, so how can it be a science? The comments are usually most vociferously made by undergraduates, and may be translated as 'why aren't you suffering like us?' There is no easy or short answer to the question of how 'scientific' psychology is. Some commentators would even argue that it is irrelevant (i.e. what is so important about labels?). However, a reasonably brief answer might be as follows. Science might be defined as the systematic exploration of an item or event by means of testing and observation, with the intent of creating a law to describe how all such instances of that item or event behave. For example, one might boil water and observe that at 100 degrees centigrade, it turns to a gas. Psychology cannot usually be so precise. For example, if a group of people are tested on how long a list of numbers they can remember, then not everyone will perform in the same way (i.e. some will remember more than others) and it is quite likely that a figure of the average performance will contain a fraction (e.g. the average number of numbers remembered is 7.4). This is odd, because clearly no individual remembers seven numbers and then four tenths of another one. Again, although psychologists can make statements that in a particular situation, most people will behave in a certain way, not everyone will (e.g. most people will avoid pain, but a minority gain sexual pleasure from being hurt). In general, the results of psychology experiments seem to be too variable for definite statements to be made, and compare badly, in some people's eyes, with the precision of the 'proper' sciences.

However, such an argument can only be made by taking a very naive view of some sciences. For example, in the boiling water example, it is highly unlikely that the temperature of the boiling water will be recorded as *exactly* 100 degrees on each occasion – there will be some variance in the measure. Again, the finding is only true for boiling water at sea level (water boiled at a higher altitude will do so at a lower temperature), and absolutely pure water at that (any impurities will alter the boiling point). So when we say that water boils at 100 degrees, we are making an assumption that sea level is the proper altitude at which water should be boiled. However, this is merely convention which states this – there is no objective reason why sea level should be taken as the measure of such things. There are convenient reasons, but these are largely (if the reader will pardon the phrase) psychological.

A more sophisticated version of the above argument is to say that Psychology does not obey the fundamental physical laws of Newton, to which, arguably, all other science can ultimately be reduced. This misses the point. Psychology is largely about how the mind works. Although the mind is arguably a product of the brain (see the Mind–Body problem in Chapter 10) and the brain can certainly be described in physical terms, mental processes are largely abstract things which are not necessarily ruled by the mathematical laws which describe physical systems. However, current work within artificial intelligence (computer simulation of mental processes) indicates that many mental processes may in fact be controlled by relatively simple logical and mathematical rules.

A further criticism of Psychology is that it has not achieved the discoveries of the other sciences (vaccinations, space travel, the atom bomb, germ warfare, etc). However, Psychology is a much younger academic discipline, being barely a hundred years old. Other sciences at the same state of development were, for example, still of the opinion that the technique for turning lead into gold was just around the corner, whilst geographers thought that any humans on the far southern half of the planet had an extra large foot which they raised over their heads to act as a parasol (hence the term *Antipodes*). In comparison, Psychology's early history does not appear too bad.

## Animal experimentation

It is unfortunate for Psychology's image that when the subject has delved into studies with a readily-discernible 'scientific' content, these have often involved experimentation on animals. The proportion of psychologists actively engaged in such research is fairly low compared with the total number of psychologists, but there is no escaping the fact that such work takes place. In some instances this simply involves observing animals in their natural habitat, or presenting animals with the sort of stimulus they encounter every day and seeing how they respond. Ethically speaking, such research is usually innocuous, but this cannot be said of some laboratory-based work, in which animals are operated upon and/or killed and dissected. Work of this kind is never undertaken lightly – other less invasive techniques will always be used in preference and in most countries there are stringent guidelines governing such research. However, many people still find such work ethically and personally offensive. Matters are not helped by the fact that work of this type tends to be performed on furry mammals such as rats, dogs and monkeys, which (aside from any cogent arguments that they are sentient beings) have an intrinsically 'cute' quality. It is an interesting comment on human susceptibilities that experimentation on a few hundred beagles raises an outcry, but that manufacturers of insect sprays can, in testing their products, kill thousands or even millions of house flies and other insects without any protest.

It cannot be denied that some psychological research and teaching is based upon animal experimentation in which animals have undergone surgery or have been killed in order to get the desired findings. The study of perception, for example, would be impossible without such work. If a person objects sufficiently strongly to animal experimentation, then it is a matter for their conscience to decide if they wish to study certain areas of Psychology, or indeed study the subject at all. The issue becomes akin to the moral dilemma facing scientists presented with the findings of the 'researchers' in some Japanese and German World War II prisoner of war and concentration camps. Through systematic torture of prisoners, key findings on human resilience to, for example, hypothermia and blood transfusions were made. Because these findings were made immorally, should they be used to aid medical research? By a similar token, although an individual may object to the methods used to discover particular details of psychological functioning, once they have been discovered, should they not be used? However, to place matters in perspective, it should be reiterated that large sections of Psychology are not based upon animal experimentation.

## Summary

Psychology is a wide-ranging subject concerned with the study of mental life by scientific means. Although other subject areas have interests in mental life, these have tended to concentrate upon mental illness (the other 'psych-' subjects) or, in the case of philosophy, on more global questions not appropriate for experimental examination. Psychology is not completely divorced from these, however, and an harmonious interaction between it and the other fields of study does take place. Within Psychology, there is a broad division into applied and academic topics – the former concerned with applying practical psychological solutions to problems, the latter observing and modelling aspects of mental performance. Although academic psychology is not necessarily concerned with practical solutions to everyday problems, there is considerable overlap and interaction with the applied fields. Psychology also draws upon the distinct disciplines of philosophy and many of the sciences.

To reiterate: in subsequent chapters, the principal topics of academic psychology will be examined in greater depth. The chapters have been arranged in what is perhaps the most comfortable reading order, but each chapter could be read as a self-contained unit with the minimum of cross-referencing.

FURTHER READING

Any of the general textbooks cited above (e.g. Coon, 1995; Crider *et al.*, 1989; Dworetsky, 1994; Huffman *et al.*, 1994; Sternberg, 1998) will provide a broad and general introduction to Psychology. Their principal advantage is that they are big, well-written, and have lots of coloured illustrations and photographs. They will not provide a quick introduction, however, since most are at least 500 pages in length. There is an interesting discussion of Psychology's relationship with other disciplines in Valentine (1992). For those interested in the ethics of animal experimentation, there is an excellent book by Marion Stamp Dawkins (1980).

# CHAPTER 2

# Intelligence

## Introduction

The purpose of *individual differences* research can be summarised quite simply: people are different, and researchers want to know how and why they are different. However, answering the 'how' and the 'why' has proved to be far harder a task than one might suppose, and has led to more ill-feeling and controversy than in any other subject in Psychology. The reasons for this are, as we shall see, varied rather than complex. For ease of understanding, it is customary to divide the study of individual differences into separate sections on intelligence and personality and this custom will be observed here. In this chapter, the nature and study of intelligence will be discussed. In the next chapter, there will be a similar discussion about personality.

## Intelligence testing

In the 1900s, Alfred Binet (1857–1911) devised the first modern intelligence test. It would be unfair to say that other people had not thought of devising measures of intelligence, but these had tended to be (by modern standards) rather hit-or-miss affairs. Binet's was the first attempt to provide a systematically-designed objective measure. Having had a varied but prestigious career (he had initially trained as a lawyer, before turning his attention to biology and psychology) Binet was working in Paris, when in 1904 he was asked by the ministry of education to devise a test which would identify those pupils who were so intellectually disadvantaged that they merited special education. This at first sight seems very simple (e.g. why not just take the children who were bottom of the class?) but there was a need to identify those who were genuinely disadvantaged from those who were able, but were not learning because of motivational problems (e.g. they were simply lazy).

In solving this problem, Binet had two major tasks – to test 'genuine' mental ability and to grade performances for level of excellence. To solve the first problem, Binet devised a set of problems which required some very basic general knowledge, but which were not reliant on school learning (e.g. does this sentence make sense? – 'Bill's feet were so big that he had to put his trousers on over his head'). If a child got these questions right, but was doing badly at school, then it could be argued that he or she had the mental capacity to learn, and that the poor scholastic performance must therefore be due to a non-intellectual cause. On the other hand, if the child did badly on these tasks and was doing badly at school, then their scholastic failure was probably due to a general intellectual deficit. That tests should assess 'raw' ability, rather than be reliant on having learnt particular pieces of information at school, has become an article of faith in individual differences research. As shall be seen, this goal has not always been attained, and in some circumstances has been abused, but the belief that intelligence tests should be *culture fair* (i.e. the questions must be equally accessible no matter what one's educational or cultural background) is fundamental to modern test design.

Having devised a test which, it is claimed, measures genuine intellectual ability, the researcher next needs to know what the test scores *mean*. In other words, the test must show how advantaged or disadvantaged a child is for his or her age. To do this, Binet gave his questions to (literally) thousands of schoolchildren of different ages and from their results calculated the score which an average child of any particular age should get. This meant that when a child was tested, his or her score could be found and could be compared with the average performance of his or her age group. A score considerably below the age group average would indicate a poor performance, and one meriting remedial help. Again, this procedure has become a ubiquitous feature of psychological tests – before being offered for general use, the average performance of the population for which the test is intended must be calculated. Without this information, it is impossible to judge how able a person is compared with people in general. It is also important that the test is given in the same way to everybody. Hence, tests contain specific instructions on how the test should be administered which must be followed implicitly by whoever is giving the test. This is to ensure that the person being tested is experiencing the test in as near-identical conditions as possible to the people who were used to draw up the 'average performance' charts. This whole procedure of calculating average performance (or *norms*) and establishing testing procedures is known as *standardisation*. In fact, the process involves more than simply working out age group averages. A responsible test designer will take the trouble to ensure that the people tested are representative of the cultural mix of the population for whom the test is intended. For example, the norms of an intelligence test intended for the general population would probably be unrepresentative if its standardisation had purely used pupils in private schools. Furthermore, the items on the test itself may be altered in the light of the standardisation process. Generally, the set of test questions which are given at standardisation is larger than that used in the finished product, and items which produce aberrant responses (e.g. everybody gets them right or everybody gets them wrong) are likely to be excluded. The choice of which items remain in a test and which are excluded is a key topic in the related study of *item analysis* (see e.g. Kline, 1993).

Binet died before he had chance to see the intelligence test become widely used, not only in the French education system, but across the world. The Binet test was taken to the USA, where Lewis Terman devised an English language version, called the *Stanford-Binet Test* (Terman was based at Stanford University) which, after several modernisations over the years, is still in popular use today. Many other intelligence tests have also been devised, and not only for use on children. Amongst the most popular are: *Raven's Progressive Matrices, Wechsler Adult Intelligence Scale (WAIS), Wechsler Intelligence Scale for Children (WISC), the AH* test series, and the *Cattell Culture Fair Test*. Formats of IQ tests differ considerably. Some, like the Raven's test, simply consist of one type of problem. The person is shown a set of shapes which are linked by a similarity (e.g. they contain parallel lines) and has to choose another shape which obeys the same rule from a set of alternatives. As the test progresses, the problems get successively harder. The test is done against the clock, so that to do well, a person must not only be accurate but also work quickly. Other measures are also against the clock and get progressively harder, but consist of several different tests (often called *sub-tests*). Examples of these included the WAIS and WISC measures. These assess different aspects of intelligence. For example a common sub-test is a measure of *verbal skills*, assessing (logically enough) ability to process verbal information. Questions may include such tasks as identifying words which mean the same thing, or spotting the word which does not belong to the same category as the others in a list (e.g. 'cat, rat, bird, man'). Another common measure is of non-verbal reasoning (often called a *performance test*) which measures logical and mathematical reasoning (e.g. what is the next number in the series? 2 5 9 14 20 _ ). A third commonly-used measure is of *visuo-spatial skills*, which is the ability to process pictorial and spatial information (e.g. being shown a flat cardboard shape and calculating if it can be folded into a particular three-dimensional figure). Some tests also measure memory for items (e.g. ability to remember lists of numbers) since this is known to be strongly related to intelligence level. Using sets of sub-tests (a collection of such tests is sometimes called a *test battery*) can have its advantages. First, it is possible to identify if a person is particularly gifted or disadvantaged at specific types of tasks. Second, in some instances calculating the IQ of a person from their average performance on several sub-tests can yield a more accurate measure than if they are tested on just one type of task. The disadvantage is that because more tests are involved, test batteries take longer to administer. It should also be mentioned that tests can be devised for being given en masse to groups (not surprisingly, known as *group tests* – the Raven's test being an example) or they must be given on a one-to-one basis (e.g. the WAIS and the WISC).

However, whatever their differences in format, all IQ tests which have entered standard use possess *reliability* and *validity*. These are complex terms (see Kline, 1993; Stuart-Hamilton, 1996, for further discussion), but essentially they mean that the test can be trusted. Reliability refers to the fact that if the test is used again on the same person it will (allowing for some random fluctuations) produce the same measure of intellectual ability. This is vital if a test is to be trusted – if a test graded someone as a genius at one test session and as severely disadvantaged on another, then clearly its value would be limited. Validity means that the test measures what it claims. In other words, performance on the intelligence test in question will predict performance on other intellectual tasks as opposed to unrelated abilities (e.g. ability to distinguish between colour shades) or nothing at all.

In addition, all tests essentially address the same questions as Binet's — what is a person's 'raw' intellectual ability, and where does this place the person in comparison with his or her peers? In addressing the latter question, a useful formula called the *intelligence quotient*, or IQ, was devised by William Stern. At its most basic, this is a score which tells one how clever a person is for his or her group. A score of 100 indicates someone who is average, a score above 100 someone who is above average, and below 100, below average. Scores only rarely go below 50 (indicating someone who is very mentally disadvantaged) or above 150 (indicating someone who is unusually good at intelligence tests).

In its original formulation, IQ was calculated as *mental age* divided by *chronological age*, multiplied by 100. 'Chronological age' simply refers to how old a person is. 'Mental age' is the age which an intelligence test 'says' a person is. Thus, if a person gets a score which is typical of an average 8-year-old, then that person has a mental age of 8 years. Multiplying by 100 simply makes the score obtained into a percentage. For example, suppose that an 8-year-old child takes an intelligence test and gets a score which is typical of an 8-year-old. The person's chronological age and mental age are both 8 and, using the above formula, it can be seen that the IQ of that person is 100. In other words, they are average. However, if an 8-year-old were tested and he or she produced a test performance typical of a 12-year-old, then their IQ would be 150 (chronological age = 8, mental age = 12, 12/8x100=150), indicating an ability considerably above average.

The IQ measure is a useful guide to a person's abilities relative to the rest of his or her age group. However, it can only be used in its original formulation using children. This is because scores on intelligence tests rise throughout childhood and adolescence, but then usually reach a plateau at about 18 years. In other words, a person of 36 is likely to have the same test score that he or she had at 18. This makes nonsense of the mental age calculation. If adults have a mental age which remains stable from 18 onwards, then the traditional IQ calculation cannot be done. For example, a person of average intelligence at 18 will have a mental age of 18, and hence an IQ of 100. However, at 36, he or she will have doubled their chronological age, but their mental age will be the same as when he or she was 18. By the traditional IQ calculation, his or her IQ is now half what it was (chronological age = 36, mental age = 18, IQ = 18/36x100 = 50). To sidestep this problem, researchers devised a new method of scoring. This essentially involves calculating the percentage of the population who will score worse than the person in question – what is, entirely logically, called a *percentile* score. Thus, a person who has a percentile score of 50 scores higher than 50 per cent of the population, and by the same token, worse than the other 50 per cent – in other words, the person is average (extrapolating from this, a score higher than 50 indicates someone with a score which is above average, etc). The percentile score is often used, but in some circumstances, the score is converted (by complex mathematical methods) into the 'traditional' IQ score, where 100 indicates average. It is also worth noting that another system in relatively common use divides classifies performances into bands of ability (e.g. very below average, considerably below average, slightly below average, average, slightly above average, considerably above average, very above average). In such instances, people are placed into an ability group rather than receiving a score on a single continuous scale.

It is important to recall that Binet devised his intelligence test to tackle a specific practical problem – namely, identifying children with extremes of intellectual ability so that they could be targeted for special education. This use of the intelligence test is relatively uncontroversial[1] – critics of the intelligence test have usually acknowledged that it has its uses in identifying whether someone has a general intellectual problem, or whether it is more specific. It is when researchers have tried to make intelligence tests more specific predictors of ability that trouble has arisen.

## Predicting everyday performance from IQ tests

Although some commentators will dispute this, it is fair to say that at a *general* level, how people score on an IQ test is a reasonable predictor of how they will perform on tasks in 'real life' which involve intellectual skills. For example, people who do well at intelligence tests will tend to do better at

---

1    Though note that some American states have restricted the use of this procedure because it was felt to be prejudicial against some African-American children.

school exams and will tend to have better-paid jobs. However, this is only at the level of a *trend* – the prediction breaks down when individual cases are involved. Thus, it is possible to think of people who are manifestly not very intellectually gifted who nonetheless have had successful careers and similarly, people who have high IQ test scores who are in poorly-paid jobs (lecturers being good examples of this). However, the fact that there are individual exceptions does not in itself invalidate the use of IQ tests, as some commentators have tried to argue. This is akin to denying a particular football team the status of best team in the league because, although they have won more matches than anyone else (i.e. there is a trend for them to win), they occasionally lose one.

Similarly, the criticism that IQ tests contain the occasional ambiguous or 'unfair' question does not invalidate their use. An example of such an ambiguous question is 'Does the sun shine at night?', which provoked an interesting correspondence in a UK newspaper some years ago. An answer of 'no' ignores the fact that although the sun may not be shining where it is night, it is shining on another part of the world where it is day. Conversely, answering 'yes' seems to indicate that the testee thinks that the definition of night is 'time when the sun comes out'. Such a question is obviously ambiguous and were an entire test made up of such questions, then it would be a poor test. However, the debate ignores the fact that isolated instances of bad questions are swamped by the majority which require unambiguous answers.

A more serious criticism of IQ test measures is that they are patently inaccurate in predicting *individual* test performance. Suppose that an individual is given an IQ test and their level of intelligence is found. If the person has a high IQ, does this mean that he or she will *inevitably* do well at another task with a high intellectual content? The answer, alas, is 'no'. It has been established (see e.g. Herrnstein and Murray, 1994) that IQ test scores are correlated with scholastic tests of similar construction, such as the US SATs (exams used in effect as university entrance exams). However, beyond this relatively narrow band of tests, IQ is a poor predictor. For example, studies have persistently found that the correlation between IQ test scores and ability at 'real life' intellectual tasks is very low. In some cases, the amount of variability in ability at real life tasks which is explained by differences in IQ test scores can be as low as 4 per cent (see Sternberg *et al.*, 1995). Again, Howe (1997) argues that some acknowledged 'geniuses' (e.g. George Stephenson of railway engineering fame) would score very badly on conventional IQ tests. In other words, a lot of an individual's performance level is predicted by things other than their ability at an IQ task. This is for many different reasons. Amongst these are the fact that the general state of the person when taking the IQ test may be different from when they are performing other tasks (e.g. the latter could be done when the person has a cold, the former when he or she is well). Again, it is assumed that the IQ test is directly measuring 'pure' intelligence. However, no-one is really sure what this is. The scope of the problem can be seen if one considers how to define 'intelligence'. The term is, like 'light' and 'food', so basic that any definition is little more than a synonym. Intelligence is used in practically anything a person does, from choosing the right paint for redecorating a bedroom to solving a problem in calculus. Given it is so universal, expecting to find a simple measure of it may, on logical grounds alone, be over-optimistic. Trying to say how well a person will succeed as a computer engineer based on how well he or she can solve a set of logical puzzles may be rather like trying to judge the performance of an internal combustion engine from the state of its spark plugs.

However, it must be reiterated that at a *general* level, IQ test scores will be a sound predictor, in that over a whole group of people, bigger IQs will *tend* to be matched by bigger scores on other measures. This shows that IQ is measuring something meaningful, in the same way that positions in a sporting league are a good indicator of general performance. But, in the same way that league position is not an outright guarantee that a team will win or lose on a particular week, so IQ test score is not a sound predictor of each individual who takes a test. In academic psychology, such individual variation can be taken in its stride – typically, psychological research is interested in looking at group differences because it is recognised that individuals are not representative of the whole population, and by doing group testing, the effects of individual variability are in effect removed. However, in individual differences research, this is precisely the point of interest. The problem becomes more than of theoretical interest when IQ tests are being used to predict abilities which have a bearing on an individual's welfare and future.

An example of the above is the Eleven Plus system in the United Kingdom, which was used by many education authorities from the 1940s to the mid-1970s. State secondary schools (i.e. for those aged 11 years and upwards) were placed in a hierarchy, with grammar schools for the most gifted, and secondary modern schools for those who were less gifted (in some areas of the country, technical schools took pupils who were just 'below' grammar school standards). Teaching in the schools was geared towards the jobs pupils were expected to attain. Thus, grammar school pupils were directed towards academic subjects and the expectation of higher education or at least a high prestige 'white collar' job. Technical school pupils were given a vocational training in engineering and similar 'applied' studies, whilst secondary modern pupils were given a more 'basic' curriculum. Hence, which school a pupil entered at 11 very much determined his or her future. Children were allocated to schools on the basis of their performance on an Eleven Plus examination, which was largely or solely composed of intelligence tests. Ergo, performance on intelligence tests determined a child's future.

Dislike of the system has largely stemmed from the fact that the system slots children into career paths at a very early age, and that 'late developers' or children who only just failed to enter the grammar school may be put off learning. Again, the system creates an unattractive air of elitism, in that a person's worth is seen in terms of their intellectual ability. In response, it can be said with some justification that the alternative – that all children are taught in the same school (called 'comprehensive' schools in the UK for obvious reasons) – can be equally divisive. Instead of children being taught in ability groups, children attend the school which is geographically closest. This means that comprehensive schools in towns and cities tend to be enclaves of privileged or underprivileged children, depending upon their location, and this is often reflected in exam results. Again, within comprehensive schools, children are often streamed according to ability (i.e. the most gifted are taught together) thereby creating an Eleven Plus system in miniature.

The debate over the worthiness of the Eleven Plus system has been debated for many years, and has polarised into a left versus right political argument (the former favour comprehensive schools). By the 1970s, the system had nearly died out, but the resurgence of right-wing government in the

1980s saw a revival in favour of grammar schools and selective education. Intelligence testing's association with this has hardly made it a darling of critics with left-wing sympathies.

Another frequently-cited criticism of the intelligence test is the cultural bias which may unfairly affect candidates from certain cultural backgrounds. A notorious case of this is the US Army selection tests of World War I. During the mass mobilisation of men for this conflict, the Army required a quick and efficient method of identifying the intellectual status of recruits. Part of this was the need to identify people of sufficient intelligence to merit training as officers. Gould (1981) observes that the tests were biased against men from impoverished backgrounds (which, alas, included, inter alia, most recent immigrants and African-Americans) because the test materials presupposed a white, middle-class background. For example, being shown a picture of a tennis match in which the net is missing and being asked to spot what is wrong with the picture will not strike the modern reader as an especially difficult question, and might be reasonably supposed to be drawing on general knowledge which everyone should possess. However, in 1917, tennis was very much a middle class preserve, and people from impoverished backgrounds would probably never have seen a tennis court (a modern analogy might be to spot an anomaly in a picture of the dashboard of a Porsche). In addition, the tests were (obviously) in English, thereby placing recent immigrants, still struggling to learn the language of their new country, at a distinct disadvantage. The net result of this was that tests made people from working class and racial minority backgrounds appear to be mentally retarded, and certainly not of officer material.

However, in one sense (and in one sense only) the tests were sound. The Army, for good or ill, was commanded by white middle and upper class men. The efficiency of an army stands or falls on the accuracy with which commands are understood by the lower ranking officers responsible for enacting these orders. It is therefore vital that they fully understand what is being told them. In this respect, the tests chose the right men for the job – a battle is no time for making allowances for an officer being basically gifted but unable to understand the language in which a command is written. However, the tests are completely wrong as a tool for indicating the *genuine* abilities of different social and racial groups. Common sense (a skill often in short supply in individual differences research) should have told researchers that the tests were flawed in this respect. Instead, many chose to believe them and use them as a political weapon to 'prove' the natural inferiority of anyone who had not been elected to the Lucky Sperm Club and been born white and middle class. Which leads us to the highly controversial topic of the nature–nurture debate.

## Nature versus nurture – the background

Any arguments which have so far been raised are but minor skirmishes compared with the academic bloodshed which is the stuff of the nature–nurture debate. The argument in essence is beguilingly simple. Because people differ in intellectual abilities, there must be a cause for this. The two most obvious explanations are the nature and the nurture arguments. The nature argument states that differences are laid down in the genes, and that people are born predestined to be of a particular level of intelligence. The nurture argument argues the opposite – namely, that everyone is born roughly equal (i.e. one's genes have little to do with it) and that the reason for differences is upbringing – more gifted people are more intelligent because they have been better educated. The arguments have been used as rallying points for political factions. The Right favours the nature argument, because it demonstrates that inequalities in society are God-given (a point which is literally believed by some) – thus, there is no point in trying to raise the lot of the poor, because they are genetically fixed to be no better than they are. It is a short step from this argument to the now mercifully defunct apartheid system of South Africa, which held that the subjugation of Black people was justified because it was genuinely believed that they were born incapable of ruling responsibly. It is likewise but a short step to arguing that women are born inferior to men, because genetically they have been prepared for rearing families and looking after the home, whilst men have been genetically prepared to be tough and ingenious. In short, the nature argument has been used to provide a 'scientific' justification for societal, racial and sexual inequality. The Left favours the nurture argument, because it demonstrates that inequalities are essentially the product of an unjust society

('Man was born free, and everywhere he is in chains' as Rousseau originally wrote, in a phrase later attributed to Engels). If inequality of ability is not a natural state, then it should not be rewarded. By the same token, racial and gender differences are illusory.

The awful consequences of extremist right-wing politicians who have used the nature argument to support abhorrent policies has been seen all too clearly in this century. Hitler and the Nazi Party murdered some nine million people, mostly Jews, because they had the 'wrong' genetic material and were polluting the racial purity of Europe.

This, alas, is not the only evil act associated with the nature argument (though in itself it is more than sufficient). One episode of shame for psychology is the move by some American psychologists to restrict the 'breeding' of 'low grade' humans who might otherwise dilute the genetic stock of the USA. It will be recalled that intelligence testing of US Army recruits had demonstrated that working class, coloured and immigrant men were of appreciably lower intelligence than the white middle classes. Despite obvious evidence that this was probably the product of faulty test design, this was taken as 'scientific' proof that breeding controls should be introduced. Bluntly, anyone who was deemed to be mentally ill or handicapped was to be sterilised. By a similar token, immigration from Europe to the USA was limited by the 1924 Immigration Act, thereby cutting an escape route for Jews fleeing Nazi Germany. Clearly these findings are an appalling indictment of a particular group of psychologists, but it is important to put them in context.

First, it is extraordinarily naive to think that psychology was the sole cause of this. Worries over immigration and the supposed enfeeblement of the US population had begun a long time before. Racism in general, and anti-semitism in particular, has been a cancer in Western society for a thousand years or more. To pretend that *psychometrics* (the measure of psychological differences) invented this is arrant nonsense. To assume that some racists would use the findings of psychometrics as a justification for their actions should not surprise us, even if we find it sickening. However, without psychometrics, it is doubtful if things would have been much different. Second, commentators often note that the first actions towards controlling the population were the Idiocy Acts of the early 1900s. Some psychologists (notably Terman, a famous pioneer of the subject) were involved in this. However, the same commentators appear to miss the rather obvious fact that the first IQ tests were not available until *after* the introduction of many of these laws. The intelligence test proved a useful propaganda tool, but it did not prompt the invention of the sterilisation programme.

The above arguments do not mean that anyone should condone what took place – far from it. It is to be hoped that it is universally recognised that anyone is entitled to a loving, caring relationship. It should also be hoped that one would not deny a mentally disadvantaged person the chance of being a parent, even though he or she would require considerable assistance, provided, on pragmatic grounds, the potential problems were thoroughly explored first. What was especially bad about the sterilisation acts was that: first, by sterilising the person they left no options; second, often the person was not told what was happening to them (e.g. they were told they were having an appendix operation); and third, the category of 'retarded' often involved people of a higher IQ than would today be classified as 'severely' handicapped. In total, several hundreds of thousands of people were sterilised by the early 1970s, when the practice was largely abandoned.

Reading some textbooks, it is tempting to conclude that all of psychology supported this shameful programme and that, in general, psychologists supported the idea of the inheritability of intelligence, the natural superiority of men over women and of white people over coloured people. This is nonsense. Consider the following quotations:

> Not only differences between individuals, but differences between groups, may be due to either heredity or environment. As regards the races, it appears certain that some physical differences are hereditary, but when we come to mental differences the matter is by no means clear, since the children in one race grow up in a different cultural and social environment from the children of another race.

> It must be understood that a sex difference is usually simply a difference on the average, with much overlap of individuals [...] in general, any sex difference is small in comparison with the range of individual variation within either sex.

> On the whole, there is little indication of a sex difference in intelligence.

The above selections are from pages 190–191 of a very popular introductory psychology text book of its day, by RS Woodworth (Woodworth, 1930). It can be sensibly assumed that Woodworth represented a 'safe' middle ground of opinion in academic circles, and yet there is none of the rabid pro-nature argument which might be expected if the pro-sterilisation lobby really was representative of Psychology in general. This in many ways makes the nature argument more reprehensible, since it clearly was not due to a collective mass hysteria of the whole profession. If the sterilisers had bothered to pay attention, they would have seen that not everybody was marching to their tune.

Commentators properly catalogue the horrors which a slavish inter- pretation of the nature argument can bring, but forget that an *extreme* version of the more liberal nurture argument can have similar results. This in no manner devalues the obscenity of Hitler's acts, but Stalin murdered more people, and for the 'nurture' argument that they were creating the wrong environment by spreading anti-Soviet propaganda (i.e. anything which remotely criticised Stalin). It should also be recalled that Hitler murdered Communists and other critics for similar reasons. More recently, Pol Pot subjected Cambodia to the Year Zero plan, which sent the country back to an intentionally simple agrarian life, removed from Westernised capitalist values. Anyone who had contact with Westerners, or could do such decadent things as read and write, was killed.

In fact, it is easy to attribute ills to academic theories, but psychologists are flattering themselves if they think dictators pay that much attention to intellectual niceties. Monsters of that calibre do not need an academic to give them impetus to think up reasons for killing people. At 'best', theories may provide a specious window dressing to policies, and there are always fools in the academic community who will court publicity and academic power by cravenly supporting extreme views, regardless of what a level-headed pragmatism should tell them.

It should also be borne in mind that, to a certain extent, the traditional allegiances to nature and nurture are flags of convenience. It is possible to present cases for political factions supporting the reverse cases. For example, the Left might argue that genetics fixes people as different. Therefore, if someone is born less gifted, it is not their 'fault', and they deserve extra help from the State. Similarly, the Right might argue that if people are born equal, but some prosper more than others, then this must be the result of hard work (by this token, someone born with privilege does so as the result of an ancestor's hard work, and why should this not be rewarded?). If someone is poor, it is because they have not worked hard enough, and, since individual effort is the basis for capitalism, why should the poor be helped when it is manifestly their own fault? These arguments are not as far-fetched as they may first appear. In the 1920s and 1930s, many of the most vociferous supporters of selective breeding programmes (whereby 'genetically inferior' people of low IQ would be discouraged from breeding, whilst the intelligent would be encouraged to be fecund) found strong support amongst the left-wing intelligentsia, including that darling of the liberal left, George Bernard Shaw (see Carey, 1992). Conversely, the argument that the poor have only themselves to blame sounds horribly familiar to students of right wing politics.

The purpose of this lengthy discussion has been to establish that the tendency of modern commentators to wreath the nature argument with all the sins of Soddom and Gommorrah because it is tied with a selection of (admittedly illiberal and unlovable) right-wing policies is largely specious. First, because nurture arguments can be equally abhorrent when pushed to an extreme, and second, because to a large extent the allegiances of nature and nurture to right and left are largely a matter of coincidence. An investigation of the worth of the two arguments more properly rests in an analysis of what scientific evidence demonstrates.

### Nature versus nurture – the evidence

The first point to be made is that neither nature nor nurture can exist in isolation. For example, people cannot become intelligent in the absence of *any* attempt at upbringing. In historical times, various kings and emperors (including James IV of Scotland and Akbar the Great, a sixteenth century Mogul emperor) have been 'credited' with arranging for orphaned babies to be reared with the least possible contact with other humans. Such 'experiments' created children with no language and (usually) severe mental retardation. In more recent times, there have been (mercifully rare) cases of *attic children.* These unfortunate individuals have been reared in virtual isolation and often physically straitened circumstances, usually because the parents (or in some cases the parents of the bullied mother) decided that the 'sinful' child should be hidden from the world. Such children, deprived of normal emotional contact and intellectual stimulation, emerge in very much the same state as their historical forebears. In some cases, it is possible that the children were mentally retarded from birth, but the fact remains that on any scale of judgement, their deprivation has made them considerably worse than they would have been if reared conventionally. Thus, the extreme 'nature' view – that people will reveal their true intellectual abilities no matter what the upbringing – cannot be supported. There must be some stimulation from the outside world for the intellect to develop. An extremist 'nurture' view cannot be supported either. It is clear that some individuals are born mentally disadvantaged through genetic abnormalities and that no amount of coaching can totally remove this deficit (though it can be lessened, and no rational person would argue against such training being given). Therefore, in some instances, the inherited component of a person's intellect will militate against any other factors.

It can thus be readily appreciated that neither nature nor nurture alone can explain all that needs to be known about differences in intelligence. Therefore, the debate shifts to one of the relative importance of nature and nurture – in other words, which is more essential? This at first seems to be a harmless academic debate, of interest only to those with a taste for arid theoretical discussions. However, the issue is still a potent one. Suppose one argues that intelligence is largely a matter of genetic inheritance, and though one acknowledges that one's environment plays a part, it is a relatively small one. If someone is of a low IQ, then what will happen if they are given the best possible teaching and the best possible environment in which to be raised? The answer is that there will be *some* improvement in intelligence, but it will not be very large. Conversely, a nurture supporter would argue that such teaching and environment would dramatically improve the person's IQ. In other words, nature supporters argue that trying to help low IQ individuals may be worthy, but in practical terms it will be a waste of time and resources – better by far to concentrate on those who already show ability.

Nurture supporters, on the other hand, would argue that intervention programmes will have a profound effect.

The debate has a clear application in instances such as applications to universities and similar posts. Suppose that woman A, from a socially disadvantaged cultural group, applies for a position and has a lower intelligence test score that woman B from a more advantaged cultural group. Who should be chosen? If we go strictly on test scores, then the answer is obviously B. However, B has had greater advantages than A. If they had both had the same opportunities (access to the same education, libraries, etc), then A might have outperformed B. Thus, A's potential might be greater and so she should be preferred. However, is this fair to B? B may not be personally responsible for the problems A's cultural group experiences, but B is being asked in effect to pay for A's misfortunes by being denied a place. Although, by the same argument, A is even less responsible for her misfortune, so why should she be penalised, just as the generations before her were? The argument can be aired *ad infinitum*, and there appears to be no easy answer. However, it is precisely this problem that bedevils any attempts at positive discrimination in favour of people from disadvantaged cultural groups. Do nothing, and the lack of action is condemned; but try to amend the situation, and there are accusations of social engineering which disadvantages the more gifted from the more powerful cultural groups.

This debate is a highly contentious one, as can be imagined, and recent pro-nature books on the subject have raised the hackles of commentators. There was a storm of protest on the publication in the USA of *The Bell Curve* (Herrnstein and Murray, 1994) which presented pro-genetics arguments on this subject in one relatively small section of a large book. More recently, a British researcher produced a highly pro-nature book which was rapidly withdrawn by its publishers following vociferous protests. Without commenting on individual cases, it is clear that pro-nature researchers run a gauntlet whenever they publish and a certain sense of righteous indignation may be detected in some of their writings. Much of the work involved in individual differences research demands very sophisticated (and hence difficult) statistical knowledge and testing of thousands of people. It must be singularly galling for researchers to labour hard at these tasks, produce their findings, and then find that anything which is in favour of genetic inheritance will be pounced upon by armchair critics, most of whom do not understand the methodology, but who lie in ambush longing to be offended (in comparison, pro-nurture researchers receive less heavy criticism, presumably because the Zeitgeist places them on the side of the angels). However, no matter how clever the researcher, anyone producing an argument in favour of inequality who does not expect a sensible protest on social grounds alone is showing a level of unworldliness unusual in even the most cloistered academic. The problem with such controversy, whether justified or not, is that it distracts from the real issue – namely, to what extent can intelligence be said to be a product of genetic inheritance?

## Studies of genetic inheritance of intelligence

Genes provide the blueprint for building the body. It is sensible to ask how psychological characteristics can be inherited, since genes only control physical mechanisms. The simple answer is that the mechanisms are not fully understood, but it can be reasonably argued that the physical state of the brain must have some bearing on the workings of the mind. For example, if a person has nerves which conduct information faster and more accurately, then this will logically enough have a bearing on the speed and accuracy with which thoughts can be processed. At first sight it is a simple matter to prove the strength of the genetic influence on intelligence. Blood relatives (obviously) carry genetic material in common. In sexual reproduction, a child inherits half his or her genes from the father and half from the mother, and this is why children often resemble one or both parents physically. If genes shape intelligence, then one can also predict that a child will resemble his or her parents in intellectual accomplishment. This is at first sight proven by considering the *correlation* (a mathematical measure of the strength of the relationship) between a child's IQ and his or her parents'. Generally, the correlation is fairly strong, thereby apparently supporting the nature argument. The case is further strengthened when one considers the correlation between a child and other genetic relatives. Siblings (i.e. brothers and sisters) share the same number of genes in common as do parents and children. It would therefore be expected that the correlation between siblings' IQs should be roughly the same as that between parents and children, and that is indeed what is found. More distant relatives share fewer genes in common. Grandparents have about a quarter of their genes in common with grandchildren, and the correlation of their IQ scores is weaker than that between parents and children. By a similar token, other distant relatives have less intelligence in common. In short, the greater the proportion of genes two people have in common, the more similar their intelligence levels. This apparently presents firm evidence for a genetic link in intelligence. However, the results are deceptive. If two people are genetically very similar, then it is also likely that they share a very similar environment. For example, siblings may have similar IQs because they have a lot of genes in common, but they also have been brought up in the same household. Likewise, children and parents may have similar IQs because not only have they been living in the same household, but it is quite probable that the parents will have tried to raise children to be similar in outlook and behaviour to themselves. More distant relatives are genetically less closely linked, but by the same token they are also likely to be leading different sorts of lives, so it is not surprising that they will be more dissimilar in intelligence levels. In short, both the nature and the nurture factions can use the evidence of similarities between relatives' IQ levels to support their case. Something more conclusive is therefore required.

The logical solution to the problem is to find instances where genetically similar people have been raised in radically different environments. If little similarity is found between them, then this argues in favour of nurture being the dominant force, whilst if they are very similar, even though they have been raised in different ways, then this argues in favour of nature. The most straightforward way to pursue this would be deliberately to separate children and have them reared in radically different lifestyles, following the precedent set by Akbar the Great and James IV mentioned above. However, for obvious ethical reasons, this is not a sensible proposition. One therefore has to find situations where such a process has happened naturally: namely, adoption. The most notable studies to adopt this approach involve studies of twins. There are two forms of twins – identical and fraternal. Fraternal twins are non-identical and are formed when the mother produces two eggs in the same cycle, both of which are fertilised. Genetically speaking, fraternal twins are as related as any two siblings born of separate births. Because they are formed from two eggs, they are known as *dizygotic* or *DZ* twins. If reared together, DZ twins tend to have slightly more similar IQs than 'normal' siblings, probably because they have been brought up in a more similar manner. Identical twins are created when the embryo divides into two identical forms soon after fertilisation. The two copies are genetically identical, and because they are formed from a single egg, they are known as *monozygotic* or *MZ* twins. If reared together, MZ twins have very similar IQs, though again, this may be because they have been reared in a very similar environment, and because they look the same, the twins will tend to be treated in similar ways. However, what would happen if pairs of MZ twins were reared apart (known as *MZa* twins)?

An extreme example shall be considered to illustrate the above question. Suppose that at birth a pair of MZ twin boys are put up for adoption. One is adopted by Lord and Lady Blankshire and after an education at Eton and Oxford, becomes a barrister in a leading London firm. The other twin is adopted by Mr and Mrs Clothcap of Gasworks Terrace, Barrow-in-Furness.[2] After an education at the local comprehensive, this twin becomes a labourer in the local shipyard. Suppose that these twins are tested for their IQ when they are adults – given their different backgrounds, will they have similar IQs, or will their life experiences have affected this? If they are similar, then the nature case is supported, whilst if they are dissimilar, then the nurture case is supported. As might be imagined, incidences of twins being separated and offered up for adoption are rare, but they do happen, and several studies (called *split twin studies*) have been performed. Generally, these have found that there is a high correlation between the separated twins' IQs; not usually as high a link as for those reared together, but higher than would be expected by chance. This provides evidence that there is a genetic factor in intelligence, but unfortunately, the strength of the link is open to question because of several serious flaws in the design of split twin studies.

---

2    For those unfamiliar with the author's place of birth – a town of 60,000 inhabitants centred around shipbuilding where a cat stuck up a tree is front page news.

The first major criticism is that there have been instances of fraud. The most notable case concerns Sir Cyril Burt, who in his day was arguably the leading figure in British psychology (in particular he was responsible for establishing educational psychology to the UK, and was a leading light in instigating the Eleven Plus system). From the 1950s onwards, Burt produced a string of papers in which he reported the findings on split twins in the UK (e.g. Burt, 1966). In these, he demonstrated that the correlation in IQ test scores of MZa twins was nearly as high as for those reared together. In other words, genetic inheritance seemed to be very important indeed and environment was having very little effect. To take the above example, whether one is the adopted child of a peer of the realm or a manual worker, one's genes will guarantee that one has roughly the same level of intelligence, come what may. However, there were several serious flaws in Burt's work which raised suspicions. The first is that the figures Burt produced were simply too good to be true. In a devastating critique, Kamin (1974) demonstrated that the figures Burt reported must in effect have been 'fixed' – they were too precise and always fell the way Burt wanted them. Real data would have been 'messier'. The second was that when the noted historian of psychology, Leslie Hearnshaw, was asked to write a biography of the now late Sir Cyril, he could find no record in Burt's papers of the data relating to the split twin studies. Such an important piece of work would have generated a lot of paperwork (particularly in pre-computer days) and yet none could be found. Similarly, researchers whom Burt claimed had helped him collect the data could not be found. Thus, the findings of Burt's split twin study were probably the product of his imagination as much as any genuine data. Burt has been the whipping boy of Psychology for some years, and a full revival of his reputation is unlikely. However, it is possible that he did collect some genuine data which were then lost (his office was bombed during World War II). This may explain an understandable urge to publish one paper based on memory of genuine figures, but it does not excuse elaborating the lie by repeatedly publishing papers based on these data, over time increasing the number of pairs who had supposedly been studied. By the time Burt was doing this, he had gained a deserved reputation from his legitimate research (though suggestions of malpractice have been made about some of this) and should have basked in his glory in semi-retirement. Perhaps the greatest irony is that later studies, which were legitimately and honourably carried out, often found the same basic correlations as Burt. In short, there was no need to cheat (for a lengthier and considered discussion of the 'Burt Scandal' see Mackintosh, 1995).

However, although studies other than Burt's were carried out honestly, there are still flaws which weaken the value of their findings. Perhaps the major criticism is that MZa twins are often not as 'split' as might be at first supposed. Although twins may have been reared separately, they may have been raised in the same geographical area or by relatives. In short, the environments may not be radically different, so a certain similarity in test scores would not be surprising. Again, there are suspicions that some supposedly separated twins in reality knew of each others' existence but lied about this to researchers, simply because they wanted the attention of the researchers (one such study involved a free holiday). In other instances, twins had in fact spent years together before separation, so that they had a lot of shared formative experiences in common. If such dubious cases are removed from analysis, then the correlations between the remaining pairs of twins are typically far lower (Kamin, 1974). In other words, a lot of the similarity between the twins may be due to an environment held in common. Thus, split twin studies, when conducted fairly, still do not provide overwhelming evidence for the nature argument.

Other studies on adopted children and the correlation of their IQ scores with those of their biological parents and adopting parents have likewise shown that genetic factors do not overwhelmingly control intelligence. Analyses of large bodies of such studies have shown that a reasonable estimate is that the degree to which people differ in intelligence is roughly equally due to genetic and environmental factors (see e.g. Mackintosh, 1995). In other words, both are just as important. Which makes an impartial observer question why all this debate has been generated over such an inconsequential finding. Neither nature nor nurture emerges from this laurelled in victory. Added to all this is the finding cited earlier that, in any case, the IQ test is not a very accurate predictor of intellectual performance. The debate has been over whether genes or environment control ability at a test which in itself is unreliable, and measures far from all that a sensible observer would wish to classify as 'intelligence'. However, this is not an excuse for complacency. Extravagant claims for the relative role of nature and nurture in intelligence will continue to be made, and for as long as there are issues such as using IQ tests to decide people's academic futures (and by extension their careers), the matter continues to require careful monitoring.

Nor are the dangers limited to old issues. Of recent concern is the Human Genome Project. This is an attempt to describe the genetic composition of humans, and identify what each gene is responsible for. This has laudable aims – many diseases are genetically controlled, and finding the precise cause of previously incurable illnesses will be of obvious benefit to medical research. However, there is a darker side to this knowledge. If genetic links can be identified, then it will be possible to identify those individuals who are in grave danger of contracting a particular type of illness. What if (as is at the time of writing being considered) insurance companies demand the right to test individuals' genes before they will accept them for life assurance policies? People with the 'wrong' genes will find themselves uninsurable. Many commentators may feel that insurance companies are already rich enough from what is after all only a sophisticated form of gambling (i.e. they rely on fewer claims being made than they receive premiums) without them stacking the odds yet further in their favour. However, what if claims are made to have identified genes for intelligence? Genetic factors are not the sole determinant of intelligence, as has been seen, but by the same token, it is arguable that some genetic combinations are better than others. Will some educational institutions try to accept only those people with the 'correct' genetic profile? What if genetic testing is done on the foetus – will aspirational parents have foetuses aborted if they do not promise to be sufficiently gifted? The battle between nature and nurture may in the future take a new, and more sinister, turn.

## What use are intelligence tests?

It might be supposed from what has been written so far that intelligence tests are by their very nature divisive and inaccurate. If they are divisive, then this is because of the ways they have been misused. They are, it must be acknowledged, inaccurate. However, it is useful to ask critics of the IQ test what they would use instead. For all that IQ tests are castigated, in most instances they are the best measures of ability available. They may not be perfect, but equally, they are less imperfect than other methods available.

## Models of intelligence

Before leaving the discussion of intelligence, it is important to study one final aspect of this large topic – namely, what intelligence is. It was mentioned above that 'intelligence' is difficult to define because it is such an all-embracing skill. Much of the work on models of intelligence has concentrated upon whether it can be accurately described as a single skill or whether it is in fact a collection of relatively independent sub-skills. This debate will become clearer if some of the key theories of intelligence are examined.

### Spearman's model

Charles Spearman was one of the pioneers of psychology and, in the early 1900s, developed a statistical technique called *factor analysis* which he used to examine the nature of intelligence. Factor analysis is complex to use, but its basic aim is very simple. Suppose (as Spearman did) one gives a group of people lots of different tests of intellectual skills. It is likely that people's scores on these tests will be fairly similar – in other words, they will correlate with each other. Factor analysis can determine if this pattern of correlations is the result of a smaller group of 'forces' acting upon them. When Spearman analysed his data, he found that ability at all intellectual tasks was at least in part explained by a single factor, which he called $g$ (for 'general intelligence'). This makes intuitive sense. From experience of school life, it is apparent that if a child is good at one subject, he or she is good at others. Thus, the child who is top of the class in English will also tend to be at or near the top in maths, French, history, etc. However, Spearman found that $g$ alone did not explain all of performance. In addition, he found that there were a number of more specialised skills (called $s$, for 'special factors') which seemed only to come into play on some of the tasks which he had given his testees. Thus, a special factor would appear to operate on the maths tasks, whilst another special factor would operate on the tests of verbal reasoning. Again, this makes intuitive sense. Although school pupils may be good at a variety of tasks, an individual tends to be especially good at just one or two, and may have a weakness in some others (e.g. people tend to be especially good at either arts or science subjects). Therefore, what Spearman was arguing was that intelligence is made up of a general all-round ability, which is in operation in any intellectual task, aided by more specialist types of intelligence which only operate within their particular domain.

### Thurstone's model

In the 1930s, Louis Thurstone raised an objection to Spearman's model. He argued that general intelligence was not required, and that a more convincing model simply consisted of a group of specialised intelligences, like Spearman's *s* factors (though Thurstone called them *primary mental abilities*). The seven primary mental abilities identified by Thurstone were: memory, number, perceptual speed, reasoning, space, verbal comprehension and word fluency (the *Test of Primary Mental Abilities*, which was based upon this work, is still in common use as an IQ test). The primary mental abilities are essentially a collection of mathematical, logical, verbal and visuo-spatial specialist skills which in combination could be used to perform any intellectual act. Thurstone's insistence that a general intelligence was not involved as well is, however, spurious. Thurstone used factor analysis to analyse his data. Unfortunately, factor analysis is not a very objective measure. The mathematical reasoning behind this is very complex indeed, but the researcher can in effect pre-determine the pattern of results he or she wishes to find from a set of data. For example, depending upon the method of factor analysis used, a researcher can decide whether one underlying factor (such as *g*) will be found or whether several factors (e.g. the primary mental abilities), each only explaining part of the data will be discovered. Thurstone chose a method which would bias the findings towards *not* finding *g*, though his data reveal that if he had chosen a different method, results analogous to Spearman's would have been found.

This finding makes some models of intelligence hard to trust. If the proof of a theory relies on a statistical technique which can be pre-weighted to find what the researcher wants to find, then this hardly ranks as objective proof. Debates over whether intelligence is the product of a single factor or of a multitude of specialised skills have persisted since Thurstone's work was published, and other researchers have made claims for anything from a handful to over a hundred specialist skills, depending upon the method of analysis used. The consensus of opinion within psychology in general probably favours a version of Spearman's model (i.e. *g* underlying all acts, aided and abetted by appropriate specialist skills) as a rule of thumb, but inevitably there is some mistrust over the methods used to prove this point.

### Crystallised and fluid intelligence

Another useful distinction which is tangential to the above is to divide intelligence into *fluid intelligence* and *crystallised intelligence*. Fluid intelligence loosely corresponds to the everyday notion of 'wit'. Namely, it is the speed and efficiency with which a novel problem can be solved. Fluid intelligence is typically assessed using the tests described above – timed and presenting the testee with problems which get harder to solve as the test progresses. *Crystallised intelligence* is, roughly speaking, 'general knowledge' – it is what the person has learnt. Tests of crystallised intelligence include such measures as vocabulary tests (i.e. providing the definitions of obscure words) and questions on the correct procedure in certain situations (e.g. 'why is it important to keep clean?', 'why should we pay taxes?'). Such questions can only be answered if the person already has the information stored in his or her mind before the test starts – they cannot be answered from first principles, as questions on a fluid intelligence test can. The concepts of fluid and crystallised intelligence are often used as useful conceptual guides by many researchers.

### Sternberg's model

Dissatisfaction with factor analytic approaches led researchers to examine other methods of assessing intelligence. The upsurge in interest in Cognition from the 1950s onwards brought with it an interest in analysing the components of a mental act. Traditional approaches to intelligence testing had looked at the relationship between the *outcomes* of mental processes – in other words, how well someone performed on one task was related to how well they performed on another. Factor analysis examined the relationship between these scores, and $g$ and $s$ factors which were found simply stated that there was a relationship between *the scores*. When researchers said that there was a specialist skill for, say, verbal ability, this was because they had found that how a person performed on one verbal test tended to determine how he or she performed on all the other verbal tests. From this it was *inferred* that within the mind, verbal skills must be organised in a manner separate from other mental skills. However, what actually took place in the mind was ignored. This is akin to watching a collection of Porsches and Ladas[3] race each other. Simply by watching them, it can be concluded that the Porsche is a faster car, and it might be *inferred* that it has a more powerful engine. However, to *prove* this, the engine has to be looked at.

The *component process approach* (sometimes called the *information processing approach*) has attracted a number of researchers, but the most often-cited is arguably Sternberg (e.g. Sternberg, 1985). Sternberg breaks intelligence down into a number of component processes, which can be broadly grouped according to the essential nature of what they do. For example, Sternberg argues that one aspect of intelligence must be the ability to acquire information – there are methods for doing this, and how well they are executed will in part determine intellectual performance. Likewise, there must be components responsible for storing the information and others for retrieving it (since intelligence in part must consist of the ability to retrieve and make use of knowledge). By means of detailed experimental analysis, it is possible to demonstrate that particular tasks require certain mental skills, and it is possible to demonstrate that people differ in the speed and accuracy with which they perform these. Intelligence can therefore be seen as the product of the combined workings of these components. Sternberg has integrated his findings into a *triarchic theory of intelligence* (Sternberg, 1985). This argues that 'intelligence' is the product of the interaction of three types of skills – *componential* (roughly akin to fluid intelligence); *contextual* (the ability to adapt to and live in one's environment); and *experiential* (intellectual skills de-

---

3    For American readers – 'Lada' occupies the same place in the British motorist's heart as 'Yugo' does in an American's – and yes, we have the same jokes about them.

rived from experience). The theory is of especial interest because it emphasises that intelligence is not simply a matter of being good at academic skills, and incorporates the idea that intellectual acts also include the ability to cope with 'everyday' situations. This theme has been adopted by other researchers, notably Gardner (1983), who argues that in addition to verbal, logico-mathematical and visual intelligences, humans possess separate skills of: musical intelligence; bodily-kinaesthetic intelligence (basically, skill in movement); and personal intelligence (ability to analyse emotions and needs in oneself and others).

## Concluding comments

It cannot be denied that intelligence research is a messy business. It is intuitively obvious that some people are cleverer than others, yet researchers seem incapable of agreeing on: (a) the cause; (b) what constitutes 'intelligence'; or (c) how to find an intelligence test which predicts performance of other intellectual skills. However, people are still drawn to studying the topic, perhaps precisely because these important issues have still to be resolved. In addition, there is the intuitive feeling that intelligence 'must' be a key component of human behaviour, and that discovering its precise nature is central to a complete understanding of Psychology. In fairness, it must also be said that research on intelligence has revealed a general set of concepts and testing methods which have achieved majority (if not universal) acceptance. Researchers generally accept that the best measure of intellectual skill is the IQ test, provided it is recognised as indicating a trend and is not taken as a completely accurate gauge. Similarly, researchers are generally prepared to accept a model of general intelligence aided and abetted by more specific skills (though whether $g$ is a product of the interaction of the specific skills or is an entity in its own right is debatable). Researchers will generally accept that differences in intelligence are attributable to a mix of genetic and environmental factors. However, these are simply consensus opinions – researchers who are active in intelligence research will often hold more extreme views. In itself, this is indicative of a healthy research atmosphere. But when such opinions are manipulated for the purposes of social engineering, then the matter becomes of concern to everybody.

FURTHER READING

Mackintosh (1995) is a fairly brief edited volume which provides a sound introduction to the Burt Scandal, and in the process covers some of the general issues of the nature–nurture debate. Kline (1993) gives a good introduction to the design of test materials. Sternberg (1985) gives a good introduction to his own tirarchic theory, and a more recent paper (Sternberg et al., 1995) provides a good critique of many of the assumptions of intelligence testing.

# CHAPTER 3

# Personality

## Introduction

Personality has been defined in many ways by different authors, but in essence it is the pattern of behaviour and attitudes which a person will usually display. Thus, a person may be thought to have a timid personality if in most cases he or she avoids arguments with others, is unwilling to volunteer or generally avoids activities in which he or she will be 'put in the spotlight'. This does not mean that a person will *invariably* display these behaviours (e.g. when physically threatened, he or she may become very stubborn and argumentative) but simply that this is their *usual* behaviour.

It may also be said that everybody has a unique personality, since to a large extent how one behaves is very much the defining characteristic of an individual's uniqueness. However, this does not mean that people do not share aspects of their personalities in common. For example, the reader is invited to consider members of their own family and friends. Although each person they think of will be different, some might be classified as being similar because they tend to be equally outgoing, whilst others may have a similar level of bad-temperedness. Therefore, the 'building blocks' which make up a person's personality will come from a common set from which others are also constructed. One of the key goals of personality research is to see how accurately people can be categorised using as few of these building blocks as possible. This follows a principle known variously as the *parsimony principle* or *Occam's Razor* (after a mediaeval philosopher who first stated the concept), which argues that given more than one explanation of an event, always choose the simplest.

It is worth noting at this point that theories of personality, in addition to trying to obey Occam's Razor, also fall into two categories – either they describe personality in terms of *types* or in terms of *traits*. Type theories essentially argue that a person either has one sort of personality or another (e.g. a person is either outgoing or they are reclusive). Trait theories argue that everyone possesses the same 'building blocks', but in different strengths (e.g. most people will want some periods of solitude, but few would want to live the life of a hermit). Perversely, both approaches echo everyday experience. People are often categorised into types, such as 'friendly', 'quick-tempered' etc. Equally, people are often classified by the answers to such questions as 'how easily does she lose her temper?', recognising that everyone can lose their temper – what differs is the ease with which this takes place. The problem is akin to considering the colours of the rainbow – it can be seen that it is composed of different bands of colour, but at the boundaries between the colour bands, one colour gradually merges into the next. Thus, although it can be seen that there are clearly bands of red and orange, it is impossible to be certain precisely where the red ends and the orange begins. In a similar way, it is possible to see personality in terms of separate types, but it must also be recognised that at the boundaries between one personality type and the next, the division is blurred (e.g. at what point does someone cease to be described as reclusive and becomes better described as outward-going?). Trait theories recognise this blurring in a manner which type theories cannot. However, trait theories cannot give a snappy answer to the question 'what sort of personality does this person have?' Accordingly, neither approach is entirely successful in itself.

The trait versus type debate runs through personality research, but it is not the only method of analysing the subject. Personality can also be seen in terms of the theoretical stance of the researcher. Different perceptions of what are the important aspects of personality (particularly its formation) have led to different researchers creating radically different models, as shall be seen in the next section of this chapter. It should be noted that a great deal of personality research has been derived from studies of mental illness. In other words, the prime motivating factor has been to gauge how *ab*normal a person's behaviour is, what the possible causes of this are, and how it might be treated. There is no logical reason why studies of abnormal personality should not also be informative about normal personality (since one cannot be defined without the other). However, it is important to bear this caveat in mind when considering models of personality.

## Models of personality

### Theories of personality before psychology

It must not be thought that interest in personality began with Psychology. Some of the earliest work in this field was done (not surprisingly) by the Ancient Greeks. The most prominent worker in this field was Hippocrates (460–377 BC), whose work was later elaborated upon by Galen (131–201 AD) – also Greek, but working in the Roman Empire. Galen's theory argued that personality was determined by the *humours* – four fluids which were hypothesised to be the mainstay of the body's functioning. These were: yellow bile, black bile, phlegm and blood. If the quantity of humours in the body was balanced, then a person had a stable personality. However, if one of them became too abundant, then problems arose. An excess of yellow bile was said to make someone *choleric* (i.e. irritable), whilst an excess of black bile made someone *melancholic* (the word has the same meaning as the modern term). An excess of phlegm made a person *phlegmatic* (which did not quite carry the modern meaning – the term implied listlessness rather than calmness) and an excess of blood made someone *sanguine* (which carried the negative value of over-confidence). The theory is an interesting one and strikes a modern chord in that it emphasises the idea of a whole body in balance. It remained popular until well into the Middle Ages, and allowed doctors to miss obvious signs that the body and mind were not so simply controlled. For example, a mediaeval manuscript records the case of a knight who had a severe head injury in a tournament and who subsequently had mood swings. This was treated by purges and bleedings (to reduce the quantity of humours) – the fact that part of his brain and skull had been removed appeared not to have been considered to be a contributory factor.

### Sheldon's personality types

A latterday personality theory which based personality on physical factors was devised by WH Sheldon in the 1940s. He argued that there were three basic body shapes, with corresponding personalities. The *ectomorph* has a 'beanpole' body shape (tall and thin), and the corresponding personality (the *cerebrotonic personality*) is one of the stereotypical 'shy academic' – reserved, and primarily cerebral in tastes. In contrast, the *endomorph* is fat, and has a *viscerotonic personality*, characterised by a rather 'laid back' attitude, and gregariousness. The final type – the *mesomorph* – is very muscular, and the corresponding *somatotonic personality* is one of seeking action and command. Sheldon argued that everyone can be categorised according to the degree to which they possessed each of the three body types, and their personality will similarly reflect this mixture. However, it can be argued that a particular personality will drive a person into a particular body shape just as plausibly as Sheldon claimed the reverse (e.g. a mesomorph may become muscular by dint of the exercise which his or her personality compels him or her to take). It is also worth noting that although the theory has a specious attraction, the appeal is built on societal stereotyping – fat people are expected to be jolly; muscular and physically fit people tend to be active, and are admired; and academics are popularly portrayed as beanpoles with a frumpish dress sense.

### Freud's psychoanalytic theory

A rather different view of personality was provided by Sigmund Freud (1856–1939), the founder of *psychoanalysis*. He created a very rich theory of human psychological behaviour, which although not part of mainstream psychology, had a profound influence on its early development (even if only in the formation of theories opposed to it). At the heart of the theory is the belief that the human personality is empowered with *psychic energy*, which when it builds up, has to be released in the form of an appropriate action (e.g. if the drive is to eat, then eating is an appropriate release). The *pleasure principle* states that there will be an attempt to do this as soon as possible, but the *reality principle* attempts to ensure that the release only occurs in a socially appropriate form (e.g. a frustrated employee may have an urge to hit his/her boss, but the drive may be channelled into being nasty to an office junior – not commendable, but preferable in terms of social survival). The psychic energy drives three forces. The *id* is a primitive collection of urges with which a baby begins life. It is capable of projecting some basic thoughts of desirable goals (*primary process thought*), but is, as might be expected, very basic in its needs. In order to cope more efficiently with the everyday world, the *ego* develops. This loosely corresponds to rational thought (*secondary process thought*), decides on appropriate goals, and attempts to keep a check on the id and the *superego*. The latter arises in later childhood, and is a collection of (often overly-harsh) ideals, and in effect acts like an internalised set of moralistic parents. If the ego feels threatened by the id and the superego, then various *defence mechanisms* are available. One example is the famous *repression*, where an unpleasant thought is blocked by the unconscious. In very extreme cases, this can result in a psychological blocking of the senses. For example, in *hysterical deafness*, the patient literally cannot hear anything. The ear and associated physical mechanisms are working normally, but the mind blocks out any incoming messages. Freud argued that the id, ego, and superego develop as a consequence of several *psychosexual* stages of development. Each is centred on an *erogenous zone* – an area of the body providing sensual (and not necessarily exclusively sexual) satisfaction. In the *oral stage* (0–1 years), sensual satisfaction is obtained primarily through the mouth. This is followed by the *anal stage* (1–3 years), where satisfaction is primarily attained through the retention and expulsion of faeces. At the *phallic stage* (3–5 years), according to Freud, a boy realises that he has a penis, and desires his mother (the *Oedipus complex*). However, he fears that this desire will cause his father to punish him by castration. This leads him to cease desiring his mother, and to identify more with his father. A girl at this stage discovers that she lacks a penis, but desires one (*penis envy*). She feels that she once had one, but that it has been cut off as a punishment. She blames her mother for this loss, weakening her identification with her, and increasing her liking for her father. Following these eventful episodes is the *latency period* (5 years to adolescence), when energy is channelled into non-sexual development of intellectual and social skills. At the *genital stage* (adolescence onwards), the individual now aims for 'mature' sexual satisfaction with a permanent partner of the opposite sex. However, 'faulty' development prior to the genital stage will lead to inappropriate behaviour in adult life. For example, a man who did not properly resolve his Oedipus complex as a child may feel drawn to seek sexual partners who resemble his mother. 'Faulty' development affects more than choice of partner, however.

For example, a baby in the oral stage who bites at the nipple will develop a 'biting' and sarcastic sense of humour in later life. Likewise, a baby who in the anal stage obtained pleasure from retaining faeces rather than expelling them will develop an *anal retentive* personality, characterised by meanness and an inappropriate obsession with detail.

The above is a very simplistic gloss of a very rich theory, which has influenced a large number of researchers in psychology as well as other fields (notably surrealist artists and the stream-of-consciousness novelists).[1] Freud's theories have been very heavily criticised for, amongst other things, being post-hoc and untestable explanations. This raises an important issue in research – namely, *falsifiability*. This has its origins in the work of Karl Popper, a philosopher with an especial interest in scientific methods. Falsifiability argues that for a theory to be proven, it must be possible, in principle, to disprove it. This sounds perverse, but an example will help to clarify matters. Consider the theory that the world was spontaneously created three seconds ago, and will disappear in a further three seconds. This theory cannot be proved – any arguments that one has memories of more than three seconds ago or that one can produce historical artefacts of ancient times could all have been part of the spontaneous creation process. Equally, one cannot look at one's watch and after four seconds have elapsed, say pointedly that the world is still here, since the world might just have been created, along with a memory of having looked at a watch for four seconds. In short, the theory cannot be disproved. However, by the same token, one cannot prove the theory either, for exactly the same reasons – namely, that it is untestable. However, suppose one developed the (unsurprising) theory that dropping glasses from a skyscraper onto the ground below will break them. This could be easily disproved – if a sample of glasses were dropped, and a significant proportion of them did *not* break, then the theory would be disproved. By the same reasoning, if all or most of the glasses did break, then the theory would be proven. In short, if a theory cannot allow for the reverse of what it predicts to be tested for, then it is not a provable theory.

---

1    Though whether Freud should be blamed or praised for this is open to debate.

By this reasoning, Freud's work cannot be proven. Statements about personality being formed by childhood development cannot be easily tested, simply because records of what actually took place in childhood are not present. Therefore, Freudian therapists help patients explore their past by carefully interviewing them about their past and through various mental activities designed to unleash hidden feelings. It is argued that although a person may be unaware of these, they are lurking in the *subconscious*, and may become apparent only through accidental slips of the tongue (*Freudian slips*) or in dreams, which must be interpreted for their symbolic meaning. For example, it was felt that rather than face the real thoughts (which might be too horrifying for the patient) dreams present them in symbolic terms. For example, Freud felt that one patient's dreams of a giraffe were indicative of a fear of having his penis cut off. However, these arguments are untestable. In the giraffe example, the patient may have had a fear of castration, but by the same token it might have been a dream about giraffes (as Freud himself acknowledged, sometimes a cigar is just a cigar). There is no empirical way in which the therapist's interpretation can be proved or denied. To take another example: suppose that a man seeks partners who resemble his mother – is this because he has an unresolved Oedipus complex? If the man is asked about his relationship with his mother, then it is possible that he might admit to such feelings. However, what if the man denies this? Freudian theory would argue that the man is denying his feelings, but 'deep down' he knows that they are true – this worries him, however, so he enters into a state of denial. In short, whether the man denies or accepts the interpretation, the Freudian analyst wins his or her case. However, by the same token, the theory is unfalsifiable. This does not (as some commentators have mistakenly argued) mean that Freudian theory is wrong – simply that it cannot be proven. Without wishing to sound blasphemous, this places the theory on a par with proving religious belief. A rational proof of God cannot be produced – whether one believes or not rests on faith.

In addition to the above criticisms, it should also be noted that Freud's theories were also sexist. For example, women are portrayed as having 'naturally' weaker personalities. Again, several of Freud's women patients reported being molested by relatives when they were children. Freud usually dismissed this as fantasising,[2] whereas modern awareness of the extent of sexual abuse of children makes it likely that Freud should have taken these claims seriously.

Some of Freud's own pupils and later psychoanalysts disagreed with sections of his theory without wishing to reject it wholeheartedly. These *post-Freudians* developed variants on Freud's approach which presented contrasting views of personality formation. It is interesting to note that Freud did not take criticism very well. Those critics who began as his followers were ostracised and Freud would (literally) never speak or write to them again. He was, for example, particularly hard-hearted about the death of psychoanalyst Alfred Adler (who devised the famous inferiority complex), who had disagreed with some aspects of Freud's theory. In general, Freud's own life was hardly a model of good behaviour. For example, he tended to have interesting memory lapses about the work on cocaine he did when a young man (at the time it was felt to be a useful medicinal drug). A full survey of the post-Freudians is not appropriate for a book of this size, but it is important that at this point the most notable member of this group is briefly discussed.

### Jung's psychoanalytic theory (analytical psychology)

Carl Jung (1875–1961) had already made his reputation as a psychiatrist before he encountered Freud's work. Jung met Freud in 1906, and the two men seem to have formed a firm bond from the start. In 1909, Jung was invited by Freud to accompany him on a lecture tour of the USA, and in 1911, he became the first president of the International Psychoanalytic Association. Regardless of this, Jung from very early on had doubts about Freud's theory, and these doubts were made explicit in his writings. This did not endear him to Freud, and in 1911 the two agreed not to correspond with each other. In 1914, Jung resigned his presidency, and in effect split from the mainstream Freudian movement.

Although his work was largely based on Freud's psychoanalytic theory, Jung played down the role of sexual forces, and believed that several factors motivated people's personality development. In particular, Jung rejected the

---

2    In fairness to Freud, the opinions of colleagues biased him to adopting this view.

idea that early childhood consists of sexual development. For example, he saw the attachment to the mother as being one of physical dependency for food, shelter, etc, rather than sexual (though some unkind Freudian supporters noted that Jung's mother was apparently rather ugly ...). Also, Jung argued that in addition to the unconscious as conceived by Freud, there is a *collective unconscious*. This is a set of inherited images (*archetypes*) of God, of heroes and heroines, etc, which have the power to shape development, but which the person is not consciously aware of (although they may appear in the guise of art, folk tales, etc). Jung also de-emphasised the role of past experience. He argued that people were not absolute prisoners of the past, but were are also shaped by future goals. This is a blow against the rather fatalistic Freudian notion that people are prisoners of their childhood, destined never to escape the results of faulty development.

Jung's model of personality is based around the premise that (regardless of how they developed) people possess four basic methods of viewing the world: the *feeling personality* (the emotional impact is of principal importance); the *intuitive personality* (the world is judged on hunches and intuitions); the *sensing personality* (the direct perception of the world as it appears through the senses); and the *thinking personality* (the primary emphasis is on abstract thought). These personality types are measured by the *Myers-Briggs Type Indicator*, first devised by Katharine Briggs and Isabel Briggs Myers in the 1920s, which is still in common use as a personality test. Jung also conceived of individuals being primarily *extraverted* or *introverted*, and being a mixture of active and 'masculine' elements (*animus*), and passive and 'feminine' elements (*anima*).

Jung's theory appears gentler and more spiritual than Freud's, and his concept of the collective unconscious attracted the attention of a wide audience. It also emphasised the active nature of personality, and the fact that it interacts with the here and now, and is not locked in the past. However, like Freud's theory, it is likewise unfalsifiable, and stands or falls on the basis of faith. One key aspect of his theory which was adopted by other researchers (who would otherwise avoid psychoanalytic concepts) was the identification of introversion and extraversion, which will be covered below.

It is difficult to judge how posterity will treat the psychoanalytic theories. Certainly Freud, Jung and the other pioneers of the subject will be honoured (in the same sense that modern chemists honour alchemists as having started the profession), and there are many psychoanalysts in practice offering therapeutic services to those who feel they have a dysfunctional personality which can be cured by analysing their subconscious and childhood (often at great expense, since such services are almost invariably only available in the private medical sector). However, whether this approach will continue to be popular (particularly as drugs for the treatment of mental problems become more efficient) is open to question.

*Phenomenological theories*

An important group of models of personality which oppose psychoanalytic theories can be described by the term *phenomenological theories*. These explicitly reject discussions of what caused the patient's condition, and instead concentrate on how the person is *now*. Amongst the most cited of these models is *Maslow's hierarchy of needs*, devised by Abraham Maslow. This argues that people have a set of needs ranging from the basic to the relatively refined, and that people can only truly fulfil the higher order needs if the more basic ones have been met. Thus, the most primitive is *physiological need* (for food, etc) followed by *safety needs, belonging and love needs, esteem needs* (all self-explanatory), *cognitive needs* (i.e. intellectual needs), *aesthetic needs*, and finally, *self-actualisation* (the full realisation of one's (positive) attributes and potential). This final goal was taken as the central point of *Rogers' self theory of personality*. Carl Rogers argues that the basic drive in personality development is self-actualisation. Central to this is the argument that the person should receive *unconditional positive regard* – an uncritical acceptance and feeling of warmth towards the person, which enables the person to be true to his or her feelings. This is not a creed of pure selfishness, however – other goals which should be obtained include *congruence* (the harmony of self with experience), and *empathic understanding* (the ability to perceive the needs and feelings of others). Therefore, the ultimate goal is that everyone should be allowed the freedom to express themselves and be true to themselves without hurting others. Rogers argues that often desires are compromised, and people are forced into doing things they may not like doing because this is the only way they will obtain affection or reward from authority figures, such as parents or teachers. This is known as *conditional positive regard* (i.e. positive responses will only be given for certain acts). Such situations can create an internal conflict (e.g. the girl likes to play soccer, but her parents forbid it, so she stops, but this creates an inner tension because her wish has been thwarted). Such conflicts mean that the person behaves in one manner because that is the one which will be rewarded (the *condition of worth*), though he or she may really want to do something different. Such conflicts, Rogers argues, retard personality development. In time this leads to problems, because the person's self image, which has been built on inconsistencies, does not match up with reality, and in order to protect the self image, the person experiences anxiety, and has to create defences. A therapeutic programme – *client-centred therapy* – which is largely based upon Rogers' theory, has been created to help the person resolve these conflicts.

A somewhat different approach to the above, though still within the phenomenological fold is the *personal construct theory* of George Kelly (1905–1967). This argued that people view the world through *constructs,* which are collections of ideas and opinions, and that in order to perceive a person's personality, his or her personal constructs have to be determined. The theory has a certain intuitive appeal: it is a commonplace observation that everyone views the same situation differently, based upon their own unique set of knowledge and beliefs (*constructive alternativism*). Several types of constructs are proposed: many are basic building blocks (*subordinate constructs*), which can be combined in a variety of ways to form *superordinate constructs.* Others (e.g. a strong stance on a particular issue) can only exist by themselves (*preemptive constructs*). *Constellatory constructs* are prejudices which shape how other constructs are designed. To allow a person to identify many of their constructs, Kelly developed the *repertory grid test.* This rather complex procedure in essence requires a person to identify two people of importance in the person's life (*significant others*) who are similar on a particular attribute (e.g. decisiveness, honesty, etc) and one significant other who is different. This exercise is repeated for more attributes, and then the results analysed to determine the construct of the individual being tested.

Overall, the phenomenological models of personality can provide a refreshing antidote to the psychoanalytic models concept that people are forever doomed to a life of dysfunctional misery because toilet training did not go quite right. However, it would be wrong to say that phenomenological models are without their faults. Two arguments will be cited. First, a lot of the suppositions about what is right for a person cannot be proven any more than the assertions of the Freudians. It must be taken on trust that, for example, self-realisation is a good thing (see Ross, 1992). Whether sections of many of the models are correct depends upon whether one shares the same value system as the models' creators. Second, the concentration on the here and now and the perennial looking to the future can be misleading. If a person is displaying an abnormal personality, then trying to alter this without asking why the person is behaving as they are may be treating the symptoms without tackling the origin, thereby allowing the problem to resurface. For example, it is possible to treat a tooth abscess with powerful painkillers – this will remove the principal problem (the pain) but the root cause (a rotting tooth) is still there.

### Bandura's theory of social learning

Another view of personality concentrates upon how aspects of personality might be created through experience. The idea that personality might be formed through formative experiences is of course nothing new, and has been a repetitive theme in religious and secular writings since earliest times. More prosaically, early work on *classical* and *operant conditioning* (see Chapter 7) had demonstrated that people and other animals can be trained to do things either by rewarding them for doing desirable deeds (*positive reinforcement*) or by punishing them for doing something which is not desirable (*negative reinforcement*). It is easy to appreciate how a rudimentary personality could be formed in this manner. A person will adopt certain behaviour patterns because these are the ones into which he or she has been explicitly conditioned. Thus, a person may be very polite because they were taught 'good manners' as a child and rewarded for displaying them. However, this cannot be a complete explanation, since there are many aspects of behaviour which people display which they have never been explicitly taught. A noted researcher in this field, Albert Bandura, (e.g. Bandura, 1989) observes that in many situations, people (especially children) learn skills simply by observing others performing them, and then copying. Often the very first attempt at imitation is very accomplished – an example of what is called *no-trial learning*. Bandura identifies various factors which influence the success of this *social learning*. Obviously, the person must attend to the to-be-copied activity, and be physically capable of replicating it (e.g. it is no use an infant watching someone toss the caber). The person must also be able to retain a memory of the task. Bandura argues that this is often done with a verbal code (e.g. 'right hand hold sprocket, then left hand turn screw') which is more flexible than a visual image. Children under five years lack this code, and so are more restricted in what they can learn. The motivation for learning and, more important, performing the task, largely depends upon whether it is perceived as rewarding. This can be learnt by *vicarious reinforcement* (observing if others are rewarded or punished for performing the same actions). In one celebrated study (Bandura, Ross and Ross, 1963) children were shown a film in which an actor went into a room in which there was a range of toys, including an inflatable doll[3] of Bobo the Clown, a popular television character at the time. The film has a slightly surreal air, in that in one variant of the experiment, the actor attacked the doll. This deed was then shown to be either rewarded, punished, or ignored. Left to play afterwards, children who had seen aggression rewarded were significantly more likely to behave violently to toys than were children in the other two conditions. There is a considerable debate over the range of learning situations for which Bandura's methods are applicable (see e.g. Pervin, 1993), but nonetheless the model presents a plausible mechanism whereby certain behaviours might be acquired.

### Eysenck's trait model
Whilst the Freudians were establishing their theories in Europe and America, rather different research was being conducted in the Soviet Union, which would eventually lead to a personality theory at odds with the

---

3    Not *that* sort of inflatable doll – the device was a popular children's toy of the time.

psychoanalytic approach. The work of Ivan Petrovich Pavlov will be discussed in detail elsewhere (see Chapter 7). For the moment, it is sufficient to note the following. Pavlov was a Russian physiologist, active around the turn of the 20th century. Whilst using dogs in experiments on digestion, he noted dogs began to salivate when they saw a particular lab assistant, who was the person who usually fed them. Normally dogs do not salivate when they see humans, but only when they see food. Therefore, Pavlov argued that the dogs were salivating because they had come to associate the assistant with the arrival of food. To examine this further, Pavlov conducted a series of experiments in which he presented a stimulus which normally would not make a dog salivate, just before the dog was fed (in the most famous version of the experiment, the stimulus was a bell, but other stimuli, such as a flashing light, were also used). At first, the stimulus did not make the dog salivate, but after a few days, the stimulus alone was enough to make the dog salivate. In other words, the dog was associating the stimulus with food. This learned association between a 'neutral' stimulus with one which 'naturally' provokes a reaction is known as *classical conditioning*. As will be seen in Chapter 7, this led to a rich area of research, but of interest here are the individual differences between the dogs in how quickly they learnt the association. Basically, not all of his dogs conditioned equally well: the dogs which were friendly and approachable took longer to learn associations than did the quieter, less approachable animals. It might at first seem that this means that the harder to condition dogs were less intelligent, but a more plausible explanation was advanced by one of Pavlov's followers, called Teplov (e.g. Teplov, 1964). In essence, he argued that the ease with which the dogs learnt depended upon the 'strength' of their nervous system. A 'strong' nervous system is one which can withstand a lot of stimulation, whilst a weak one can only stand a small amount of stimulation.

This argument is related to the phenomenon of the *inverted U function*. Essentially, this argues that increasing the level of stimulation at first causes an increase in the strength of a response. Further increases will cause a further increase in response until a peak is reached. If stimulation becomes any stronger, then the response begins to fall.[4] For example, suppose that a dog is conditioned to respond to a bell. If the volume of the bell is increased a bit, then the response becomes stronger (i.e. it will salivate more). However, if the volume is increased too much, then instead of salivating more, the response will diminish. The amount by which stimulation has to increase before this fall takes place differs between individuals. In other words, some people have to have a big increase in stimulation before they show a decline in response, whilst others will show a drop after only a small increase in stimulation. Those that require a big increase are said to have strong nervous systems, whilst those who require only a small increase are said to have weak nervous systems.

After a considerable amount of further analysis and experimentation, the concept of strong and weak nervous systems was adopted by Hans Eysenck (1916–1997) in his model of *introversion–extraversion*.[5] It is clear from everyday experience that people vary in the degree to which they are gregarious and outward-going. At one end of the spectrum are introverts (socially withdrawn and shy) and at the other are extraverts (outward-going and gregarious). How does this relate to strong and weak nervous systems? It follows from what has been said that people with weak nervous systems cannot stand as much stimulation as those with strong nervous systems. To reach the strongest level of response before it begins to fall, weak nervous system people require only a little stimulation. Therefore, weak nervous system people will tend to avoid situations where there will be too much stimulation. Conversely, strong nervous system people need lots of stimulation before they reach their peak, so they will tend to seek out stimulation. Eysenck argued that introverted people had weak nervous systems, whilst extraverted people had strong nervous systems. Hence, introverts need relatively little stimulation – if they get over-stimulated, then they run the danger of going 'over their peak'. Therefore, they tend to be fairly withdrawn. Extraverts, on the

---

4    It is called an inverted U function, because a graph plotting strength of stimulation on the x axis and strength of response on the y axis will produce a curve looking like an upside-down 'U'.

5    Pedantically speaking, 'extraversion' is the correct spelling, but 'extroversion' is in wide use, particularly amongst American researchers.

other hand, seek excitement in order to boost their levels, and so tend to be outward-going. Again, because introverts need relatively small amounts of stimulation to reach their peak, any stimulation they receive will tend to strike home at a higher level than extraverts. This means that in a fairly routine thing like a conditioning task, introverts will tend to condition better, simply because they receive the signals which they are supposed to learn at a higher intensity. In most instances, introverts tend to condition rather better than extraverts (Monte, 1987). As the source for this nervous activity, Eysenck cited the *ascending reticular activating system (ARAS)*, a complex system of nervous pathways running through the brain, which originate in the *brain stem* (an area of the brain which 'sits' on the top of the spinal column). The argument over the precise function on the ARAS is debated, but there is general evidence that stimulating this area in non-human primates increases the ease with which they can be conditioned.

Eysenck's model of introversion–extraversion presents an example of how apparently complex personality patterns such as the level of gregariousness can be determined by a very simple mechanism. He expanded upon his theory by arguing that personality is also shaped by a further dimension, reflecting the degree of *neuroticism* a person possesses. Basically, this is a measure of the degree to which a person responds to situations calmly. A person with a high level of neuroticism will tend to worry and fret over even the smallest thing which goes wrong (or is perceived to go wrong) in their world. Conversely, a person with a low level of neuroticism will tend to have a 'devil may care' attitude and resolutely not worry over anything. Eysenck argues that people's personalities can be broadly categorised by their degree of neuroticism and extraversion–introversion. Indeed, he argued that using these two measures, it is possible to create the four personality types of the humours. People who are introverted and emotionally stable are said to be phlegmatic; introverted and unstable corresponds to melancholic; extraverted and unstable equals choleric; and extraverted and stable produces a sanguine personality. Thus, it is possible to create personality types using a trait measure. Eysenck also added a further personality trait – *psychoticism* – which describes how emotionally 'cold' and unaffected by emotions a person is.

A measure of the three traits of extraversion–introversion, neuroticism and psychoticism – the *Eysenck Personality Questionnaire (EPQ)* – is in wide use. A notable feature of this questionnaire is the *lie scale*. If a person is taking a personality test, then he or she may well wish to make good impression. It is possible to check for this by using a lie scale, which asks the person to identify him- or herself with a series of impossibly virtuous statements (e.g. 'I have never lost my temper'). A person who identifies with all or most of these statements is arguably trying to create an artificially good impression, and procedures are available for adjusting test scores accordingly.

On a more general note, it is easy to perceive personality test scores as value judgements, but this would be inappropriate. Arguably, an extreme level of any trait is undesirable – someone who is painfully shy or worries unnecessarily is obviously at a disadvantage, but someone who is outward-going to the point of embarrassment[6] or who refuses to heed any warning signs is also not behaving very sensibly. However, the majority of people fall somewhere between these extremes, and it should not be inferred that one sort of personality is 'better' than another.

*Other trait theories*

Eysenck's is perhaps the simplest of trait theories in common usage. It attempts to describe personality in terms of three elementary scales. It might be intuitively supposed that three basic measures are rather too few to describe the richness of personality, and indeed other researchers have produced models containing many more traits. Cattell (e.g. Cattell, 1965) argued that personality can be seen in terms of a large number of *surface traits*. These are behaviours which manifest themselves in certain specific situations. However, Cattell argued that these can be grouped into clusters, based on shared features. For example, separate facets of personality all involving the degree to which a person is outgoing might be grouped together because they share an underlying theme of level of extraversion. Cattell argued that surface traits could be condensed in this way to 16 *source*

---

6    E.g. contestants on certain television quiz shows, habitues of karaoke bars who go there *when sober*, etc.

*traits*, which were the most fundamental 'building blocks'. It was the workings of these, he argued, which principally determined personality. The sixteen traits (or *personality factors*) include measures of degree of reserve; degree to which a person thinks in concrete or abstract terms; degree to which a person is self-sufficient (as opposed to being a 'team player'); and degree to which a person is tense. Cattell devised a measure of these traits, which he called the *16PF Test* (the 'PF' stands for 'personality factors'). This creates a personality profile of the testee, in which the relative strength with which they possess each trait is presented. Trying to 'take in' what a profile containing 16 separate measures means can be difficult, so it is possible to interpret the data mathematically to identify what personality type a person possesses. This provides a verbal description of the likely strengths and weaknesses of the person, as well as an indication of the sorts of professions and occupations in which that sort of personality is prevalent.

The 16PF is not the only personality measure which attempts to classify personality on a sizeable number of scales. Others include the *Minnesota Multiphasic Personality Inventory (MMPI)* which was originally devised for identifying forms of mental illness, and produces 10 scales indicating the degree to which a particular aspect of personality may be unusual. The *California Personality Inventory (CPI)* is derived from this, but is primarily intended for 'normal' rather than mentally ill people.

*The 'Big Five' model*

In recent years, attention has focused on a theory of personality which argues that personality is best described as composed of five central traits. For obvious reasons, it has become generally known as the *Big Five model*. The five traits are: *openness, conscientiousness, extraversion, agreeableness* and *neuroticism*, and the model is sometimes referred to by the acronym *OCEAN*, after the traits' initial letters. [7] Openness (O) measures the degree to which the subject is prepared to seek out and cope with the unfamiliar, and by a similar token, the degree to which a person is willing or capable of thinking deeply about

7    It should be noted that some commentators use slightly different terminology, and describe 'extraversion' as *surgency*, 'neuroticism' as *emotional stability*, and 'openness' as *intellect*.

something. Conscientiousness (C) measures the degree to which the subject is organised and reliable, whilst extraversion (E) measures very much the same trait as described in Eysenck's theory. Agreeableness (A) measures the degree to which the subject is prepared to 'go along with' a situation, and accordingly has extremes of gullibility at one end of the scale and cynicism at the other. Neuroticism (N) measures, in a similar manner to Eysenck, the degree of emotional stability a person possesses.

The Big Five model was first conceived following an analysis of English words used to describe personality. At the heart of this lies the *fundamental lexical hypothesis*, which argues that if a feature of human personality is important, then it will have a single word to describe it. This would appear to be generally true of most languages, which have a core vocabulary of words describing roughly the same concepts (John, 1990), though there are certain exceptions. For example, as Bryson (1990) notes, English does not possess a precise single word synonym of the German *schadenfreude* (taking pleasure in other people's misfortunes), nor for the fantastically useful Scottish Gaelic *giomlaireachd* ('having the habit of dropping in at mealtimes'). Notwithstanding these quibbles, there appears to be some support for the fundamental lexical hypothesis. If people are asked to rate English words describing personality attributes, and the ratings are subjected to a factor analysis, then it has been demonstrated that five factors are found, corresponding to the five traits of OCEAN (e.g. Goldberg, 1990). This is not just a feature of English nor indeed other Indo-European languages, since evidence for the Big Five has also been found in other tongues linguistically remote from English, such as Finnish and Estonian (Tartu, 1995).

The concept of a core of five personality measures is not, however, very new. Earlier researchers had made similar claims, and Kentle (1995) has demonstrated that many of the early pioneers of personality research, active at the time of World War I, made claims which could be regarded as precursors of the modern theory. Nor should it be supposed that the Big Five model is necessarily a better measure of personality than earlier ones. Perhaps the most established test of OCEAN is the *NEO-PI*, originally devised by Costa and McCrae (1988), and subsequently revised. People (obviously) differ in their personalities, and the amount of this difference which can be 'explained' by people's scores on the NEO-PI is roughly equal to that explained by their performance on other popular personality tests, such as the EPQ, 16PF and the MMPI (see Kline, 1993, and Pervin, 1993). In other words, the NEO-PI is no better nor worse than other measures. In total, this means that the OCEAN model may explain personality more elegantly than some other models, but it is not necessarily any more accurate.

## Measuring personality

So far, methods of assessing personality have been touched upon tangentially. However, it is important that the reader is aware of the contrasting methods of testing personality which are available to the psychologist.

### Psychoanalysis

Freudian methods essentially involve assessing people on an individual basis. Psychoanalysis is a very 'labour intensive' method – typically, each patient must be assessed on a one-to-one basis, often over a period of years. This is because it is argued that the patient will not easily reveal the contents of his or her subconscious. To tease out the hidden thoughts, the therapist may use any of a series of tests and exercises. These include the famous dream analysis, in which the patient is asked to describe their recent dreams. It is argued that although conscious awareness of 'dark thoughts' may be hidden by the patient, dreams allow them to be presented in the form of a symbolic play. The case of the dream of the giraffe has already been cited above as an example of this. Another method is to instruct the patient to say the first word which enters their head when given a word by the therapist. The rationale is that the patient may be tricked into saying what they 'truly' associate with a particular word (thereby indicating their subconscious wishes) before they have a chance to 'cover up' and present a more socially acceptable answer. To take a (deliberately) simplistic example, if a male patient says 'mother' when presented with the word 'sex' then this might be construed as an interesting indicator of the man's problems.

## Personology

However, detailed individual testing is not confined to Freudian and post-Freudian analysts. Work by Henry Murray in the 1930s and beyond created the concept of *personology* (e.g. Murray, 1938), which argues that the valid study of an individual's personality is a detailed analysis of the individual's life history. Personological approaches are undoubtedly excellent if a detailed examination of an individual is what is required. However, within the general run of personality research they are not of great value, simply because they are too time-consuming to be a practical proposition. Furthermore, by concentrating on what is unique about the individual, they ignore the traits and types which a person may hold in common with others. Personology is not wrong as much as inappropriate in many situations.

## Observation

In certain situations it may be desirable to judge a person's personality by their behaviour rather than by direct questioning. For example, a person may be mentally ill, and questions may be misinterpreted or answered evasively or in a bizarre manner. Observation of 'real life' personality is a powerful tool, but in itself it can be misleading, because of *observer bias*. This means that the observer may simply see what they want to see and disregard other important information because it does not fit their preconceptions of what is 'wrong' with the observed person. This does not have to be done maliciously – however, people tend to be selective in judgements and perception in all circumstances. To counteract this bias, *behavioural checklists* may be used. These are report forms in which the observer must record a series of observations as requested by the checklist. This ensures that the person reports a range of behaviours and not just the ones which he or she thinks are important. In some instances, observers may be asked to use *rating scales*, in which they grade the degree to which a particular attribute (e.g. ease of responding to a member of the opposite sex, level of aggression shown, etc) is displayed. The checklists are designed so that potentially important information is not overlooked.

*Interview*

By similar reasoning to above, interviews may be constructed so that they are *structured* or *semi-structured*. In the former case, the interviewer must take the interviewee through a series of questions in a set order, noting the reply to each in turn. A semi-structured interview allows for the interviewer to follow up the interviewee's responses by asking further questions in reaction to what he or she has said. These methods make interviews more formal than an *unstructured interview*, in which there is no fixed agenda. However, the imposition of a structure enables the interviewer to predetermine that important topics will be covered (in an unstructured interview they may get forgotten in the heat of discussion), and also ensures that if more than one person is being interviewed, each will receive the same questions. This is important if, for example, the interviews are part of a job selection process.

*Self-report questionnaire*

A problem with observational and interview techniques is that whilst they can elicit a useful indication of what a person's 'surface' personality is like, they give little indication of the forces which shape it. This is the main reason for the self-report questionnaire, and the prime examples of it have already been mentioned, such as the 16PF, the EPQ, etc. Self-report questionnaires are designed for a person to answer by themselves, and are called self-report for the obvious reason that they require the person to report on him- or herself. Usually they are in the form of a paper and pencil test, but computerised versions, in which the person sees questions presented on a VDU and must press a button in response, are on the increase. Questions in a self-report questionnaire usually require a person to answer either 'yes', 'no' or (in some tests) 'unsure' to a series of statements. These typically present descriptions of behaviours indicative of particular personality attributes. For example, a person who replies 'yes' to a lot of questions such as 'are you the sort of person who likes to go to parties?' is likely to be an extravert. Similarly, someone who replies 'yes' to lots of statements such as 'is the world a miserable place?' may be suffering from depression. As mentioned earlier, test designers also often incorporate a lie scale to ensure that people do not provide impossibly virtuous (and untruthful) answers in the hope of making a good impression.

Self-report questionnaires are usually created around a particular theoretical stance. Hence, the Eysenck test measures the personality traits which Eysenck feels are central to his model of personality. Likewise, Cattell's 16PF assesses those traits which *he* feels are central to *his* model. In fact, as has already been seen, no matter what the reasoning behind them, most of the mainstream personality tests are about equally good at predicting personality (see e.g. Pervin, 1993).

Not all self-report questionnaires are concerned with measuring the whole personality, and several have the more specific aim of measuring particular aspects of personality. For example, the *Bem Sex Role Inventory* is a measure of the degree to which a person holds 'traditional' male and female values (e.g. a stereotypical male value is to be forceful, and a stereotypical female value is to be nurturing). There is no 'natural law' which states that men must solely hold 'masculine' values, and women 'feminine' ones. Indeed, the author of the test argues that it is useful to have an *androgynous personality* (see e.g. Bem, 1974) in which more positive aspects of both genders are present (e.g. to be nurturing without being subservient, forceful without being aggressive, etc).

Another, and more controversial, example of a more specialised measure is the *honesty test* (also known as *integrity test*). It is well-established that companies suffer from employee theft, ranging from relatively innocuous appropriation of small amounts of stationery to wholesale theft of products. The effects of such behaviour go beyond the workplace – companies recover their losses by charging higher prices for their products. Therefore, in the long run, everyone suffers because of employee dishonesty. For this reason, testing that potential and existing employees are honest is in principal a sensible policy. In practice, it is fraught with difficulties. If someone is honest and admits to past misdeeds, will he or she be at a disadvantage compared with someone who has been more dishonest in the past and has convincingly lied on the test? Evidence on the usefulness of the honesty test is mixed. Cunningham, Wong and Barbee (1994) report that allowing for some exaggerated responses, the test is basically fair. In a similar vein, Bernardin and Cooke

(1993) report that an honesty test was an accurate predictor of future thefts by employees. Other researchers have been less supportive. For example, Guastello and Rieke (1991) argue that honesty tests can be easily faked, whilst Saxe (1991) reports that they are a poor predictor of future honesty. Therefore, for the moment the jury is out on the worthiness of such measures.

### Projective test

A final form of test to be considered takes a different form from others so far mentioned, and has its roots in psychoanalysis. Most tests require a person to answer questions set by the tester. In *projective tests*, the person is shown a picture or an object, and is asked to describe the thoughts it inspires. The most famous example of this is the *Rorschach Inkblot Test*, in which the person is shown a series of inkblots not unlike the 'paint butterflies' most children learn to create in art classes.[8] The inkblots are abstract in shape, but, in the same manner that it is possible to see pictures in clouds or the flames of a fire, it is possible to imagine pictures in the blots. People encountering the test for the first time are often alarmed at the amount of sexual imagery they can see in the blots. This is normal.[9] The test is less concerned with what pictures people see as the variety of types of pictures (e.g. does the person seem only to see pictures of animals?), where the pictures are seen (e.g. the does the person see them only on features at the edges of the blots?) and whether the person only looks at the pictures from one angle. The inkblot test was devised for use in psychoanalysis, and was intended to elicit thoughts normally suppressed (by reasoning similar to that for the other psychoanalytic tests mentioned above). A test similar in aims and rationale is the *Thematic Apperception Test*. The testee is shown a picture by the experimenter and must make up a story based upon it. For example, a picture of a man and a small child standing together which elicited a story about child abuse might give cause for concern.

---

8    I.e. put some paint splodges on one half of a piece of paper, and before it is dry, fold the wet paint side on to the dry; press down hard and then unfold. Some of the paint will transfer to the dry side, thereby creating a symmetrical design.

9    Though salivating with excitement is probably not.

# Causes and continuity of personality

*Nature versus nurture*

As with intelligence research, there is controversy over the degree to which personality is determined by nature or nurture (see Chapter 2). The debate has followed roughly the same path as that for intelligence. However, to save the reader the tedium of repeating the same arguments and counter-arguments, a consensus opinion is that approximately half the variability in personality is due to genetic factors, and half to environmental (see e.g. Pervin, 1993 for an overview, or Bouchard *et al.*, 1990, for details of a specific study). Some of the most persuasive evidence has come from studies of adopted twins and siblings and the relationship between their scores on personality tests and those of genetic and adopted relatives. If a person has test scores which are similar to those of genetic relatives, but with whom he or she has not lived, then this points to a genetic factor underlying intelligence. Similarly, if a person has a similar personality to someone he or she has grown up with, but who is not genetically related, then this indicates an environmental cause of personality. Some of the genetic factors underlying personality appear to be remarkably strong. For example, Bouchard *et al.* (1990) found that certain personality measures were held in common by monozygotic (*MZ*) twins reared apart as strongly as by MZ twins reared together. This, however, should not be surprising. It has been noted that the apparently complex extraversion–introversion trait might be controlled by a very simple mechanism governing the general state of activation of part of the nervous system. Accordingly, it would not be surprising to find a genetic factor.

In certain circumstances, the relationship between personality and nature–nurture may be rather complex. For example, Lyons *et al.* (1995) provide evidence that the level of antisocial behaviour may be primarily attributable to environmental factors in teenagers, but in adults, it may be more strongly attributed to genetic causes. A similarly complex picture is provided by Bergeman *et al.* (1993) who demonstrated a strong genetic component governing responses to questions about Openness and Conscientiousness on the NEO-PI, but a stronger environmental influence on measures of Agreeableness. The explanations for these findings are relatively complex, but they demonstrate that personality is not simply a combination of genetics *and* environment, but a complex interaction of the two.

*Person–situation debate*

A concept related to the nature–nurture debate is the issue of *person–situation* (or *trait–situation*). Essentially, this concerns the degree to which a person's personality and behaviour patterns are an intrinsic part of the person, and how much they are due to the situation in which the person finds him- or herself. For example, it is clear that people tend to be very formal and 'on their best behaviour' at job interviews, but the same code of conduct would be considered odd or even impolite at a birthday party. It is therefore clear that the situation can shape behaviour. Equally, it is clear that relative to each other, people differ in personality across situations. For example, an introverted person will tend to be withdrawn across most situations relative to an extraverted person. Thus, some 'basic' aspects of personality remain with a person across situations. This is *not* necessarily the same as the nature–nurture argument. If a person has a long-lasting trait, then this does not means that it is genetically created – a perfectly plausible case can be made that it is the product of early upbringing. For example, there is considerable evidence that the first-born child in a family is more likely to succeed in certain competitive careers. This is probably because parenting methods are more likely to emphasise rewards and punishments to the first-born child, whilst later offspring may escape quite such close attention (see Coon, 1995, for a review).

Again, it can be demonstrated that personality changes over the life span. Although it does not usually change by a great deal once adulthood is reached (e.g. McCrae and Costa, 1990), nonetheless, there will be some shifts. For example, Smith (1992) demonstrated that if the same people are given a personality test and then re-tested at a later point in their lives, the longer the gap between test sessions, the more their test scores have changed. This may at first sight appear to prove the situation argument – namely, that people's personalities alter with changing circumstances. However, it be equally plausibly argued that it would be foolish to have an overly-rigid personality which could not change to meet different circumstances. Accordingly, part of a genetic programme could allow the person to alter their behaviour to accommodate change.

In reality, it is difficult to judge how either side of the person–situation debate might be conclusively proven. To take a deliberately extreme example – showing that a person remained the same across every conceivable situation might prove the 'person' argument, but it could equally show someone with a *very* strange character (e.g. would someone who behaved in just the same way at a funeral, a sports match, and a wedding be considered 'normal'?). Similarly, the demonstration that someone had a different personality for different occasions could not be taken as proof of the 'situation' argument. It has already been noted that it is expected that people will behave differently from 'normal' on some occasions, because societal pressure and custom dictates this. Therefore, acting differently in different situations may be a consistent feature of personality.

FURTHER READING

McCrae and Costa (1990), Monte (1987), Pervin (1993) and Ross (1992) provide useful introductions to more detailed discussions of the key issues raised in this chapter.

# CHAPTER 4

# Social Psychology

## Introduction

Many branches of psychology are concerned with the individual. Either they are concerned with how and why he or she is different from others (e.g. individual differences, mental illness) or how the mind of the individual works (e.g. memory). However, humans are also social creatures, and social psychology is the study of how people interact socially. Arguably, most psychology students are initially attracted to the subject because of one of the applied branches, but it is social psychology which later captures their attention. In part this may be a reaction against the perceived arid nature of many of the other branches of the discipline, with their emphasis on detailed examinations of aspects of mental behaviour which are in everyday life uninteresting (e.g. how we recognise shapes, how we remember lists of numbers, etc). In contrast, social psychology covers many topics which are fascinating in themselves, such as how we make friends and fall in love, or why people join particular groups or cults. In this chapter, an overview of some of the most popular and frequently-cited topics will be given. As with any introductory chapter, not all areas will be covered and those left out are not necessarily of less importance. For those readers interested in pursuing matters further, a reading list is provided at the end of the chapter.

## Conformity, compliance and obedience

One of the key questions in social psychology is the extent to which people will follow other people's wishes. Clearly psychologists have not found a foolproof method of doing this, or the world would be controlled by psychologists. However, it would appear that several core methods describe many instances in which people can be made to follow a desired path. These are often categorised into *conformity* (adapting one's behaviour to 'fit in' with a particular group's code of conduct), *compliance* (adapting one's behaviour following a *request* by another person) and *obedience* (adapting one's behaviour following a *command* by another person).

## Obedience

If a list were ever compiled of 'Psychology's Greatest Hits', then Milgram's conformity experiment (e.g. Milgram, 1965) would undoubtedly be in the Top Ten. The experiment (like many others in certain branches of social psychology) resembles a practical joke in very poor taste, and is conducted as follows. Person A is participating in a 'learning experiment' along with person B. A and B are told that one of them will take the part of the teacher and one of them the learner. Lots are drawn and A is made the teacher and B the learner. B is strapped into a chair which can be made to give electric shocks. A is given a mild shock to demonstrate how painful this can be. A is then put in an adjoining room where he can hear B but not see him.[1] A reads out questions to which B must respond. Every time B gives a wrong answer, A is told to give him an electric shock. As the experiment progresses, A is told to give increasingly large shocks, even though there are 'danger' signs on the equipment warning A not to go past a certain strength of shock. B has been calling out that the shocks are hurting him. If A demurs, he is told phrases by the experiment's organisers along the lines of 'you must continue' or 'the experiment must be completed'. B continues to give wrong answers – will A go past the stated safe limit and give B a dangerously large shock?

Given this bald statement of the experiment, people new to Milgram's experiment argue that person A will refuse at a fairly early stage in the experiment. The thought of giving painful electric shocks, especially for something as trivial as a 'learning experiment', is abhorrent. People who argue this are in good company, since psychiatrists and other knowledgeable professionals Milgram approached before running the experiment argued very much the same thing. However, in the original study, *nobody* dropped out until the level of shock reached 300 volts and, incredibly (for once the word is not being misused), 65 per cent gave the maximum possible shock of

---

1    In the original experiment, all participants were male.

450 volts. Lest readers suppose that Milgram had inadvertently chosen a group of psychopaths to act as teachers, the experiment was subsequently replicated using other groups of people in a variety of permutations and cultures. Nor is the effect restricted to men. Women subjects were subsequently found to perform in much the same manner.

At this point it should be stressed that person B was never in reality given shocks. He was a confederate of the experimenter and the drawing of lots was rigged so that he always became the learner. The protests and cries of pain uttered by B were acted out. However, person A *did not know this*. As far as he was concerned, he was inflicting pain on B. Why?

Milgram's initial impetus was a fascination with why so many Germans could have participated in Nazi atrocities. It is one thing not to protest about mass genocide through fear of becoming a victim oneself. However, it is quite another to become a participant. Many people in the Allied nations consoled themselves with a comforting myth that some flaw in the German character made people blindly obey whoever was in power and that 'it couldn't happen here'. What Milgram proved was that a distressingly high proportion of people anywhere are capable of obeying orders simply because they have been told to do so. No single argument can account for all of this phenomenon. However, certainly part of the issue is that people tend to obey authority figures. Several experiments (see Bushman, 1984) have demonstrated that people are more likely to obey a request from a person in uniform than if the request is from the same person wearing 'ordinary' clothes. For example, a firefighter or even a person wearing a 'uniform' (though with no specific indications of which service it represents) asking for a small amount of money from passers-by will more often than not receive it, whilst the same person in other clothing will tend not to receive the money.

It is easy to mock such behaviour, but we should be aware of what we are mocking. Much of society's structure is built upon an implicit respect for authority figures, and obeying orders *per se* is not necessarily wrong. For example, if we disobey uniformed personnel's requests for a small amount of help, are we similarly going to disregard police warnings that there is a bomb in the building? Often, 'classic' social psychology experiments work by showing what happens when a social practice which is normally a sound rule of thumb is pushed beyond morally sensible limits. Be that as it may, this does not entirely explain the behaviour of Milgram's volunteers. Although a predisposition to obey orders may explain why people started the experiment, it does little to account for why they carried on with it – the excuse that 'I was only obeying orders' has rung hollow since the Nuremberg trials. Part of the explanation may be that the participants thought that they were not ultimately responsible for their actions. In other words, they carried on with their task because somebody else had given them permission, and if anything went wrong, it was the other person's fault. If people are made aware that *they* are to blame *as well*, then willingness to continue with the experiment diminishes. Again, the more the participants were aware of the consequences of their actions, the less willing they were to continue. Thus, if the participant could only hear person B, they were more willing to go to the limit than if they could see him, and if he had to put person B's hand directly onto a metal plate to administer the shock, then willingness was even less.[2] A final point to note is that people are less willing to continue if others also refuse. If the experiment was run with confederates joining person A as 'co-experimenters', and the confederates refused to continue past a certain point, then only a minority of people continued to the maximum shock level (see Milgram, 1974).

The evidence therefore indicates that it is relatively easy to get people to obey orders, but explaining why is rather more complex. Before concluding this discussion, it should be noted that since Milgram ran his experiments, ethical codes of experimental conduct have been made much stricter, and it is doubtful if many institutions would today support this research.

### Compliance

In obedience studies, a direct command is given to people and the critical measure is whether this command is obeyed. Compliance is a subtler matter. Here a *request* is being made, which the recipient is at liberty to disobey or ignore. If the request is intrinsically sensible then, not surprisingly, a person is likely to agree. For example, asking people to come to a sale because all

---

2    Though 30 per cent of people still went to the maximum voltage.

goods are reduced to ten per cent of their original price is likely to meet with an enthusiastic response. Again, if the service being offered is rare, this also will, sensibly enough, be attractive. Even so, there are other instances where a reasonable request will not be met with a universal response (e.g. requests by health authorities for people to give up smoking). If sensible requests are not uniformly met, what hope is there of persuading a person to respond favourably to an unreasonable request? Research has shown that several options are available.

The first is *reciprocity*. This works on the principle that people dislike feeling that they owe somebody else something, and so have to offer something back in return. This is neatly seen in the behaviour of some religious groups who hand out a 'gift' of a flower or a cheap paperback to passers-by, and then ask for a small contribution in return. The passers-by are made to feel uncomfortable that they have received something and are now 'in debt', so to restore the balance and remove this feeling, they give a donation. Even a few pence will more than pay for the flower or book. Again, there are the familiar 'free gifts' offered 'just' for trying out a product and which are 'yours to keep' even if you decide to return the product itself.

Like other techniques, reciprocity has its limits, particularly because it may not always be feasible for the 'seller' to offer something (e.g. the response sought may be too big for a simple gift to act as an inducement). However, there are many more weapons in the seller's armoury. For example, another common method is the *foot-in-the-door* technique. In this, people are first made a modest offer which it would be hard to refuse. If this is complied with, then a much bigger request is made. A classic study of this was made by Freedman and Fraser (1966), in which a male interviewer 'phoned women at home as a representative of 'a consumer group'. He then asked a few innocuous questions about soap brands and rang off. Several days later, he 'phoned again, this time asking if the woman would permit a team of people to visit her house and make a thorough inventory of all her belongings, and be given freedom to go through cupboards, drawers, etc. About half of the women agreed, compared with about a fifth who were only 'phoned once and just asked the second question. Subsequent studies have found similar, if less pronounced results, and the general explanation is that the effect is probably due to enhanced self-image – helping at a modest level makes people think they are 'good helpers' so they are more likely to comply with future requests which will provide further evidence of this status (see Baron and Byrne, 1991).

The reverse to the above is the *door-in-the-face* technique. In this, the initial request is a large and unreasonable one, which the seller makes knowing that the recipient will refuse. The seller then makes a second and smaller request to which the recipient is more likely to accede than if simply given this second request only. A frequently-cited instance of this is a study by Cialdini *et al.* (1975). People were stopped in the street and asked if they would act as unpaid counsellors to a group of juvenile delinquents for the next two years. This request was (naturally) refused, so it was followed up with a milder request – would the passers-by be willing to take the said group on a trip to the zoo? About half the passers-by agreed (compared with about a fifth who were only asked the second question). Explanations for the effectiveness of the door-in-the-face technique vary, but the most plausible argument is that it is again a question of redressing an imbalance. People feel that they 'owe' the person making the request a favour for having turned them down, and so they are more amenable to offering a smaller favour by way of compensation.

Other techniques are more or less directly concerned with selling. For example, the *that's not all* technique is an example of what sales people sometimes call the 'clincher' or the 'sweetener'. Suppose that a consumer is indecisive about buying a particular product and *then* discovers that it comes with an extra gift; is this more persuasive than knowing from the start that the product and gift come as a complete package? The answer, surprisingly, is 'yes'. The term comes from the familiar sales patter of advertisers who introduce a product, eulogise about its qualities and price, and then add 'but that's not all folks – you also get …'. Like so many issues in compliance research, why this technique works is open to debate. Baron and Byrne (1991) suggest that people feel more obliged to accept the product when the seller makes what is seen as a concession (i.e. there is an induced feeling of imbalance which can be rectified by buying the product). Another possibility is that the extra item or service being offered has a greater impact when it is added to

the advantages of the basic product which the consumer has already calculated than if it is considered from the start as part of the initial package.

Another technique operates in the opposite manner to this. The *low ball
technique* offers the consumer a product and only when agreement is near is
the consumer told about the 'hidden extras' which will increase the price (e.g.
that tax is not included in the initially quoted cost) or that the product has
limitations (e.g. electrical goods which will need a mains adaptor not included in the package). Such techniques clearly work, since many computers
and some items of hi-fi are advertised in just this manner (in the UK at least).
Presumably, the consumer is so close to completing a deal that withdrawal
will create a feeling of imbalance (again, the financial cost of the extras is usually not very great in proportion to the total cost of the item being sold).

As can be seen, methods of eliciting compliance are varied in their approach, and each is likely to be particularly effective in specific situations. It
must also be noted that more general variables also play an important role in
persuading people. For example, a well-groomed individual is more likely to
persuade people to buy cosmetics than an ill-groomed one. Again, people are
generally more likely to be responsive if the person doing the persuading is
working for an altruistic cause, such as a charity. This may seem an obvious
point, but it is worth noting that, under some circumstances, techniques
which fail when used to promote an ostensibly commercial concern work
when the same requests were made on behalf of a charitable concern (e.g.
Patch, 1986). This issue of *legitimacy* (i.e. the perceived right of the agent to
be making requests) permeates much of the compliance literature.

### Conformity

The methods so far discussed have all directly presented a person with an
order or request. In conformity, the method is more tangential – in this case
we are interested in what makes a person come to share the beliefs and
behaviours of others. As with many other areas of social psychology, what is
of primary interest are instances of exaggeration of 'normal' behaviour. Many
instances of conformity are clearly a matter of 'common sense'. For example,
people obey basic rules of driving such as always driving on the correct side
of the road because to do otherwise is dangerous. Again, people are usually

peaceful and law-abiding because of fear of punishment and a general appreciation of the pragmatics of democracy. However, other conforming behaviours are less obvious. For example, why should British lawyers have to wear wigs and gowns in court? Why should a married couple both adopt the husband's surname? In such situations, pragmatics cannot provide an answer.

In a classic study by Asch (e.g. Asch, 1951), a group of people was given a 'perception experiment'. The people were shown a line and next to it three other lines, one of which was the same length as the first one. The task was to decide which of the three lines was the same length. Since the three lines were of palpably different lengths, and it was possible to compare them against the other line, the task is under normal circumstances very easy. However, as with Milgram's work, there is a strong 'practical joke' element in the experiment. The group of volunteers consisted of confederates of the experimenter, with the exception of one genuine test subject. Each member of the group in turn was asked to judge which lines matched, with the test subject giving his or her judgement after several others. For the first few trials, everyone gave the correct answer. Then, uniformly, all the confederates began to give the same wrong answer. What should the genuine test subject do – stick to his or her guns and give the true answer, or defy the evidence of their eyes and give the same answer as the rest of the group? Asch found that about a quarter stuck to their guns, but the rest went along with the group response at least some of the time.

Why are people often so willing to follow a group norm, even when it is against their better judgement? Many reasons have been suggested, and none by itself probably suffices. To a certain extent, the effect probably relies upon the culture in which the person is raised. The greater the emphasis on collective effort, the more likely people are to conform. There is also evidence that different generations may have different levels of conformity. For example, Perrin and Spencer (1981) found practically no conformity when they ran an exact replication of Asch's experiment on students in the early 1980s (other studies have tended to find some, but not to the extent found in the original study).[3] Again, there is a general wish to belong to social groups, and if this involves some sacrifice of individuality in order to fit in, then so be it. Another consideration is the size of the group. The more people who are added to the group, the greater the conformity – but only up to a certain point. Adding more and more can result in diminishing returns: adding more people does not appreciably raise conformity any further. A final consideration is that the group must speak with one mind. Even a single dissenting voice can cut through a conforming urge. Asch found that putting a dissenting confederate amongst the group caused the test subject to conform on fewer occasions – even if the dissenting confederate was portrayed as severely myopic.

## Interpersonal attraction

Work on conformity, compliance and obedience can leave one with a rather bleak view of social activity. By looking at relative extremes, it implies that social intercourse is little more than manipulation. Of course this is not true, and it should be stressed that much of our interaction is based upon sensible pragmatics. This capacity for itemising pleasurable social activities and making them seem mechanistic perhaps reaches its zenith in work on *interpersonal attraction* – quite simply, the study of how people become attracted to each other and form emotional bonds.

The causes of initial attraction and the strength of feeling held are many and varied. Some factors play a role before the first meeting takes place. For example, level of arousal can help determine how attractive a person appears. In a famous experiment by Dutton and Aron (1974), the rather unusual location of a deep valley gorge was chosen. There were two bridges over this gorge – a high and a low one, crossing the former being the rather more frightening experience. Two groups of male volunteers were made to cross

3    It is possible that participants in these replication studies were more aware of the deviousness of psychology experiments than students in the 1950s. In other words, they do not conform because they are aware that the 'perception experiment' is a ploy right from the start. The author's own experience of trying to replicate the experiment is that students 'smell a rat' almost at once.

one or other of the bridges. Whilst on the bridge, they were interviewed and tested (e.g. writing a brief story about a picture) by a female researcher, who gave the men a 'phone number if they wished to inquire later about any aspects of the study. Those men who had met the researcher on the high bridge (and hence were in a more aroused emotional state) were far more likely to contact her afterwards (the primary motivation was *not* to talk about the experiment).

A rather more obvious candidate for attraction when first meeting is physical attractiveness. It is obvious that within a particular society, certain types of appearance are favoured more than others. However, taste is fickle and changes across time and between cultures. For example, in western culture, over the last fifty years, the 'ideal' woman's body shape has fluctuated between the 'voluptuous' Marilyn Monroe-type figure to very thin 'waifs'. Across cultures, different parts of a woman's body are most highly admired, ranging from the nape of the neck, to breasts, to feet, to buttocks, to ear lobes. Such a variety of values demonstrates very clearly that admiration based on looks is something shaped by societal whims and is a hollow desire. However, whether one approves or not, physical appearance *is* important, at least in establishing early attraction, although once in a relationship, attractiveness becomes less important (see e.g. Buunk, 1996). People may assume that physical attraction only applies to sexual relationships, but this is not true. Generally, the more physically attractive a person is rated by others, the more likely it is that his or her non-sexual friends are also rated as attractive.

Although physical attractiveness is an important factor, the reasons why it is so are not fully understood. There are obvious reasons why someone who is palpably physically or mentally unhealthy may not be everybody's choice of a partner, because there are clear practical disadvantages in many such relationships. However, why some physical characteristics are preferred above others seems largely a matter of taste. Some commentators have argued that certain physical shapes convey an evolutionary advantage. Thus, a woman with large breasts may indicate that she is capable of suckling young, whilst a thin rather than a fat man might be a better hunter. These arguments are often largely spurious at a detailed level, both in their own terms (e.g. breast size has little to do with milk capacity and arguably fat people are a better option because they can survive for longer on less food) and also because different cultures drawn from the same gene pool can have radically different ideas of beauty. A more general argument stems from the argument that physically attractive people are likely to have physically attractive offspring. Anyone wanting to increase the chances of their genes surviving down the generations should therefore breed with as attractive a person as possible so that their offspring will also be attractive and stand a better chance of mating. This argument is plausible in many animal species where breeding is in response to a ritualised mating display and breeding success largely depends upon physical appearance at this one event. However, human interaction and breeding rituals are less dependent upon single displays, so such a simplistic explanation is unlikely to be as valid. If nothing else, practically everybody who chooses will eventually form some type of sexual relationship, and not everybody can be physically attractive.

Regardless of the reason, people tend to have partners and friends of a similar level of physical attraction. Why this should be so is yet again open to discussion. The most likely explanation is one of balance. People tend to feel happiest if there is an equilibrium between what the two people are perceived to bring to the relationship. Thus, if one person is very attractive and the other is not, then a feeling of dissatisfaction can be created. Interestingly, if there is an imbalance, this is felt badly by both the attractive and less attractive partner (Buunk and VanYperen, 1991). This may also be the best simplistic explanation of why when there is a disequilibrium, one partner often 'compensates' for lack of physical attractiveness by being more abundantly blessed with other traits, such as a particularly sharp intellect or 'good' personality. There is of course a grave danger with any work of this nature to assume that relationships can be reduced to a level of barter ('I can't be friends with you because our aesthetic appeal scores are too far apart', etc). It is therefore important to stress that what has been said so far is only a *general description*, not a prescription of what 'must' take place.

Upon first meeting, the initial verbal exchange can be crucial. Some people spend a great deal of time thinking up an opening line – a largely wasted activity, since few men or women find a supposedly 'witty' chat-up line appealing. Generally, an innocuous greeting such as 'hello' will work as well as anything (e.g. Kleinke, Meeker and Staneski 1986). Another point worth noting is that even if a 'witty' remark is successful, how does one follow it up?

As can be seen from the above examples, the factors involved in initial attraction are varied, and this is not a complete list (see e.g. Baron and Byrne, 1991 for further discussion). However, for any of them to work, two people have obviously to meet. Small wonder then that one of the biggest factors in attraction is *propinquity* – in other words, the amount of contact two people have with each other. It is obvious that for two people to be attracted, they must meet, but the simple act of encountering each other regularly can have a major effect. Several studies have illustrated this point by demonstrating that students who have rooms near each other are more likely to become friends than students with rooms some distance apart (e.g. Festinger, Schachter and Back, 1950). This holds true even allowing for such confounding variables as being on the same degree course, etc. Part of the reason for the attraction is probably that people living in a particular building are likely to have something in common because, be it that they chose to live there and/or because they are attending the same institution. However, simply the act of repeatedly being exposed to each other's presence (the *mere exposure effect*), is also likely to increase liking. Practically anything not actually aversive becomes liked more the more frequently we are exposed to it (e.g. Moreland and Zajonc, 1982).

It is easy to overplay the propinquity argument, however, especially when considering romantic relationships. The findings that people tend to marry[4] partners living within a relatively short distance or that they work in the same building *might* prove the propinquity case, but they also demonstrate that people with similar social status tend to marry each other (since people in the same socio-economic group tend to live in the same areas and have similar status jobs). One of the more interesting demographic statistics is that with the advent of railways, the average geographical distance separating

---

4    The term is used throughout as a shorthand for 'form a stable live-together relationship', since it still is the commonest form this takes. No negative judgement is intended towards people in other forms of relationship.

couples before marriage doubled. In other words, given the opportunity, people will search for partners further afield. Therefore, being in frequent contact with another person is not enough to guarantee a lasting relationship. Indeed, if a person is socially reserved, then propinquity may actually be aversive.

Discussions of why people stay with each other after the initial attraction are varied. As has been noted, friends and partners tend to be of similar attractiveness, but there are many people who are equally physically attractive, and not all of them are friends. Generally, people tend to be equally matched on not just looks but also many other key factors, such as attitudes, social status and height. At a symbolic level, this becomes an exercise in economics and balancing the books. Partners weigh up their assets and liabilities against those of their partner and a gross discrepancy may lead to the ending of the relationship. Against this is weighed the investment already placed in the relationship. If this is heavy, then leaving may mean surrendering too many assets for it to be economically feasible (e.g. Levinger, 1980). Successful relationships are often those in which partners recognise that there are times when the balance will be biased towards the other partner, but in the long term the equilibrium will be restored.

A problem for some people new to Psychology is that this reduction of romance to a very mechanical level can be off-putting. Aesthetics aside, there are reasons to be careful about how much weight we put on such research. First, although it describes the typical types of relationships, it cannot be taken as prescriptive that this is what should always be the case. Again, a lot of what is written is little more than received wisdom dressed up in more exact terminology. For example, finding that happily married couples tend to be similar is not, in the cold light of day, all that surprising.

## Groups

A need to belong is not just restricted to emotional relationships – generally, people are also members of groups. The definition of 'group' differs between authors, but the general consensus is that it consists of two or more people; the said people have a common purpose or interest; and the said people interact with each other. The latter condition (about interaction) is important, since it distinguishes a group from a *collective*, which is merely a set of people who have a common interest but who do not interact (e.g. all the stamp collectors in the world are a collective of stamp collectors, but amongst their number, only those who meet together to, for example, discuss their hobby, might be called groups). As with other social behaviours, there are obvious reasons why groups are a good idea. Strength in numbers, the enjoyment of socialising with people with the same interests, the collective effort being greater than the sum of individual endeavours, etc, are amongst many reasons which can be cited. However, what are less obvious are the forces binding groups together and instances where group behaviour can go wrong.

Some of the key reasons for joining a group have already been given. To a certain extent, the same factors in modified form help keep a group together (*cohesiveness*). People with similar interests, bound to a group with sets of regulations (written or unwritten) of correct behaviour, are given a sense of 'belonging' in a way which non-members by definition cannot share. Generally, and not at all surprisingly, the greater the emotional bond between members, the more clearly defined the goals and interests of the group, etc, the stronger the cohesiveness (this also generally means that smaller groups are more cohesive than large ones).

Cohesive groups are a necessary part of social existence and are generally beneficial. However, cohesiveness can go wrong, in some cases horribly so. *Cults* are an extreme example of this, in which members are united by an unquestioning obedience to a leader or set of rules, going well beyond normal levels of cohesiveness, since many of the *norms* (i.e. accepted or required behaviour to remain in the group) are not what would be considered rational in a 'normal' group (e.g. signing over one's personal wealth and property to the cult). People are bound not just by shared beliefs, however, but also by a dependency upon the cult for support (removal of personal property and means of financial support creates a real need for the cult to provide even the most basic aspects of sustenance). Why people should join cults is often baffling to outsiders, especially since many members are palpably intelligent and articulate. Theories abound, but a generally accepted principle is that members prior to joining were questioning their own beliefs or 'purpose in life' and felt insecure. Cults, by providing security and removing the need to think about what to do (the cult will tell one what to do, and will feed, clothe and house one) remove all this uncertainty. That the individual abnegates all personal wealth, identity and freedom, may to some people be an acceptable sacrifice (see e.g. Stevens, 1979). Whether this is ultimately morally wrong is a debate beyond the confines of psychology, though arguably the principal concern is the degree to which the leaders of the cult materially benefit from this behaviour (e.g. a cult in which all the followers practically starve, whilst the leader accrues millions in a Swiss bank account, is clearly wrong; but a cult in which everyone makes genuine sacrifices and works towards a morally worthy goal is another matter).

The cult is of course an extreme form of the group – readers worried that their monthly stamp collectors club meeting will turn them into unquestioning zombies are somewhat wide of the mark. However, within more 'normal' groups, behaviour borne out of cohesion can be harmful. An obvious example of this is *group prejudice* (Allport, 1958), in which a group decides that it dislikes some or all categories of non-members, and this view must be expressed by all group members, regardless of the level to which they personally believe this prejudice. Such behaviour may initially have a grain of validity. For example, groups may develop a prejudice against others out of an understandable if misplaced pride in their own worth. Again, groups united by misfortune may become prejudiced because they blame non-members for their suffering.

However, whatever its origins, group prejudice is in itself irrational and harmful. Indeed, the origins can in some instances derive from no more than arbitrarily being assigned to a group. In a famous study by Sherif *et al.* (1961), boys attending an American summer camp at Robbers Cave were arbitrarily assigned to two groups – the 'Rattlers' and the 'Eagles'. Within a couple of days, the two groups were engaged in bitter (and physically violent) rivalry, even though the reason for group membership was no more than essentially arbitrary assignment. Group prejudice can in part be overcome by forcing members of different groups to cooperate with each other. For example, in the Robbers Cave study, the two groups were forced to work together to repair the water supply to the camp (actually damaged by the experimenters), without which both groups would have lacked water. However, prejudices can still be deep rooted. In part this goes beyond the question of groups to the nature of individual personalities. It has long been argued that some individuals are inherently more prejudiced than others. An early measure of this was the *F Scale* (the 'F' stood for 'fascism'); later measures, to capture the concept that left-wing people can also be intolerant of others, have tended to use more politically neutral terms such as *dogmatism, authoritarian personality,* etc. These all argue the same basic point – namely, that some people more strongly believe in such phrases as 'it's them or us', and the need for the 'firm smack of government' than others do. People high in this trait also are more likely to detect plots threatening their way of life and immorality amongst people not in their group. Not surprisingly, prejudices in general are usually higher in such people.

Groups can also be harmful to themselves as well as to individual members. An example of this is *groupthink* (e.g. Janis, 1982). This refers to a collective decision-making process in which policies are decided by going along with the consensus opinion and ignoring or trivialising any viewpoints or factual arguments which run counter to this process. Such collective folly has been argued to be behind many political and commercial disasters (e.g. launching a new product which fails to sell in an embarrassingly big way). Janis argues that groupthink can be minimised by ensuring that all voices, including dissenting ones, are heard, and that plans are scrutinised by a 'Devil's advocate'.[5]

From the evidence presented above, it would appear that all groups are a dangerous thing. However, this is not the case. Many groups are necessary and work well. The above arguments demonstrate some instances of what *might* go wrong when insufficient vigilance is exercised and intrinsically rational procedures get out of hand. For example, group prejudice can stem from a basically rational drive for cohesiveness. Again, not all collectively-made mistakes can be attributed to groupthink. Sometimes democrati-

---

5    The term is derived from the Roman Catholic procedure in deciding whether to canonise a
     person – the Devil's Advocate is an official who examines the evidence to see if the person in
     question was *not* truly holy.

cally-made decisions can be wrong, not through overlooking evidence, but because negative factors could genuinely not have been foreseen. Groups are generally rational, in spite of their potential faults.

## Aggression

The discussion of prejudice above leads to the more general issue of aggression – behaviour intended to harm others. Like most social behaviours, this has its origins in a rational act. In violent times, it may be necessary to defend oneself and others against attack, and few cultures would decry the use of aggression in such circumstances, even in extreme forms (the so-called *norm of reciprocity*). At a less extreme level, we may use verbal arguments which may hurt others in order to get our own way. If that goal is palpably for the greater good, then such aggression can again be seen to be a rational behaviour. However, everyday experience indicates that aggression is far more commonly iniquitous and often irrational. Using violence to fend off a violent attack might be logical, but the original attack probably was not. Likewise, shouting at a child who has run into the road might be understandable, but hurting the child for a minor misdemeanour is not.

However, the fact that aggression, whilst being highly undesirable in some cases is understandable in others makes the issue of where we draw the line between 'good' and 'bad' aggressive acts difficult. This is not aided by the argument that aggression is a 'natural' act. This was perhaps most famously expressed by Konrad Lorenz (1903–1989), a famous ethologist [a person who studies animal behaviour], in his book *On Aggression* (Lorenz, 1966).[6] The full argument is a complex one, but in part argued that aggressive behaviour in humans may be an evolutionary necessity which 'must' be expressed. Lorenz's sympathies with the Nazi party early in his career (which, in fairness, he later recanted) did not help his case, which was (mis)interpreted as justifying violent behaviour as a necessary release of 'natural' urges. However, at a less extreme level, the concept that there might be a general drive to be aggressive is one which might be accepted by many commen-

6    See also Chapter 11.

tators. Like other psychological traits, this may have a genetic component: in other words, some people are born more aggressive than others. However, this only explains why some people may be more predisposed to *become* aggressive; it tells us little about the nature of aggression itself or the triggers which cause a specific aggressive act.

Explanations of triggers of aggressive acts are legion. One of the most often-cited is the *frustration–aggression hypothesis*. This essentially states that aggression occurs when a person is seeking a particular goal and is frustrated in this attempt. However, the hypothesis in its simplest form has difficulty in explaining why the same level of frustration produces aggression towards others in some situations and less violent reactions in others. Therefore, a modification was introduced – the *cue-arousal theory* (Berkowitz, 1974). This argues that frustration gives rise to a state of anger. The anger predisposes the person to behave aggressively, but the precise form his or her behaviour assumes depends upon the situation the person finds themselves in (the *cues*). This can be illustrated with the *weapons effect* study (Berkowitz and LePage, 1967). Participants took part in a 'learning study' in which they were given shocks by another 'participant' (actually a confederate) when they gave incorrect answers. In reality, the shocks were not given in response to the actual performance, but served the intended purpose of getting the participant annoyed; the more shocks he or she received, the more annoyed they were. When the roles were reversed and the participant got the chance to shock the confederate, more shocks were given the more annoyed the participant was. However, the number of shocks given could also be manipulated by the situation in which the participant found him- or herself. In the test room some items were within view on a table – these were either guns (which obviously could be said to be violent cues) or badminton rackets (neutral cues). Participants gave more shocks when they saw the guns than when they saw the badminton rackets. In another experimental condition, participants were not made angry with shocks before being given the opportunity to shock the confederate. In this case, the presence of the guns had no effect. Subsequent studies have usually (though not always – see Mummendey, 1996 for a summary) found that the presence of violent cues increases aggressive behaviour. Therefore, aggressive behaviour is typically mediated by the cues to hand.

This argument leads into the obvious question – why are some cues more effective than others in eliciting aggression? In part this may be attributable to basic physiological responses. People who feel physically uncomfortable or disoriented may in some cases be more *prone* to be aggressive (hence one reason why alcohol consumption is often related to aggressive acts). In addition, people may learn to associate some cues with aggressive behaviour. For example, in the weapons effect study, guns and badminton rackets can only have the effect they do because people have learnt what these items are for – there is nothing intrinsically threatening or neutral in their visual appearance per se. Again (and not surprisingly), if people have found that aggressive behaviour has been rewarded in the past, then they are more likely to repeat it again. Thus, some poorly socialised children may grow into violent adults, because they have never been adequately taught that using aggression to gain goals is wrong. Again, if people have been exposed to situations in which they have seen others rewarded for violent behaviour, then social learning theory (see Chapter 7) dictates that they are more likely to use aggression themselves.

This in turn leads to the issue of whether exposure to media violence (and television and video sources in particular) leads to aggressive behaviour. The general indications are that over the short term, exposure to a violent programme (and particularly one in which aggression is rewarded and/or the effects of violence on the victim and his or her family are not shown) leads to an increase in violent behaviour. Evidence on the long-term effects (i.e. after several years) of exposure is more equivocal. People who have watched a lot of violent television programmes tend to be more aggressive, *but* such people may in any case be predisposed to be aggressive. In other words, they might watch violent programmes because it matches their tastes, rather than be made violent because they have watched aggressive programmes (see Mummendey, 1996).

If views of aggression make gloomy reading, then studies of behaviour designed to help others (*prosocial behaviour*) can be equally depressing. An often-cited example is the *Kitty Genovese murder*. The eponymous person was a young woman murdered in a New York street in 1964. More than thirty people heard her cries but did nothing. This is cited as a prototypical example of *bystander apathy* – the failure to take action when intervention is needed. A large number of reasons have been cited for this behaviour. Of these, a key argument concerns the number of other bystanders present. In general, and contrary to what might be logically predicted, the more bystanders there are, the lower the probability that *any* of them will offer assistance (Darley and Latané, 1968). Bystanders, when interviewed, often assume that someone else is bound to take action, so they do not bother. When the number of by-standers is small, presumably it becomes apparent to the bystanders that one of *them* must take action if any action is to be taken at all. In other words, the *diffusion of responsibility* is so limited that it is clear where the responsibility for action lies. This does not necessarily mean that bystanders are uncaring. However, there can be a strong reserve against taking action when others are present. For example, several experiments have shown that when faced with an apparent emergency (e.g. smoke entering the room, cries for help from an adjacent room), people are more likely to respond when by themselves than when in a group. This occurs even when (as in the case of smoke entering a room) the individuals themselves are perhaps at greatest risk.

Thus, in both aggressive behaviour and in its antithesis, behaviour is less obvious and clear-cut than 'common sense' explanations would predict.

## Social perception

*Social perception* is the study of how we infer people's attributes from their social behaviour. It thus forms a contrast with the topics covered so far in this chapter, which are largely concerned with how people interact with each other. There are many ways in which we interpret other people. One frequent method is through analysis of *nonverbal communication*. Essentially, this is any information a person reveals about his or her state other than through the use of words. Such information can range from the explicit (e.g. deliberate use of gestures) to the unconscious (e.g. a dilation of the pupils may indicate a heightened level of sexual interest[7]). A wide variety of studies has been done on this topic. In the 1970s some of these became popularised in the study of

---

7    Or that the room is dark.

*body language*. It is well-established that certain body postures can indicate a particular state of mind. For example, people who are very much in agreement tend to adopt similar postures when talking to each other (this is usually done unconsciously). It follows from this sort of research that it might be possible to judge if a person is sexually interested in you just by correctly interpreting their posture and other non-verbal signals. Thus, a plethora of pop psychology books promised definitive guides to cutting out time talking to uninterested people, enabling one to concentrate on those where there was a chance of things going further (perhaps not surprisingly, the books were largely aimed at heterosexual men). Unfortunately for any hapless swain lulled by the promises, the reality is that such signals are often difficult to interpret except under laboratory conditions (hardly analogous to the local disco) and, with a few exceptions, are not invariably shown by every individual on every occasion.

This does not mean that body signals in general are unimportant; far from it. To take the example of *personal space*, it is clear that practically everyone has an invisible layer of space around the body (typically about 18 inches) which should not be entered except during periods of physical intimacy. Friends are allowed within the next space outwards (usually up to about 4 feet away – the distance varies between cultures) and strangers are typically kept at a greater distance still. These unwritten rules are held very firmly. Violation of personal space brings feelings of discomfort that someone is standing 'too close'. In situations where personal space must be infringed (e.g. in a lift/elevator) people will deliberately gaze upwards into middle-distance rather than look directly at each other – the intimacy implied by a direct gaze whilst standing that close would be considered too much of an infringement.

Again, it is worth noting that another important aspect of non-verbal communication – namely, facial gestures – is universally recognised in every culture. The main facial gestures of happiness, surprise, fear, sadness, anger, disgust, and interest, are recognised with roughly equal accuracy the world over (see Argyle, 1983). Cultures vary in their choice of other, more specific, gestures (e.g. compare the American use of one finger versus the British use of two to indicate a hostile reaction). However, at least a rudimentary vocabulary of non-verbal signals is effective and widely-understood.

Another topic of especial interest within social perception is *attribution*. This has a wide variety of applications, but of particular interest is the interpretation of a person's state based upon their actions. Observers have a tendency to assume that anything a person does (particularly a mistake) must be due to his or her internal state, rather than external circumstances. For example, if a waiter trips and drops a tray of drinks, we assume that he is clumsy, rather than that, for example, he tripped over a loose rug. This is an example of a *fundamental attribution error*. Conversely, if observers themselves make mistakes, then they are more likely to attribute these to external agencies. Thus, if we drop a tray of drinks, it was due to someone being stupid enough to make the floor unsafe to walk on. This dichotomy between attributing other people's faults to their internal state and our own to external factors is known as the *actor–observer effect*.

If further proof is needed of the fickleness of social perception, then the work of Asch (1946) on *impression formation* is worth considering. Asch gave people a list of words describing an individual, and then asked people to rate this person's personality. If the list of words was: *intelligent-industrious-impulsive-critical-stubborn-envious*, then the person was rated far more positively than if he or she was described as *envious-stubborn-critical-impulsive-industrious-intelligent*. The two sets of words are of course identical – all that differs is the order in which they are presented. Observers tend to be swayed very strongly by the first few pieces of information they encounter and tend to make subsequent information fit the impression already formed. This is one reason why the advice to dress smartly for a job interview is worth heeding.

FURTHER READING

The study of social psychology covers a lot of ground, and in this chapter we have considered just a few of the topics which form part of the traditional core of the subject. In recent years, the subject has branched out into a wide variety of new areas, and has taken on board many new techniques of study, such as discourse analysis and evidence of textual sources as indices of psychological states. Readers wishing to study further are advised to consider a good general textbook on social psychology. Two amongst many worth considering are Hewstone, Stroebe and Stephenson (1996) and Baron and Byrne (1991). The latter is from a North American perspective, the former from a European view (though there is a considerable overlap between the two). As with any general introductory textbook, the final recommendation to some extent rests upon which book the reader finds most readable.

# CHAPTER 5

# Language

## Introduction

It is generally felt that language is one of the key attributes which distinguishes humans from other species. Although other animals possess at times very sophisticated methods of communication (see Chapter 11) none matches the level of attainment of human language. The study of psychological aspects of language (*Psycholinguistics*) is a large and complex area, involving a lot of jargon which can at first sight be daunting. However, the basic concepts are really not very difficult. What follows is an introduction to some of the key topics, which have been kept as jargon-free as possible.

## Language development

The legend of St Rumwald states that he began professing his faith at birth, 'and died but three days old, after addressing a long sermon to his parents' (Elliott, 1975, p.2).[1] Few of us can claim such linguistic virtuosity, but it is remarkable that, within the first few years of life, we can acquire a rich and complex language; not just its vocabulary, but also its labyrinthine rules of grammar and subtleties of expression.

Early vocal activity consists of a gradual shift from what are often called *basic biological noises* (crying, gurgling, etc) in the first two months of life,[2] to increasingly sophisticated sounds. The next three months see the introduction of cooing and laughing sounds, before the appearance at about five months of *babbling*, in which more rhythmic utterances and phonemes (see

---

1   The probable explanation is that Rumwold was a pagan king who converted to Christianity on his death bed, and thus was 'born again': the legend is an obvious corruption of this.

2   Note that these are *average* ages – there is considerable variety between individual infants.

below) can be heard. These refine further into *melodic utterance* at about nine months, when utterances become more 'sing song' in their quality and sound more 'language like' in overall structure (even if no sense can yet be made). Thereafter the first words become apparent, and the acquisition of a mature speech and linguistic system begins.

Essentially, there are four principal systems a child needs to master. The first is *phonology*, or the sounds used in the language. Any spoken word can be broken down into its constituent *phonemes*. A phoneme might be defined as 'the smallest unit of speech whose substitution or removal from a word causes a change in the word's sound' (Stuart-Hamilton, 1995a). Thus, substituting the 'b' sound in 'bat' with 'g' makes 'gat'; substituting 'b' with 's' makes 'sat', etc.

Babies can distinguish between at least some phonemes from birth, though distinguishing between subtler distinctions, such as 'th' and 'f' may take until school age to master (see Ellis and Beattie, 1986). *Production* of phonemes takes rather longer to accomplish. Some sounds, such as 'p' and 'm' are generally mastered by the second year, but many others may not appear until the child is past four years of age. There are also considerable differences between individuals in the age at which these sounds will be produced. In some instances, one child may produce a particular phoneme two years before another shows the same sound in his or her speech. Books on child care rightly stress to parents that worrying about a child's early apparently 'immature' speech may be unfounded – in most instances, speech will reach a level of 'normality' by the time the child is about five years of age. It should also not be supposed that because a child does not pronounce a word in a mature fashion, he or she does not know the difference between phonemes. This is best illustrated by the *fis phenomenon* (Berko and Brown, 1960). The authors report a young boy talking about his toy fish which he called a 'fis'. When asked 'is this your fis?' the child would reply 'no, it's my fis'. Only when asked 'is this your fish?' did the child reply 'yes, it's my fis'. The child could clearly *hear* the difference between 'fis' and 'fish' even if he could not pronounce it himself.

The second linguistic system a child must acquire is *syntax*, or the grammatical rules which govern the language. Amongst their earliest utterances, children begin to offer single words which are often intended to convey more than one word in their intent. Thus, the single word 'milk' may not just indicate the liquid but also a more complex wish, such as 'I need milk'. Following from this, the average child begins at about 18 months[3] to use two word phrases which more obviously convey an elaborate meaning (e.g. 'milk gone' 'nappy wet' etc). This is followed at about two years with *telegraphic speech*, in which the verbs and nouns are included, but 'function words' such as 'a', 'and' etc, are absent (like the telegrams of yesteryear which were charged by the word; missing function words can be easily mentally 'filled in' by the reader, so they were omitted from the message[4]). Hence such sentences as 'want dinner now', 'mummy where going?', etc. Generally, phrases become 'filled out' and adopt a mature form by the time the child is about four years old. Along the way (at about three years) the typical child begins to use phrases with more than one clause. Children are also fairly sensitive to grammatical rules, resulting in instances of *over-generalisation*. This occurs where a child attempts to use a grammatical rule learnt in one circumstance in an inappropriate setting. The child is not necessarily 'wrong' in doing this. Having heard phrases containing 'you are' a child who says 'I are' has clearly learnt a rule (but not the right one). Again, adding 'ed' to the end of verbs to denote the past tense is a rule which generally works in English, but not always (e.g. 'runned'). Over-generalisation disappears as the child learns the many exceptions which must be applied to irregular verbs and similar linguistic delights.

A third and similar linguistic system is *pragmatics* – an understanding of intent and, typically, social aptness. Everyday language can rarely if ever be interpreted at a purely literal level. The English cliché to a visitor arriving after a long journey – 'would you like to wash your hands?' (a euphemism for 'would you like to use the lavatory?') – is a case in point. However, the use of pragmatics is not just restricted to use of euphemisms; often it is used to convey information without spelling out every little detail. Thus, if asked 'shall

---

3    There are *large* individual differences in ages at which children being to use different linguistic forms; nearly all are 'normal'.

4    E.g. Dorothy Parker's famous telegram from Venice to her editor – 'Streets flooded. Please advise'.

we go to the park?' a reply might be 'it's still raining'. It may be correctly inferred from this reply that the speaker feels that going to the park is unwise
because the ongoing precipitation in the air will cause clothes, skin and hair
to become soaked with water, thereby making the experience uncomfortable and unenjoyable. It may be further extrapolated that if it stops raining,
then the removal of this physical obstacle to enjoyment may also remove his
or her objection. However, the speaker does not need to say this – the implication of the three words 'it's still raining' is sufficient to indicate all of this.
Thus, the full content of a statement may be much greater than its words (its
*pragmatic implicature*). Pragmatics also allow people to compensate for some
errors in speech. For example, in 1963, the American President Kennedy
gave a speech in West Berlin in which he declared 'Ich bin ein Berliner' ('I am
a Berliner'). For reasons too lengthy to elaborate here, this was welcome support at a time when West Berlin was feeling besieged by the USSR and its
satellite powers. Unfortunately (as cartoonists in the German press had great
pleasure with the following day), 'Berliner' means 'doughnut' in colloquial
German. However, the crowd listening to the speech accepted the pragmatic
implication of the declaration, and, as archive film of the event shows,
cheered loudly.

Because the pragmatics of language are often subtle, it may take a long
time for a full grasp of implicature to develop. Indeed, it is arguable that to
some extent, nobody will gain a total insight into all pragmatic meanings of
all utterances they encounter, because the references being made are too obscure. Some works of fiction, for example, rely for their effect, not upon the
surface message, but their pragmatic meaning. Poetry and some of the more
esoteric works of prose (e.g. James Joyce's *Ulysses*) are cases in point.[5] A further example is humour, which often relies upon shared references for its effect. This is why much risqué humour leaves children and some innocent
adults baffled. However, the shared knowledge can be on other topics. For
example, the author has in his possession a cartoon which is meaningless un-

---

5    It speaks volumes about both Joyce and his critics that for many years the supposedly standard
     edition contained some glaring typographical errors, which not only were unnoticed, but
     actually praised by some commentators as fine examples of his prose style.

less the viewer has a knowledge of World War I poetry. A British Army officer in the trenches is briefing his men before a raid, and is holding up a picture of a church clock showing the time to be ten to three. The caption reads, 'all right gentlemen, synchronise your watches'.

Such subtleties of production and interpretation are largely a product of knowledge acquisition, and will obviously take many years to develop. However, the mechanisms for using pragmatics are established at a remarkably early age. When a child first beings to talk, early conversations between adult and child can be very one-sided, with the adult both initiating topics and continuing them by introducing new ideas. Children at this age may not even address their replies to the adult, but rather to no-one in particular. However, by about three years, the child can demonstrate at least rudimentary conversational skills. Once a topic is raised, the child is willing to offer statements which push forward the conversation. Consider the following exchange between the author's wife, Ruth, and daughter, Kate (aged 2 years 6 months). The two of them are playing a game involving coloured shapes and two dice:

KATE: tell me which dice

RUTH: it's up to you

K: that and that – you have that one, and I'll have the yellow one

R: let's have all the shapes here

K: you have to turn them upside down

R: you've to sort out the colours as well

K: you start

R: I'll have a green rectangle

K: my turn.

As can be seen, Kate is perfectly capable of producing responses and statements which push the conversation along. This is one of the first stages in pragmatics: recognising the structure and intent of language and being able to manipulate it. Other skills include the ability to request repetitions of sections of speech which were either misheard or not understood. Also, children grasp the ability to recognise that different listeners will have different knowledge bases and expectations. Thus, children will usually describe an item in appropriately simple terms to a younger child, whilst using more complex terms and vocabulary when addressing an adult.

The final linguistic skill to be considered is *semantics*, or word meaning. An often-quoted calculation is that at eighteen months, an average child has a vocabulary of about 25 words; at six years, this has risen to 15, 000. If these figures are correct, then simple arithmetic shows that between these two ages a child learns an average of between 9 and 10 words *per day*. Calculations of vocabulary size are always problematic (e.g. does one include derivatives of root words?) and it is nigh-on impossible to catalogue *every* word a person uses. However, even if the numbers are wrong, subjectively it is readily apparent that vocabulary growth is still impressive.

Even at this phenomenal growth rate, children may still have difficulty finding *le mot juste*. Therefore, where a word for an object is not known, the child may *overextend* – that is, use a word for an inappropriately wide range of situations. Hence, having learnt the word 'dog' the child may for a while use it not only to refer to dogs, but also to other animals or even objects which resemble part of a dog (a famous anecdote in psycholinguistics concerns a child who referred to black olives by his pet dog's name, because the olives resembled the dog's nose). Typically, overextensions are limited to the first half of the second year.

## Theories of language development

It is apparent from the above that language develops in children so that, by the age of five or six years (the age when most children in industrialised countries go to school) they are capable of reasonably mature speech. *How* this takes place is open to debate. The simplest explanation is perhaps that offered by Skinner (see Chapter 7) who argued that language is largely acquired through conditioning. Children copy from those around them, and if they use language correctly, this is rewarded through praise or simply the results of making oneself understood. Learning begins with relatively simple words and phrases, upon which more complex linguistic structures can build.

However, simple imitation seems unlikely given the evidence of overextension presented above. If a child hears that the correct past tense of 'to run' is 'ran', but persists in using 'runned', this indicates that he or she is obeying a more deep-seated rule, rather than learning language parrot-fashion. Furthermore, everyone seems to acquire language to a fair degree of complexity, regardless of intellectual level. If language were purely a matter of learning, then one would expect perhaps much wider variability in linguistic abilities than we actually find. These and other considerations led Noam Chomsky (e.g. Chomsky, 1965) to argue that language acquisition is governed by a genetically-inherited process called the *language acquisition device (LAD)*. The full LAD model is a complex thing, but its essence is relatively straightforward. It is clear that statements can have different surface appearances and yet mean the same thing (e.g. 'the boy kicked the ball' and 'the ball was kicked by the boy' mean the same but sound different). Chomsky argued that the meaning of utterances is based upon their *deep structure*, which in essence is a representation of their meaning, ignoring their surface appearance. Chomsky devised a set of procedures or rules which were used to transform a statement from its surface appearance into its deep structure, which he called a *transformational grammar*. This is, according to Chomsky, innate and is the central component of the LAD. Furthermore, everybody possesses the LAD; this explains why children across all cultures tend to learn their native tongue at roughly the same rate and why (as far as it is possible to make these comparisons) the pattern of acquisition seems to be very similar across languages as well.

Chomsky's ideas have met with criticism, not least because neither linguists nor psychologists have been able to establish how the LAD might work. In studies of comparative psychology, genetically controlled behaviours have been discovered (see Chapter 11), but these tend to be either very or relatively simple in their effects. Certainly nothing as complex as the LAD has been found. Again, although the idea of an innate device controlling acquisition may explain why language acquisition is more than simply rote learning, the place of reward and environmental effects cannot be ignored. For example, it is readily apparent that children raised in highly literate households are likely to be themselves more literate and have a richer vocabulary and set of linguistic skills. Again, there is evidence that learning by imitation may be facilitated by the use of *motherese* – the simplification of language through repetition and regular structure which many parents and adult caregivers use with young children. It therefore seems likely that imitation and environmental effects may play a bigger role than Chomsky originally envisaged. However, given the general complexity of language, its intimate role not just in communication but also in intellectual and social life, it is difficult to see how it would be possible to tease apart the various factors using an ethically-permissible experimental study.

## Reading

At roughly the age when most children have mastered at least the basic aspects of mature speech and comprehension, a new task is presented — namely, learning to recognise and produce a visual codification of language. In other words, the child must learn to read and write. Psychological research has tended to concentrate upon reading, and the same will be done in this chapter.

To understand reading, one must first understand the nature of written language.[6] A variety of methods exist for representing words and concepts. Historically, the earliest method is the *pictogram*, in which a word or concept is represented by a picture (the system is found in many preliterate cultures in the form of cave and rock drawings, etc). Thus, a narrative is composed of a series of pictures indicating what happened. These drawings may be a literal attempt to represent what happened, or they may be stylised. In some cultures, this stylised form transmuted into a more formal writing system composed of *logograms*, in which each symbol represents a different word or concept. Chinese writing is composed of logograms.

The logogram has a great advantage in that what the word sounds like does not matter. The logogram means the word, no matter how it is pronounced. This is of great value in countries such as China where the pronunciation of words in different dialects may be wildly at variance with each other; although the pronunciations are different, the written word is the same for all. However, there is an enormous disadvantage to a logographic

6    See also the section on letter recognition in Chapter 9.

system; namely, a different symbol is needed for each word. Although some Chinese logograms look like the item they represent (e.g. 'quickly' looks like a running man), many do not, and are essentially arbitrary symbols. Hence, logograms have to be rote learned, which in turn means that even a skilled Chinese reader has a relatively low reading vocabulary, because of the effort and difficulty in not only learning these abstract shapes, but then retaining them in the memory.

In contrast, the *phoenecian* system (named after the Phoenecian culture which invented it, and from which we also derive the word 'phonetic') has no symbols for individual words.[7] Instead, each word is described by a set of symbols, or letters, which attempt to represent the sound of the spoken word. Thus, the word 'sat' is composed of 's' 'a' and 't' sounds and the letters 's' 'a' and 't' are written in appropriate sequence to represent these. As the reader will already have surmised, written English uses the phoenecian system, as do all Indo-European languages. The advantage of the phoenecian system is that the level of rote learning should be less than in a logographic system. Once a person has learnt the alphabet of letters, he or she should know what sound each letter represents. From there, it is a relatively simple matter to decode what written words mean. All the reader has to do is to read the letters out loud in sequence, and the sound of the word should be apparent.

Of course in reality, reading is not that simple. The first problem concerns the spelling of words. Some languages such as Russian are fairly regularly spelt. In other words, the spelling conforms to regular rules. Other languages, such as English, have a higher proportion of *irregular words*. For example, words like 'boy' or 'sat' are regularly spelt. On the other hand, words like 'yacht', 'demesne' or 'misled' disobey the rules usually applied to letters presented in those sequences, and are pronounced radically differently from logical expectation. This is not the 'fault' of the phoenecian system as much as an abuse of it. Reasons why English in particular seems to delight in so many abstruse and wayward spellings are largely historical. To a certain extent, it is because English has accepted a great many written words from other languages. Their spelling may be perfectly regular and logical in the language

---

7    With the exception of a few latter-day examples such as '@', '&', etc.

from which they have been appropriated (e.g. 'charabanc') but do not correspond with English spelling rules. Another factor is popularly ascribed to Caxton, who employed Dutch printers; when typesetting, they had a tendency to use continental spellings for English words, so that 'yot' or 'yott' became 'yacht'. However, whatever the reason, English, along with some other languages, has a written form which in part conforms to a set of logical rules, but also in part is composed of irregular words. This means that in order to read effectively, a child must not only learn to read using the phoenecian method, but must also be capable of recognising irregular spellings and remembering the words they represent.

Theories of learning to read have tended to go hand in hand with theories of teaching reading. Essentially these fall into two camps. The *phonics method* advocates teaching reading by emphasising the alphabet and encouraging the child to read words letter by letter and 'building up' the sound of the words from this. The *whole word method* argues the opposite. It advocates that English has too many irregular spellings for the phonics method to work. Instead, children are taught to recognise words by their shape and visual appearance, with scant attention being paid to the individual letters.

Arguments for and against either method have been taking place for most of this century, with cyclical swings in favour of one method or another. Thus, successive generations of children have tended to be taught by either the whole word or the phonics methods. It is surprisingly difficult to judge which scheme is better. This is best explained by example. Suppose that reading scheme x is taught at one school and reading scheme y is taught at another. Suppose we find that scheme x produces better results than scheme y. Can we conclude that x is a better scheme than y? The answer is 'not really'. It is possible that x is better than y, but a lot of other factors unrelated to the schemes may also have played a part (e.g. the children taught under scheme x may have had a better teacher, may have come from more supportive homes, etc). The available evidence has generally found phonics to be better than whole word (see Ellis, 1993 for a summary). However, this is a general finding and cannot be said to apply with any certainty to individual schools or even classes.

Related to this issue, there has been considerable interest paid in recent years to the issue of *how* phonic skills might be of use in learning to read. It can be reasonably argued that a child cannot benefit from learning how to read words by a phonics method unless they are aware of the phonological structure of language – a skill usually known as *phonemic awareness*. Suppose that a child is told that the letters 's', 'a' and 't' represent the sounds in the spoken word 'sat'. This will only make sense to the child if he or she can *hear* these separate sounds in the spoken word. This may seem blindingly obvious to an adult, but many pre-school children have great difficulty in performing this task. For example, Bradley and Bryant (Bradley and Bryant, 1983, Bryant and Bradley, 1985) examined whether pre-school children who had difficulties in performing a phonics task subsequently became poor readers. They did this using an 'odd one out' task (Bradley, 1984) in which the child was given a list of words which all began or ended with the same sound, with one exception (e.g. *bag, bar, sad, ban;* or *bat, hat, sat, ran*). The child had simply to detect which word sounded 'different'. Bradley and Bryant found that children who performed badly at this task tended, when examined at a later age, to be poor readers as well. This finding applied even when other confounding variables such as intelligence level had been taken into account. Furthermore, if a child who had poor phonics skills was trained in them, then their reading improved. Stuart-Hamilton (1986) demonstrated that once a child starts to read, those high in phonics skills tend to have a better 'style' of reading; they tend to make fewer errors, and the errors which are made tend to be more 'adult-like'.

## Developmental dyslexia

Although most children will learn to read with relatively few problems, reading can cause severe difficulties for a small group of people who suffer from *developmental dyslexia*. The term 'dyslexia' basically means 'having difficulty with reading'. As will be seen, people can also develop problems with reading following physical injury to the brain. Developmental dyslexia indicates a problem with reading which becomes apparent as the child develops, in the absence of physical injury, and in spite of adequate intellectual skills. Reading, like any intellectual ability, varies between individuals in the competence with which it is performed – in other words, some people are better readers than others. Generally, this goes in tandem with their general intellectual skills. A person who is intellectually gifted will also tend to be a good reader, and vice versa. However, in some instances, a person's reading ability may be much lower than is predicted by their IQ, and which cannot be explained by other, 'obvious', problems such as deafness, eyesight problems, unusually fraught home life, etc. Definitions vary between authorities, but a widely-accepted rule of thumb is that a child is classified as dyslexic if his or her reading abilities are more than two years behind his or her chronological age (e.g. a girl aged 9 might be classified as dyslexic if her reading skills were worse than the average performance of a 7-year-old child) in the absence of any other explanatory symptoms. It is important to stress that dyslexia is not just 'poor reading'. For example, a child who read well below average for his or her age but who also was not very gifted in intellectual skills would not be classified as being dyslexic by most authorities.[8]

Researchers are uncertain about the precise causes of developmental dyslexia. Certainly there would appear to be nothing grossly 'abnormal' about brain structure, the nervous system, etc. However, the fact that dyslexic children appear to be born with the problem implies that there may be a subtle difference which current test methods cannot detect (though see Ellis, 1993). A few years ago, the suggestion was made that dyslexic children may have slightly unusual eyesight, making reading difficult. Trials of special corrective spectacle lenses claimed some success in improving some dyslexic children's reading standards, but the results overall were inconclusive. Again, claims are sometimes made that a dyslexic child's visual perception in general has difficulty in coping with shapes in general and letter shapes in particular, and that they may, for example, see letters in reverse (e.g. read 'b' as 'd'). However, this argument is not universally supported by the evidence, and such anomalous behaviour may be a product of reading level rather than a cause of it.

---

8    This does not of course negate concern for that child, but remedial treatment would be most appropriately directed in other ways.

There is, as was seen above, evidence that poor phonic skills may predict reading difficulties. However, not all dyslexic children necessarily have a primarily phonic problem. It has been argued for many years that 'normal' readers differ in 'reading style'. At one extreme are the *phoenecian readers*, who read everything by building up words from letter sounds. At the opposite extreme, *Chinese readers* read everything by its visual shape, without regard to the sounds the letters in the word represent. Few people have such extreme reading styles, but instead have a mixture of both phoenecian and chinese tactics, with some people favouring one style over the other. Wilding (1990) has persuasively argued that developmental dyslexic people likewise show a similar range of styles. Some will tend to makes errors showing they are primarily using visual tactics and reading by the overall shapes of words, ignoring the individual letters (e.g. reading 'misled' as 'misted' because they look similar). Others will tend to read primarily by phonics and ignore visual information (e.g. reading 'misled' as 'myzled'). Yet others will use a more balanced mixture of these methods. Thus, there may not just be one type of dyslexic reader. All have a lowered reading ability, but the reason why may differ between individuals. Ellis (1993) in a summary of studies, provides further support for this argument.

## Acquired linguistic deficits

Although dyslexia is most common from birth, it is also possible to lose some or all linguistic skills as a result of brain damage. The brain is composed of a set of interacting sections, each of which performs a set of specialised functions (see Chapter 10). Several areas of the brain are known to be involved in language production and comprehension. These are usually contained in the left cortex[9] of the brain. Two sections of the cortex heavily involved are *Wernicke's area*, which is located (*very* roughly speaking) in the temple region above the left ear, and *Broca's area* (again very roughly, above and slightly back from the left eye). Damage to Broca's area leads to slow and laboured speech, which may be grammatically impaired; however, speech

---

9    Most right-handed people have their language areas in the left side of the brain; left-handed
     people tend to be divided between left and right.

comprehension is normal. This pattern of linguistic impairment is known as *Broca's aphasia.*[10] In contrast, damage to Wernicke's area (causing *Wernicke's aphasia*) causes a loss of comprehension, but relatively normal speech is preserved. From findings such as these, it is possible to conclude that Wernicke's area is involved in comprehending language, and Broca's area in producing speech.

Damage to other sections of the 'language centres' of the brain cause other specific problems. In *phonological dyslexia*, the patient loses the ability to read by the phoenecian method. In *surface dyslexia*, the patient can no longer read by the chinese method. In *deep dyslexia*, the patient may have difficulties with both phoenecian and chinese styles, and have difficulty in interpreting the meanings of words. Many further types of acquired linguistic disorders have been found, each further mapping out the functions of different areas of the brain (see Ellis, 1993, as a very useful starting point). What can be said with certainty is that the functions of language are mapped onto different areas of the brain.

## Language and thought

So far we have viewed language in terms of its acquisition and disorders, without considering its function. Language, like any form of animal communication (see Chapter 11) must in part be an energy-saving device. One has only to think of the difficulties encountered when trying to explain something to someone who does not speak the same language. Even the simplest request or instruction requires an elaborate and time-consuming mime (e.g. consider how one would ask the way to, for example, the nearest supermarket without using words). Communication of all but the most basic pieces of information would be impossible without language. However, it is of course much more than this. Language, because of its ability to express complex thoughts, is a primary tool in social bonding and interaction.

---

10    'Aphasia' means loss of language; typically in cases of aphasia, language is not totally lost, but is severely impaired. If 'aphasia' is preceded by another term (e.g. 'Broca's aphasia', 'Wernicke's aphasia', etc), this refers to a specific pattern of language loss/impairment, rather than a loss/impairment of *all* forms of language.

Indeed, some key developmental psychology theories, such as Vygotsky's (see Chapter 6) argue that our whole development is built around, and structured by, linguistic development and the need to use language as a method of social bonding.

However, vitally important as language as a social tool is, perhaps the greatest attention has been paid to the interaction between language and thought. At one level the connection between the two skills is obvious – thought is only constricted by the limits of ability and imagination – it is not tied to physical limitations. Language is similarly liberated and makes an ideal medium for expressing thoughts. However, how much further does the link go?

The most extreme view is perhaps the *Sapir-Whorf hypothesis*, named after the linguists (Edward Sapir, 1884–1939, and his pupil, Benjamin Lee Whorf, 1897–1941) who devised it. This contains two key and oft-quoted principles. The first is that of *linguistic determinism*, which states that thought is determined by language. The second is *linguistic relativity*, or, that speakers of different languages have different systems of thought, because of differences in the structure of their respective languages. In an oft-cited example, most languages have a limited range of words for snow, but Eskimos have lots of names for it.[11] Therefore, because the Eskimos have more names for snow, they can identify more types of snow than people from other cultures. Note that there is a strong directional argument in the above statements: thought is shaped *because* of the language. This is often now termed the *strong Sapir-Whorf hypothesis*, because it is so dogmatic. However, it also seems untenable on logical grounds alone. For example, how can a language produce different terms for items unless they are first *thought of*? If a person decides to invent names for different types of rain, there are no grounds for doing this unless these types of rain can be seen and thought of. Making up different names will not in itself make different types appear.

---

11  Actually, this is a myth – Eskimos do not have lots of extra words. A better analogy might be industrialised cultures having lots of words for different types of cars and non-industrialised cultures having only one or two.

The strong Sapir-Whorf hypothesis is further weakened by the finding of *linguistic universals*. These are sets of words for key concepts which seem to exist in all languages. Much of this work has been on colour names. Most languages have a basic set of colour names which describe the same small set of colours,[12] indicating that the same cognitive criteria seem to be shaping languages everywhere. Rather stronger proof of this came from the work of Rosch (1973). She tested the Dani tribe of Papua New Guinea, a pre-industrialised people who possessed only two words to indicate colour. Given such a limited vocabulary, the Sapir-Whorf hypothesis predicts that the Dani should have great difficulty distinguishing between types of colour. However, memory for different colours was done well, and the Dani's choice of 'most typical' colours (e.g. most typical red from a range of shades of red) was identical or near-identical to the choices made by English-speakers. Therefore, language in this instance has little effect on thought.

However, a *weak Sapir-Whorf hypothesis* is more plausible. This states that although thought is not caused by language, it is heavily influenced by it. Consider the case of car names. In British English, there are many ways of describing a car. It can be done in terms of manufacturer (Volvo, Volkswagen, Ford, etc); type (saloon, hatchback, sports car, etc); year of make (British cars have license plates which display the year of manufacture); or more facetiously (e.g. 'penis on wheels' for a sports car; 'jelly mould' describing the standard and rather dull shape of many conventional saloons; 'rep car' for the standard sort of vehicle given to travelling salespersons, etc). It is possible to describe a car using these terms with exquisite precision and (it being Britain) with an element of snobbery, if so desired. Thus, by a combination of precise terms and pragmatics, the description can have great force and shape the listener's thoughts. In contrast, a person from a non-industrial society might only be able to describe a car in far more basic terms, thus providing far less information. In this sense, language is able to shape thought to a great extent.

However, this only describes language on a day-to-day basis. A person in a pre-industrial society may rarely see a car or any other form of vehicle; therefore, a single word is sufficient for their needs. Describing a car as a 'car'

12    Typically the primary colours plus black, grey, pink, brown, orange and purple.

should not cause confusion because in his or her world, a car is such a rarity that it is unlikely that there will be more than one to be seen, and hence a confusion in description is unlikely. If more cars appear, then arguably a larger vocabulary will be created to describe them (witness the growth in car names in English over the last 100 years since they were invented). Therefore, it is perhaps best to conclude that language is a useful vehicle for expressing the distinctions important within a culture.

However, this is by no means a trivial effect. It has been noted in the chapter on memory (Chapter 8) that Loftus and colleagues (e.g. Loftus, 1979) demonstrated that eyewitness reports of events could be seriously distorted by the language used (which in turn triggered contrasting schemata). For example, if people saw a film of a car crash, they were likely to estimate a higher speed for the cars if asked what happened when the cars 'smashed' into each other, rather than 'bumped'. Again, use of sexist language may at times seem innocuous. Using terms such as 'man' or 'he' to denote all humans may seem innocuous, but there is clear evidence that listeners and readers tend to presume that statements presented in this way refer more to males than to females (e.g. Schultz, 1975). Deliberately using non-sexist language may at times be labourious, but the effort is necessary. Although formed by thought, vocabulary can turn the tables and influence it to a very great degree.

FURTHER READING

Andrew Ellis's (1993) textbook *Reading, Writing and Dyslexia* is an excellent introduction to these topics. It is very much based around a cognitive view of the subject. A more general view of linguistics (including most of the topics covered in this chapter) is offered by David Crystal's *Cambridge Encyclopaedia of Language* (Crystal, 1996). Most general introductory texts carry a useful survey of the language and thought topic. There is also an excellent survey of language in Sternberg's *Cognitive Psychology* (Sternberg, 1996). For readers interested in the whole issue of reading from a cultural and historical perspective, there is a highly readable and scholarly work by Alberto Manguel called (not surprisingly) *A History of Reading* (Manguel, 1996).

# CHAPTER 6

# Developmental Psychology

## Introduction

In theory, 'developmental psychology' means the study of psychological changes across the whole lifespan. In practice, the term is generally reserved for the study of infancy, childhood and adolescence (see e.g. Stuart-Hamilton, 1994 for a discussion of later life changes).

## Stage theories

A major theme in the study of child development is the extent to which a child is born thinking in the same manner as an adult. This is at first confusing – children palpably do not act like grown-ups, so why should we infer that they think in the same way? This calls upon a very old debate, not just in psychology, but in philosophy as well. The full antecedents of the debate need not concern us here, but can be amply demonstrated by the contrasting theories of Locke and Rousseau. John Locke (1632–1704) was an English philosopher who argued that a child is born thinking like an adult, but lacking all knowledge of the world. The infant's mind is thus a *tabula rasa*[1] upon which experiences can be written. In essence, the difference between a child and an adult is simply that the adult knows more. In contrast, Jean Jacques Rousseau (1712–1778), a French philosopher active a few decades after Locke, argued that children and adults not only differ in knowledge, but also in the manner in which they think. Rousseau argued that babies and young infants are only capable of interpreting the world in terms of the effects it has on their senses. In other words, the conception of the world does not extend much beyond what can be seen, heard, tasted, smelled and touched. Older children are capable of more 'intellectual'

---

1    Latin for 'blank slate'; the term, incidentally, is not Locke's, but dates from a later commentary.

thought, but they still cannot think in genuinely abstract terms – the world is thought about in a fairly literal sense. It is only in adolescence, Rousseau argues, that we come to be able to think about things in a genuinely abstract manner.

People often wonder what is meant by 'abstract thought' in this instance. One example is the ability to represent physical entities by symbolic means and to create predictions governing not just what has been seen, but likely future examples of the same phenomena. A good instance of this is the use of algebra – this cannot be properly appreciated unless one realises that an algebraic formula is symbolically representing a particular function, and that the symbols can be manipulated regardless of the items they represent. Another, less mathematical example which is often cited is the 'goldfish question'. What if water were opaque? What would goldfish be like? All sorts of answers can be given to this question (eyes that could see in infra-red, would the goldfish have evolved a coloured skin, etc, etc). The important point is that someone thinking in an abstract manner will see this as an invitation to hypothesise. A person not thinking in the abstract will be confused about the disruption to normality and protest something along the lines of 'but water isn't opaque'.

The Rousseau argument is thus that children not only acquire knowledge, but they also change their very method of thinking as they mature. The Locke argument is simply that development is principally a matter of acquiring knowledge. This may at first seem a rather abstruse question, but it has important implications for, inter alia, education. If children are thinking in a radically different manner from their adult teachers, then this implies that a different learning approach is needed than if it is the case that children solely lack knowledge.

## Piaget and his critics

In modern psychology, the debate has seen its most famous flowering in the work of Jean Piaget (1896–1980) and his critics. Piaget's theory of development is a rich and complex one, and has its origins not in psychology, but in attempts to integrate biology with formal logic (the idea is not as bizarre as this description sounds). It is important to remember that Piaget did not consider himself to be a psychologist (indeed, after he became famous, he had an application to read for a PhD in psychology turned down), a point we shall return to later.

Piaget, like Rousseau, argued that development occurs in stages, each characterised by a method of thinking fundamentally different from that of an adult (hence why Piaget's theories and others like it are often called *stage theories of development*). There are three main periods of development: *sensori-motor* (0–18 months); *concrete operations* (18 months – 12 years); and *formal operations* (12 years+). The ages given in parentheses are approximations of the ages of development for a 'typical' child – Piaget was happy to admit that some children will mature faster and some slower than this. A curious phenomenon is that since Piaget ran his central experiments some 50 years ago, children on average have been able to 'pass' his experiments at increasingly younger ages. However, this is not very important to the theory – what matters is not the age at which they do it, but the inevitable progression from one stage to the next. Children do not skip stages and once a higher stage is attained, then 'regression' to an earlier stage is impossible under normal circumstances. The nature of these stages, is, like Rousseau's, one of a progressively more adult-like and abstract thought.

*Sensori-motor stage*

Piaget argued that a baby can only understand the world in terms of its senses and basic movements. Thus, that which can be sensed exists, that which cannot does not exist. Hence, a toy exists for as long as the baby can see and touch it. However, if it drops out of the crib, so it cannot be seen, then it ceases to exist in the baby's mind. This of course is radically different from an adult manner of thinking – if we drop an item out of sight, we are still aware that it exists *somewhere* even if we cannot presently detect it. Piaget demonstrated this point in a set of elegant experiments. In one of these, he gave a baby a toy to play with. If the toy was taken from the baby but left in full view, then the baby reached for it. However, if the toy was covered over (though still within reach of the baby) then the baby did not reach for it. Literally, as every commentator cannot resist noting at this point, 'out of sight, out of mind'. Some observers might sensibly argue that all this demonstrates is that the reason the younger babies 'failed' was not that they did not know where the toy was, but that they had not yet learnt to lift off covers. However, this simple explanation does not account for the *A not B error*, which first shows itself at circa 10–12 months. By this age, the infant will lift up a cover to find a toy. However, suppose that the following experiment is conducted. The infant sees the toy hidden at one position ('position A') a few times, and reliably retrieves the toy. Now the infant sees the toy hidden at a new position ('position B'). Where will the child search for the toy? If the child is thinking like an adult, then it should go to position B. In fact, it will usually go to position A (i.e. where the toy has been habitually seen). Piaget takes this finding as evidence that infants are governed by actions rather than mental representations (i.e. they tend to repeat the action which got results on previous occasions rather than follow a more logical mental process). Not until about 18 months, he argues, do they begin to govern their actions by thought, at which time mistakes such as the A not B error disappear.

*Concrete operations stage*

This is a lengthy and complex voyage of discovery in Piaget's theory. Essentially, the child enters the stage thinking about the world from too limited a perspective, but leaves it capable of regarding a variety of situations from a balanced intellectual viewpoint. This is best explained through two of his most famous experiments.

The first of these is the *conservation task*. There are many permutations of this, but in the best known, the child is presented with two balls of modelling clay of equal size and shape. The child is asked if the two balls are the same, and agrees that they are. One of the balls is rolled out by the experimenter into a sausage shape, and again the child is asked if the two balls contain the same quantity of clay. Children under the age of about seven years tend to say that the quantities have changed. Why they say this is a complex part of Piaget's theory, but one explanation is that the children fail to concentrate on sufficient aspects of the problem. Thus, the child may look at the two clay shapes solely in terms of their height. Hence, when one piece is rolled into a sausage, its height is diminished and so clay is 'lost'. If the child is concentrating on width, then clay is perceived as being 'added'. When the child learns that a change in one dimension is met by a compensatory increase or decrease in another (e.g. a loss of height is matched by an increase in width), then the child attains an insight into conservation. Piaget demonstrated that this phenomenon does not only apply to knowledge of quantity, but also other factors such as volume, number, etc.

In another study, Piaget examined *egocentrism*. This does not refer to selfishness, but rather the child's immature view that whatever he or she can see is the viewpoint of everyone else as well. Piaget demonstrated this with the *three mountains task*. In this, the child is presented with a table-top model of three mountains, each with a characteristic peak (one is snow-covered, one has a cross and the other has a hut on it). The child is placed at a particular position next to the table and shown a range of pictures of the mountains taken from different angles. When asked to pick a picture which represents his or her view, then the child can do this, showing that they understand the 'purpose' of the picture. However, the child is now shown a doll sitting at another position beside the table. When asked to choose the view the doll can see, the child below circa eight years cannot do this, and will often choose the view which shows their own viewpoint again. In other words, the child literally cannot adopt another person's viewpoint.

The concrete operations stage is, as stated above, a rich and complex one, but the cardinal feature is a gradual adoption of a more sophisticated level of thought. What is also clear is that the way in which the child performs the experiments is radically different from the way an adult would perform them.

*Formal operations*

In the final stage of development, children entering adolescence begin to demonstrate genuinely abstract levels of thought. Several experiments were devised to demonstrate this. One such example was the *balance experiment*, in which participants were given a beam balance. From either side of the balance hung hooks at regular intervals away from the pivot. The distance of each hook from the pivot was indicated. Participants were also given a set of weights, and were asked to add weights to either side to make the balance. This sounds easy, until one realises that the weights were unequal. Thus, suppose one were given a 200 gramme and a 400 gramme weight – how could one make them balance? The answer is that the 200 gramme weight needs to be hung twice the distance away from the pivot as the 400 gramme weight. This is because the force pulling down on a beam is calculated by the formula force = weight × distance from pivot. Thus, a weight which is half the weight of another one has to be twice the distance from the pivot for the forces to be equal (on paper, this sounds complex, but in practice the rule is easily demonstrated). Piaget found that children lacking formal operations would quickly give up on the problem. However, once into formal operations, children would methodically explore putting weights at different distances to see which solutions worked and which did not. From this, they would then devise rules to define situations which worked. In other words, they abstracted a rule governing the situation.

It may strike the reader that formal operations sound rather difficult, and indeed, Piaget acknowledged that not every individual would attain formal operational thought. However, the point to be made is that this was seen as the pinnacle of intellectual development.

It is difficult to judge what to make of Piaget's work. Certainly, his output of published work was vast, with seemingly endless discussions of particular points of his theory. On this point, he might be accused of sacrificing quality for quantity, because many individual pieces of work tend to be badly-written. Notwithstanding this, Piaget provided what is arguably the richest and most complete 'big theory' which the field of psychology has yet seen. However, this does not mean that it is necessarily right, nor that it is particularly original nor that it shapes future directions for developmental psychology.

*Was Piaget right?*

The extent to which Piaget is valid rather depends upon the allowance one wishes to make for what the child 'really' understands about the concepts being tested. This is easily explained by example. Take the case of the three mountains experiment. In this, Piaget demonstrated that young children cannot adopt another's viewpoint. However, if one considers the experiment again, one can see that the task Piaget set the child was very difficult. The reader is invited to consider the room in front of them – without moving, imagine what it looks like 120 degrees to the right. As can be readily appreciated, this is not easy. In a study of older adults (many of them educated to degree level) Stuart-Hamilton and McDonald (1996) found that an appreciable proportion could not do the three mountains task. Clearly, such people are, in Piaget's terms, beyond the concrete operations stage, yet they displayed supposedly egocentric behaviour. This means that the children in Piaget's experiment may have failed his test, not because they were egocentric, but because the task was simply too hard for them, and their failures *looked like* egocentrism.

This begs the question of what happens if children are tested on a task which is not too difficult for them, but which still requires a lack of egocentrism to do it properly. One such instance is the *policeman experiment* (Hughes, cited Donaldson, 1978). In this task, the child is shown a set of four walls arranged in a cross shape. For the sake of convenience, we will imagine the cross arrayed like a compass, with a north, west, east and south wall. The child is told that a doll is hiding from a policeman. If the policeman is placed at the end of the north wall, where must the doll hide to avoid being seen? The answer is of course the south-east or south-west segments of the cross. Suppose that a second policeman joins the first and stands at the end of the east wall. Where must the doll now hide to avoid being seen by both police-men?[2] It was argued that this task can only be done correctly if the child understands that the doll must avoid being seen by another person. In other words, the child must imagine the viewpoint of another person (the police-man). Hughes found that children as young as three or four years of age could reliably get this task correct. This seems to indicate that children lack egocentrism, in contradiction to Piaget's argument. The reason for this, it was argued, is because the test is far simpler whilst assessing the same basic skill.

Does this mean that Piaget's findings that children lack mature skills is purely the product of bad experiments? Certainly that was the abiding view in much of psychology in the 1970s and early 1980s. Piaget's principal ex-

2    The answer is the south-west segment.

periments were examined in turn and each was found to be too 'complicated' – when the same skills were assessed using experiments more accessible to a child's intellect, then children performed far better than Piaget predicted. However, this raises the inevitable question of the degree to which the experiments of Piaget's critics are a fair simulation of Piaget's. In some cases, it might be argued that the 'easy' experiments are *too* easy. For example, is the policeman experiment really a measure of adopting another's viewpoint? It is possible to perform the test by 'simply' thinking about lines of sight. One has to recognise that a viewer is at the end of a line of sight, but one does not have to have aware in any details of what the viewer actually *sees*. Again, other researchers found that, bizarrely enough, getting a glove puppet or toy to do the manipulation of materials in an experiment (e.g. the *naughty teddy experiment* by Hughes, ibid) improved the child's performance of a Piagetian task. Does this mean that if the context in which the experiment is run is altered, then the child displays more mature reasoning? In other words, children failed Piaget's tests because the adult experimenter put them off? This is an interesting proposition, but it is also possible that using puppets and toys distracts the child from concentrating on the task, so their responses to questions may be meaningless since they have not fully attended to the true demands of the task.

These criticisms lead to a typical response in textbooks that Piaget had some fascinating theories, but was an awful experimenter. This is only partly fair, however. What Piaget did and which many of his detractors did not is interview each child about *why* they performed as they did on his experiments. In other words, he did not simply infer the child's thinking from their performance, he also asked them to explain their reasoning. Piaget's theory is as much based upon the child's own understanding of the world as it is about their actions in it. Leaving aside the thorny issue of whether children can be reliably trusted to explain their thinking, this brings us to the heart of the issue: namely, what criterion do we take as an indicator of mental ability in children – what they can *do* or what they are *consciously aware* of? By the time children can successfully perform the traditional Piagetian tasks, they can also, almost without exception, do the tasks set by Piaget's critics which supposedly test the same skill. In addition, they can also explain *why* they behave as they do. So not only can they perform the skill, they also are fully aware of its nature. Conversely, when a child can 'only' do the critics' tasks, but not Piaget's, they might be claimed to be performing the skill only under certain circumstances (regardless of the reason why this is the case). Which do we infer as a fair indicator of ability?

To compound the problem, there is also the question of the extent to which we wish to regard Piaget as a psychologist. Piaget's studies are very much of how *knowledge* is acquired. Indeed, the name he gave to his area of research is *genetic epistemology* – the study of the growth of knowledge. In other words, he is looking at what is acquired rather than who is acquiring it. A study of changes in children's clothing as they grow older relies to some extent upon the bodies the clothing will cover, but is primarily concerned with socks, shirts, etc, rather than, for example, ligaments and skin. Looked at in this manner, many of the criticisms of Piaget's theories become irrelevant, or at least side issues, because they concentrate on the child, not what he or she is acquiring. To use the analogy just given, it is like criticising a theory of children's sock design by looking at skin colour. There may be some relevance, but it is unlikely to be central. Indeed, much of Piaget's work is a study of children as acquirers of knowledge rather than as living social beings (this does not mean that Piaget was bad with children – far from it). There is little in Piaget's huge published output on the child as a social creature. His work on, for example, children co-operating on defining rules or on the development of moral sense, is very much couched in terms of its part within the growth of logical and intellectual development.

## Vygotsky

This is often contrasted with the work of Lev Vygotsky (1896–1934), a Russian researcher who was developing a similarly complex theory before his premature death. Vygotsky argued that the child develops because of social factors which in turn motivate intellectual development. For example, he argued that speech begins as a method of social communication before becoming 'internalised' as a method of thinking (e.g. a young child may use speech as a method of 'thinking aloud' before this speech becomes an inner speech purely of thought). Again, he argued that children can appreciate the intellectual activities of slightly more developed children, and the degree to which a child can 'see ahead' and appreciate more advanced thought processes is called the *zone of proximal development*. Thus, development in part occurs because of this interaction with others, with younger children emulating older ones.

This is radically different from Piaget's argument. Piaget saw development as being essentially generated from *within*: a child moved from one stage to the next essentially because their existing logic became too inconsistent to explain their observations. Vygotsky's argument is very much more dependent upon thought developing through social interaction. Not surprisingly, Vygotsky emphasised the importance of education in fostering development. Piaget was much more dismissive, arguing that often by teaching children how to think, development was stifled, since the child does not learn to think for him- or herself. This contrast between the two theories can again be seen in the relative importance placed on language. For Vygotsky, language and thought were intimately bound up with each other. For Piaget, language was largely seen as an expression of thought, nothing more.

The relative merits of Vygotsky's and Piaget's theories is a lengthy debate (see Van der Veer and Valinser, 1991 for an introduction). To a certain extent, the comparison is in any case unfair, since Piaget lived a long life and developed a very comprehensive (and at times impenetrable) theory, whereas Vygotsky died young before his ideas had perhaps fully formed. However, there seems to be considerable evidence that culture shapes development rather more than Piaget (who felt development took place regardless of culture) would have liked (see Dworetsky, 1996). However, much of what passes for 'Vygotsky's' theory is an extrapolation by later commentators, and further discussion will be avoided at this point.

It is probably politic now to leave the issue of 'big theories' of intellectual development (see Butterworth and Harris, 1994, for an introduction) and move to other areas of study. There is a danger that one's view of developmental psychology can be swamped by the idea that the subject is a matter of Piaget's all-embracing theory and reactions to it, and that other topics are footnotes to the 'big question'. In fact, discussion of Piaget's model and similar attempts to create an all-embracing theory, though important, are just one of several equally active and relevant areas of research (see Burman, 1994).

Many such areas could be covered, since practically any aspect of psychological life has to develop. Indeed, think of a mental attribute and it is likely that someone has studied its growth, from musical skills to sexuality. However, we will concentrate upon three commonly-cited areas of study – infancy, attachment and moral development, since together these give some insight into the breadth of the subject.

## Infancy

As we have seen, Piaget gave an account of infant development which stressed what the infant cannot do rather more than what he or she can. Indeed, before the 1960s, many researchers felt that studying babies' intellects was largely a waste of time because it was felt they were too 'limited' to be worthy of study. However, a series of elegant and ingenious experiments demonstrated that babies come ready-equipped with, or acquire very soon after birth, a set of quite sophisticated skills. Aside from the findings reported below, the reader should also consider the remarkable ingenuity of the researchers who created experiments to test infants who cannot speak or even move much, and who created such complex insights from such unpromising material.

The earliest demonstrations were by Robert Fantz (e.g. Fantz, 1961) who created the *preferential looking technique*. The premise behind the experiment is a simple one. If as adults we say that we prefer one thing over another, then clearly, we can tell the difference between the two items in question, otherwise we could not express a preference. Babies (obviously) cannot verbally express a preference, but they may do so in other, non-linguistic ways. Notably, if shown two objects, they may spend longer looking at one rather than the other. This can be taken to indicate that they prefer one to the other, and hence that they can tell the difference between the objects. An obvious objection to this is that the item being looked at more often happens to be in the way of where the baby just happens to prefer staring vacantly into space. This can be easily discounted by presenting items in different locations within the baby's field of vision – if the baby is simply staring vacantly into space, then he or she will not move their eyes to stare at the objects, but in fact, this is what they do, indicating that they are looking at the objects.

In the most famous example of his work, Fantz gave babies the choice of looking at two items from a set of three: a face; a random pattern made of the same facial features jumbled up; or a very basic pattern of one block of light and one block of dark. Fantz found the babies preferred the first two displays, but consistently looked slightly longer at the face. Although Fantz found evidence of this face preference in young (under one month) babies, current evidence suggests that very young infants prefer patterns in general, and it is not until about three months that a special preference for faces over patterns is apparent. Nonetheless, the results are remarkable in that they show that babies are capable of perceptual skills which had not previously been suspected. It should be noted at this point that there is a logical problem with the preference technique. If an infant shows a preference, then he or she can obviously discriminate between the stimuli. However, what if the infant spends an equal amount of time looking at both stimuli? An absence of a preference *may* mean that the infant cannot tell them apart, or it could mean that the infant *can* tell them apart, but does not have a preference (e.g. one might spend an equal amount of time looking at a bowl of strawberry and a bowl of chocolate ice cream – the difference between them is known, but one is not preferred over the other). Whilst this criticism of the preferential looking technique is logically correct, nonetheless it can be argued that it is rather implausible.

Other versions of preference studies in infants have been performed to elicit other pieces of information. For example, there is the variant known as the *habituation study*. This is based on the premise that babies become quickly bored with items they have encountered before (i.e. to which they are habituated), and this behaviour can be utilised. It is best described by example. Suppose an experimenter is interested in examining how well babies can distinguish between different colours. The experimenter presents a stimulus (e.g. a blue card), and the baby looks at it until he or she has habituated to it, and turns his or her attention elsewhere (i.e. he or she stops gazing at it). The experimenter presents a new stimulus (e.g. a card in a slightly different shade of blue). If the baby shows renewed interest (i.e. it is looked at more than the old stimulus at the end of *its* exposure), then the baby clearly perceives the item as a new object, and hence can tell the difference between the old and the new (in the example, he or she can distinguish between the two shades of blue). However, if the baby is bored by the new object (e.g. does not look at it) then it is argued that he or she does not perceive it as a new object (i.e. he or she thinks it is the return of the old 'boring' stimulus), and hence cannot tell the two stimuli apart. By varying the degree of difference between the stimuli, it is possible to measure how sensitive the baby's perceptions are. For example, if a baby looks more at a sky blue card after being shown a royal blue card, then he or she can tell the difference between sky and royal blue. On the other hand, if a pale blue is followed by a very slightly paler blue and the baby does not react to it, then arguably he or she cannot tell the difference between the two shades of pale blue.

A variation on this technique is to present the new stimulus in conjunction with the old, and measure whether the baby spends longer looking at the new stimulus. This is called the *habituation-novelty technique*. The measure used to gauge interest need not be the length of time spent looking. Other measures include measuring the heart rate of the baby – a change upon the arrival of a new object indicates that the baby is excited by the change, and hence, presumably, he or she can tell that something new has arrived. The same criticism as the one aired above – the baby may notice the change but simply not choose to react to it – can be raised with these studies, but again, to press this criticism is probably being unnecessarily churlish.

A further permutation of the idea is the *nonnutritive nipple sucking technique* or *nipple technique*. In this, the infant is given a dummy[3] to suck which is attached to sensing electrodes. Typically, sucking at one rate will produce one stimulus, sucking at another rate produces another stimulus. The infant rapidly learns this and if he or she subsequently sucks consistently at one rate to produce a particular sort of stimulus, this indicates that the infant prefers this stimulus, and by extension, can tell the difference between it and the alternative on offer. Use of the nipple technique has led to one of the more ingenious

3   For American readers – a pacifier.

studies in infant psychology. It has often been anecdotally supposed that some babies are aware of their surroundings whilst still in the womb. Certainly the unborn infant can be shown to react to fairly basic stimuli. Shining a bright light on the pregnant mother's stomach for example, may evoke a movement from within. DeCasper and Spence (1986) arranged for some mothers in the later stages of pregnancy to read out loud the same passage of text (from a Dr Seuss book) every day. The babies, when born, were placed in the nipple sucking apparatus, which would play either the story their mothers had read out loud daily before birth, or a different, but similar, story. Remarkably, the infants consistently preferred the 'familiar' story, even if read by a stranger. The explanation for this can only be that the infants had heard the story being read out loud whilst in the womb and had memorised enough about it to recognise it when born. Subsequent work has demonstrated that *prenatal cognition* is in fact fairly sophisticated and that infants in the later stages of gestation are learning more than has previously been supposed.

Before leaving the topic of infant perception, one further study needs to be mentioned because it has (justifiably) attained the status of a 'classic'. This is the *visual cliff* (Gibson and Walk, 1960). The origins of the experiment lie in a rich and complex (and controversial) theory of perception, but the study can be taken in isolation. The apparatus is essentially a (safety) glass-topped table. The glass is non-reflective. Under one half of the it (the 'solid' half) is a checkerboard pattern flush with the underside of the glass. On the floor under the other half of the table (the 'drop' half) is the same checkerboard pattern. Looked at from above (i.e. when placed on the apparatus), the 'solid' half looks safe to stand on, while the 'drop' half looks to be several feet below the level of the 'solid' half. There have been many permutations of this experiment, but in the original version, baby animals old enough to crawl (in humans, circa 6 months) were placed on the 'solid' half, and their behaviour observed. In the case of humans, the baby's mother stood at the end of the 'drop' half and encouraged the baby to crawl to her. Babies would crawl to the edge of the 'solid' half, but would usually refuse to crawl on to the 'drop' half (though in reality it would be perfectly safe to do so). This indicates that the baby can perceive (and fear) depth from visual information alone, and acted against a variety of contemporary theories which argued that babies this young could not do this. A problem with the original design was that babies had to be capable of moving themselves, limiting the study to relatively old babies. Later studies overcame this by moving babies belly down across the apparatus using a trolley, and measuring the babies' physiological reactions (which were typically of surprise and/or fear, indicating that they perceived the depth).

## Moral Development

As noted above, Piaget conducted some important research on moral development, though largely from the viewpoint of intellectual development. He argued that there are four major themes in the development of a moral code: the concepts of rules, right and wrong, lying, and justice. Underlying these is the basic concept of the transfer from *heteronomy* (blind obedience to an authority figure) to *autonomy* (developing a moral code of one's own). As part of the evidence supporting this, Piaget observed children at play (the most often cited example is marbles, though other games were used as well), and identified several stages of awareness. At under two years of age, the child is governed by *motor rules* – the child plays without any sign of what an adult would call 'rules', beyond those imposed by physical limitations. Following this (roughly, 2 to 6 years) are *egocentric rules* – the child imitates the play of older children, but lacks an understanding of the social interaction of true game playing. *Cooperation rules* (7 to 10 years) follow – the child obeys the rules, which, when the child is interviewed are declared to be unchangeable and necessary. Play now involves genuine social interaction. In the final stage of *codification rules* (10 years and beyond), the child recognises that rules can be altered by mutual consent of the players to suit particular situations. In tandem with this, the developing child changes his or her concept of the purpose of rules. In the earliest stage (under 2 years) the child is only aware that play is not a compulsory activity. Subsequently (2 to 8 years) he or she regards rules as sacred (sometimes literally God-given) and inviolate, before (8 years and beyond) recognising that rules can be adapted to suit the mutual consent of the players.

On the issue of knowledge of what is right and wrong, Piaget argued that children begin in a state of *moral realism* – a belief that the letter rather than the spirit of the law is paramount, and that a person's behaviour must be judged by its consequences rather than its intentions. Piaget supported this by citing experiments in which subjects were given stories in which, for example, a child doing a good deed accidentally broke many things, while a naughty child doing something bad only broke a small item. Children under seven years usually argued that the former child was naughtier, because the effects of his/her actions were worse. Children over seven years tended to argue the opposite. This move towards what would generally be considered a more humane and tolerant approach in Western cultures is also seen in the development of the concept of 'a lie'. At five years and under, children tend to have only a vague idea that a lie is 'a naughty word'. Between about five and seven years, this concept has changed to rather draconian notion that a lie is anything untrue (including accidental errors). By eight to ten years, this has relaxed to a concept of anything untrue, excluding accidental errors. Only at ten years or older does the child recognise that a lie is a deliberate intent to deceive. Moral realism again plays a role. Children possessing the trait tend to judge a lie by its effects. Hence, they find an act where unintentional misinformation is given and major difficulties arise to be more reprehensible than a deliberate lie whose consequences are relatively minor. Moral realism maintains a stronger hold in the development of the concept of lying than in the concept of right and wrong, and it is not until ten years or older that it is fully shaken off.

Given what has already been said, the pattern of development of the concept of justice should not be surprising. Piaget argued that there are three main stages in the development of the concept of this idea. At under eight years, a just decision or command is that given by an authority figure. Between about eight and twelve years, the child argues that a just reward/punishment should be divided equally between all deserving it; no individual should have more nor less than his or her fair share. Not until he or she is twelve years or older does the child assess each case on its own terms. Piaget measured this by observing children's judgments on a series of stories in which a child receives extra work from an authority figure, because another child has not done his/her allotted share.

A problem with Piaget's model is that it is rather limited, since the range of moral dilemmas with which he faced children were relatively small, and largely concerned with the allocation of reward and punishment. In addition, it might be argued that there are many more shades of morality than simply judging if something merits punishment. Accordingly, Piaget's work was ripe for development, and the key figure in doing this was Lawrence Kohlberg (1927–1987; see e.g. Kohlberg, 1976). From his student days, most of Kohlberg's work was concerned in one form or another with moral development. Indeed, probably uniquely for a well-known psychologist, he was a one-idea thinker. His key study presented subjects with imaginary moral dilemmas. For example, subjects were told that a man steals a drug to treat his sick wife, because the pharmacist was charging an extortionate fee – should the man have stolen? Again, in a wartime scenario, who should be sent on a suicide mission which would ensure the survival of a company of soldiers – the unpopular troublemaker, or the diseased man who does not have long to live? Kohlberg analysed subjects' reasons for their answers rather than the answers themselves (in other words, whether they were 'yes' or 'no' to the question of should the man steal, or which man was chosen for the suicide mission is relatively unimportant compared with the justifications given for the decisions), and classified them into stages of moral development. **Stage 1:** the *punishment and obedience orientation* – subjects unquestioningly believe that something is wrong if a law or an authority figure prohibits it. **Stage 2:** the *instrumental relativist orientation* – the subject acknowledges that there may be two sides to an argument, and will tend to choose the one which provides the greater benefit. There is also a tendency to a 'tit for tat' philosophy of cooperation. **Stage 3:** the *interpersonal concordance of 'good boy – nice girl' orientation* – a justifiable action seems to be judged by whether it accords with accepted norms of 'good' or 'nice' behaviour (e.g. whether society would judge someone's 'heart is in the right place', even if their actions contravene the letter of the law). **Stage 4:** the *law and order orientation* – subjects appreciate both arguments, but ultimately (and sometimes with great regret) side with whoever is more within the letter of the law. **Stage 5:** the *so-*

*cial-contract legalistic orientation* – the subject can appreciate that some laws are wrong, and must be changed if there is a consensus in favour of this. Nonetheless, even if a law is stupid, it must be obeyed until overturned by constitutional means. **Stage 6:** the *universal ethical principle* – the recognition that there are general rights and principles which transcend a country's statutes if the two are in disagreement.

The six stages can be categorised into three levels – the *preconventional level* (stages 1 and 2); the *conventional level* (stages 3 and 4); and the *post-conventional level* (formed from stages 5 and 6; also known as the *autonomous level*, or the *principled level*). Kohlberg, with echoes of Piaget, argued that subjects proceed through the stages in an invariant order, and that stages cannot be 'skipped'. Also, subjects are attracted to the stage of reasoning one above the one they presently hold. The preconventional level is the one most often held by children, who usually do not advance into the conventional level until their late childhood/early teens. The post-conventional level is not usually acquired until mid teens (if at all – the majority stay at a lower level, and a minority never advance beyond stage 1). However, there is a considerable variability in the age of acquisition. Kohlberg's early work was criticised for being too vague, particularly in details of scoring. In reply, a standardised testing procedure was devised (note that Stage 6 is very rarely attained). Kohlberg's theory has been criticised – some of his findings are vague, and some commentators have questioned Kohlberg's admiration of some moral arguments, in particular the stress on abstract ideals above any emotional consideration. Perhaps most pertinently, since Kohlberg's work largely concentrated on the responses of male subjects, it is questionable that it is a truly representative theory, and indeed later commentators (e.g. Gilligan, 1982) have argued that women and girls may have radically different approaches to the same dilemmas. Though empirical evidence for this is mixed, it is fairly damning that claims for 'universal ethical truths' are based on such a biased sample.

## Attachment

Other researchers in social development have taken a more applied approach and have concerned themselves with the mechanisms of *attachment* – the process by which emotional bonds are formed between individuals, and in particular, the bond between parent and child (without wishing to sound sexist, such research almost inevitably means 'mother and child'). Discussion of this topic has traditionally revolved around the work of John Bowlby (1907–1990), and, separately Harry Harlow (1905–1981). Both sets of research have aroused fierce debate.

Bowlby's work (see especially Bowlby, 1969, 1973, 1980) draws upon an eclectic mix of disciplines, but especially psychoanalysis. At its heart is the concept of *monotropy* – the argument that attachment is primarily directed at just one other person (almost invariably the mother). The starting point for his work in the 1940s was a set of contemporary findings that children raised in orphanages had appreciably lowered IQs and other psychological problems when compared with children reared in 'normal' families (it is now known that many of the studies Bowlby cited were seriously flawed). Bowlby's own work on juvenile delinquents (e.g. Bowlby, 1944) found that children deprived of their mothers were more likely to display a lowered emotional and, in effect, moral sense (*affectionless psychopathy* – though note that later researchers largely failed to replicate this finding).

This work later flowered into a wider theory cataloguing the effects of a disrupted bond between parent and child. Part of this work derives from studies of children separated from parents because of hospitalisation, in which a characteristic three-part behaviour pattern was observed: *protest* (at separation); *despair* (at parent not apparently returning); and *detachment* (an emotional apathy). When re-united, the child would often display an intense *separation anxiety*, fearing that the parent would go away again. Clearly this is undesirable (indeed, Bowlby's findings led to improved facilities in many hospitals so that mothers could stay with hospitalised children). Extrapolating from this, it is sensible to argue that any child should have a secure attachment with a parent.

Unfortunately, some of what Bowlby wrote (or rather more often, what his critics *thought* he wrote) can be presented as offering a rather old-fashioned view of women. It is almost inevitable that the main figure in a baby's life will be his or her mother. Should the mother be always available for the child? What if she is a working mother? Will her daily absences from the home lead to the child having an abnormal pattern of development? Such arguments are obviously grist to the mill to anyone convinced that the only place for a woman is in the home. Attitudes like this are reprehensible and (thankfully) are on the wane, but at the time of Bowlby's early work in the 1940s, they were a mainstream view (to gain an idea of the historical attitudes, at that time in the UK, under many regional educational authorities' rules, women teachers were sacked if they got married). Bowlby himself was not guilty of such out and out sexism, but there is no doubt that his findings could be *interpreted* as supporting it.

Aside from this consideration, Bowlby's argument can be attacked on more 'scientific' grounds. For example, Rutter (1981) argued that Bowlby did not distinguish between *privation* (a *loss* of an attachment figure) and *deprivation* (*never* having experienced an attachment figure). Rutter argued that it is the latter which is likely to cause later psychological problems, rather than simply experiencing a break from an attachment figure. In other words, the problem is not simply one of the 'quality' of attachment. Again, there is the issue of the reasons for separation. A variety of studies have established that if the reason for the separation is something extrinsic to the bond between parent and child (e.g. illness forces one or other to go into hospital), then, in spite of Bowlby's (understandable) concerns, the *long term* effects are typically not very harmful. On the other hand, if the reason for the separation is the bond itself (e.g. the mother does not really want the child and cannot cope with him or her), then in the long term there may be problems, but arguably these are more the product of the situation rather than the breaking of the bond *per se* (see Holmes, 1993). Again, the evidence points to children being quite content and functioning normally if they form attachments with several different adults (e.g. not just the mother and father but also adult workers at a creche, etc). Therefore, the general consensus of opinion is that attachment does not have to be solely between the child and its mother, nor does it have to be unbroken. However, attachment in *some* form is necessary.[4]

---

4    Though there is some evidence that social skills may take a slightly *different* form; however, the evidence is somewhat muddied by confounding variables; see e.g. Dworetsky (1996).

The work by Harlow (e.g. Harlow and Zimmerman, 1959; Harlow and Harlow, 1969) is also concerned with attachment, in this case the behaviour patterns of rhesus monkeys. The researchers took infant monkeys from their mother and reared them in isolation. In one of their best-known experiments, the researchers raised the monkeys with two artificial monkey-like figures in the cage. One of these was a 'monkey' made out of wire which was very robotic-looking and which dispensed milk through a teat. The other was a 'monkey' which had no practical function, but was covered in soft material, and was 'cuddly' and looked 'cute'. Since the robotic figure provided the infant with food and the cute figure held no practical function, it might be expected that the infant would spend most of its time near the robotic figure.[5] However, the reverse occurred – the infant would go to the robotic figure when it was hungry, but otherwise spent its time near the cute figure, and if it perceived danger, it would cling to the cute figure (Harlow and Harlow, 1969). From this it can be surmised that attachment in part seems to consist of a need for a tactile comfort, and that the drive for attachment is more than a simple case of learning to keep contact with whoever is providing food. A further key finding is that the monkeys reared by these artificial mothers usually catastrophically failed as adult monkeys. They were typically unable to integrate socially into groups of adult monkeys, would be bullied, and would fail to mate. These concepts were adopted by, inter alia, Bowlby, who used them as evidence of the importance of good parenting in social development. However, notwithstanding the importance of the findings, the ethics of Harlow's work must be questioned. Aside from the fact that the infant monkeys were reared devoid of a conventional level of care and grew up to have an abnormal and disadvantageous adult life, one must also consider the impact on the mother monkeys of having their babies taken away from them after birth. Whether the findings, interesting as they are, were worth the distress and suffering it caused the monkeys is questionable.

Not all work on attachment has been as controversial. For example, a noted series of studies have arisen from an experiment devised by Ainsworth

---

5    Surprisingly, both Freudian and behaviourist theories make this prediction (i.e. that attachment is a matter of conditioning to the food provider).

(a colleague of Bowlby) and Bell (1970), called the *strange situation*. The design is relatively simple. A mother and infant (typically of toddler age) are placed in a room with chairs and some toys. Shortly afterwards, a woman (and a stranger to the child) enters the room. Thereafter, there are several stages (each lasting a couple of minutes or so), where various permutations of the adults remain in the room. The principal intent of the experiment is to see how the infant reacts when the mother leaves the room and he or she is left either completely alone or with the stranger, and how he or she reacts when the mother returns. Three types of behaviour were originally reported: *secure attachment* – the infant protests mildly when the parent leaves, and is comforted by his/her return; *anxious/avoidant attachment* – the infant appears relatively unaffected by the events, and generally avoids the parent upon reunion; and *anxious/resistant attachment* – the infant shows exaggerated responses (e.g. bawls his/her head off, and clings to the returning parent without being very consoled by her return). Subsequent studies have suggested that a fourth category can be identified; namely, *insecure/ disorganised attachment* – the infant produces a set of contradictory responses (e.g. approaches the parent, but avoids eye contact – see Main and Solomon, 1986). Such a catalogue of attachment types is useful for what it can tell us about parenting styles (many researchers believe that the cause of an insecure attachment is 'faulty' methods of holding and caring for the baby) and the infant's temperament (many other researchers believe that some infants are born destined to be insecurely attached). Furthermore, it would appear that the level of attachment displayed in infancy is a good indicator of temperament in later years, with children who were securely attached infants being rated as having greater social skills and confidence (e.g. Dworetsky, 1996; Waters, Wippman and Sroufe, 1979).

FURTHER READING

From the work described above, there can be little doubt that developmental psychology encompasses a wide range of topics. What has been reported is not by any means the full set of topics which form the central corpus of a traditional degree course or textbook. Issues such as cross-cultural differences in development (e.g. different cultures tend to emphasise the nurturing of different skills); sex differences in development; drawing skills;

play; classroom skills (e.g. reading and spelling) all have a key role. Throughout its history, the general trend in developmental psychology (as much of psychology in general) seems to have been a move from big theories attempting to explain all of development in one simple package to compartmentalised studies of specific skills and behaviours, and a concomitant rise in the reading required to gain mastery of the topic as a whole.

For those whose interest has been whetted, the following titles may be of use. Atkinson *et al.*'s (1996) general introduction to psychology contains within it some good sections on developmental psychology. A relatively brief book which concentrates on the core developmental psychology curriculum is by Butterworth and Harris (1994). A larger book on lifespan development, by Turner and Helms (1995) can also be safely recommended, as can Dworetsky (1996). An interesting and alternative view of the literature is provided by Burman (1994). For those wanting a general guide to commonly used developmental psychology terms, then there is Stuart-Hamilton (1995a).

# CHAPTER 7

# Learning Theory

## Introduction

Learning and memory are often treated as synonyms, and not without reason, since arguably one could not exist without the other. Learning is clearly impossible if what is learnt is not then remembered, and equally, what is remembered cannot be interpreted without the knowledge acquired by learning. However, for all this interdependency, research into the two skills has usually followed different paths. In this and the succeeding chapter, we will consider studies of learning theory followed by memory.

## Classical conditioning

The concept of learning is synonymous in many people's minds with the research of Pavlov and his dogs salivating at the sound of a bell. Ivan Petrovich Pavlov (1849–1936) was a Russian physiologist, active at the turn of the 20th century, and with an especial interest in the physiology of the digestive system (for which work he was awarded the Nobel Prize in 1904 – *not* for his psychological research). Most scientific discoveries are the result of systematic exploration, but occasionally a finding does result out of a chance mishap, and the story of Pavlov's discovery is one such instance.

Pavlov was examining the gastric and salivary secretions from dogs as they digested food. This involved the delightful task of extracting the said fluids and analysing them. When we see food (and especially if we are hungry) we salivate. It was found that the dogs would at times begin to salivate for what at first seemed to be no apparent reason, since there was no food available. Pavlov observed that the salivation occurred when a particular assistant was in the room, and this assistant was the one who habitually fed the dogs. At what turned out to be a pivotal moment in psychology's history, Pavlov was faced with a choice – investigate the phenomenon or sack the assistant. Thankfully for the assistant and us, he chose the former option. Pavlov's reasoning ran something like this. Dogs salivate when food is about to be presented. It was apparent that there was nothing particularly appetising about the assistant himself which was making the dogs think of eating him. Therefore, the dogs must associate the man with food, and when they see him, they salivate because they anticipate that he has food for them. The important point is that normally the man would not cause the dogs to salivate, but by dint of being associated with food, the normal reaction to the food (i.e. salivation) was applied to him as well. Pavlov then made the necessary but vital leap of logic. If the assistant can become associated with food, could other non-appetising things also become linked?

Pavlov conducted a series of experiments in which this question was systematically examined. In the most famous of these, he rang a bell just before the food was presented to the dogs, and carefully observed what happened. Before the experiment, the bell had not caused any reaction from the dogs, but after several days of the bell ringing just before the food arrived, the sound of the bell alone was enough to get the dogs salivating. In other words, they had learnt to associate the sound of the bell with food. The same result was found when instead of a bell sounding, a light was flashed on and off: after several days, the light flashing alone was enough to start the salivation.

All these instances have something in common: there is a stimulus which naturally causes a reaction (in this instance, food causing salivation). The experimenter makes the dog associate the natural stimulus with a new stimulus which previously did not cause the same response. After several experimental trials, the dog associates the new stimulus with the old, 'natural' stimulus to such an extent that it responds to the new stimulus in the same way as to the old (i.e. it salivates). This is called *classical conditioning* – learning a response to a stimulus which in itself would not elicit the response, because the stimulus is associated with another stimulus which normally elicits the response. The old stimulus is known as the *unconditioned stimulus* (because it pre-existed) and the response to it is known as the *unconditioned response* (for the same reason). The new stimulus is known as the *conditioned stimulus* (because this is what the animal is trained or conditioned to respond to) and its response is known (logically enough) as the *conditioned response*.

Readers may be wondering why dogs salivating at bells is so important, and indeed if the phenomenon was restricted to the canine world, Pavlov's findings would be an interesting footnote in the history of psychology. However, what was found was that the same general phenomenon can be demonstrated in practically any other animal, including humans. Think of a species, and someone somewhere has probably conducted a conditioning experiment on it. The basic thesis is that a great many of our responses to items and events are the result of them being associated with other items which elicit a particular response which is then transferred to the new stimulus. For example, in humans there is an intriguing sexual problem called *fetishism*. A patient with this condition might be politely described as having a profound difficulty in attaining sexual gratification other than from an inanimate object or specific bodily area. Typically the patient is sexually attracted to only one type of item, which can have a recognisable sexual element (e.g. lingerie, stockings, etc), but can also be non-sexual by societal standards (e.g. prams and car exhaust pipes). Since this book is intended in part for readers under eighteen, a detailed description of that the patient does with the object of their desires will be avoided, though one can speculate on what went through a police constable's mind upon finding a man with a fetish problem *in flagrante delicto* with a car exhaust pipe (reported in the UK media a few years ago).

Why should people become attracted to such things? One explanation is derived from conditioning theory. The argument at its simplest is that when we are sexually aroused, we associate our arousal with the event and the items we encounter in it. In some instances, these associations become sufficiently strong that they can act as sexual arousers in themselves. For example, in the case of the man with the car exhaust fetish mentioned above, it was reported that, as an adolescent, stuck in the back seat of his parent's car in a traffic jam, he became sexually aroused and at the same time noticed fumes coming out of car exhausts. This association became stronger as the years went by until a fetish developed. In a similar, though less spectacular manner, most people develop 'mild fetishes' through association. These can vary between cultures. For example, in Britain, a woman's cleavage is often considered attractive by heterosexual males, whilst in some Far Eastern cultures, this honour is reserved for the nape of the neck. This, it can be argued, is because cultural values tell people that certain things are 'sexy' and by dint of repeated exposure to this connection, people come to find them attractive.

An obvious question to ask is: if such associations can be acquired, can they also be removed? In most cases, the answer is 'yes'. Pavlov found that if he stopped presenting food after the bell had rung, then at first the dog salivated, but over time, the salivation decreased until the bell no longer elicited a response. In more technical language, the animal became *deconditioned*: it learnt that the conditioned stimulus no longer predicted a reward, and so the conditioned response was weakened. Another, and less pleasant deterrant is *negative reinforcement*. In this instance, the animal receives a punishment after exposure to a stimulus. Take the case of a patient with a fetish. In the past, clinicians have tried to remove fetishes by showing the patient pictures of the fetishistic object, and giving them painful (but non-dangerous) electric shocks. The idea is that the patient will learn to associate their fetish with pain rather than sexual excitement, and thus be deterred from it.[1]

## Operant conditioning

Another type of conditioning is *operant conditioning*, the chief protagonist of which was Burrhus Frederick Skinner (1904 –1990). Broadly speaking, operant conditioning is training a subject to perform a particular act by rewarding him or her for doing it, or, training a subject to stop performing a particular act by punishing him or her. Operant conditioning is not news to anyone who has ever tried to train a pet dog. When training a dog to sit on command one rewards it when it sits on command. Similarly, one (non-violently!) punishes a dog when it chews the carpet. The dog associates particular acts with reward and/or punishment, and over time, it will tend to do the rewarded acts more and the punished acts less. In other instances, subtler forms of reward and punishment might be used. One such example is *partial reinforcement*, in which a behaviour is rewarded on only some occasions. Perversely enough, in many instances this is more effective than

---

1    In fact (ignoring for a moment the ethical considerations of such treatment), such experiments met with mixed results.

rewarding on every occasion. For example, if a laboratory animal has been trained to perform a response which is only intermittently rewarded, and the reward is then totally withdrawn, the animal will persevere in making the response for far longer than will an animal which has been rewarded on every trial. A common example of this in everyday life is in gambling. Slot machines and lottery scratch cards do not provide a reward every time you use them. They reward the user sporadically (e.g. one of the current UK scratch cards produces a prize an average of roughly one in five occasions), but just enough to keep the punters coming back for more.

Methods of testing learning in a laboratory have, naturally enough, to be rather more rigorous than the above examples. Prior to Skinner, perhaps the most celebrated attempt had been made by Edward Thorndike (1874–1949). He built a series of ingenious 'puzzle boxes' (e.g. Thorndike, 1911). A kitten was placed in the box, which would not open until it had performed a particular act (e.g. pulled a particular string inside the box). Thorndike observed that on day one the kitten's movements were random until it happened to chance upon the appropriate action which released it. On subsequent days, the kitten got faster and faster at releasing itself – clearly, it had learnt how to open the box. Thorndike formulated a series of rather obvious-sounding laws of learning to describe what he found in this and similar experiments. Perhaps the best-known of these is the *law of effect*, which states that a behaviour is more likely to be repeated if it is rewarded, and less likely if it is punished. Other laws include the *law of disuse* (the less frequently a stimulus and response are linked, the weaker the association between them becomes) and the *law of exercise* (the more often a behaviour is used, the higher the probability it will be used in the future).

Skinner devised a piece of apparatus which was less 'home made' in appearance than Thorndike's and which, until the advent of the computer, was perhaps the commonest piece of laboratory equipment in psychology departments. It is known, naturally enough, as the *Skinner Box*. There are variants in design, depending upon the animal being tested and the experimental conditions. However, its most typical form consists of a cage, on one wall of which is a chute and hopper, through which food is delivered to the animal. There is also a mechanism for the animal to operate, such as a small lever to be pressed or a button to be pushed or pecked (typically, a lever is used when a rat is being tested, a button when a bird is tested). There may also be a means of delivering a stimulus, such as a light or a buzzer. How the apparatus works can be demonstrated by example. Suppose that we wish to train a rat to press a lever when it hears a buzzer sound. If and only if the rat pushes the lever after the buzzer has sounded, it will be rewarded, in the form of a piece of food dropping into the food hopper. Typically, the rat is deprived of food prior to the experiment so that it is hungry. This will make the reward of food more powerful (food provided after the rat has had a heavy meal is hardly likely to act as an incentive).

It can be demonstrated quite easily that using basic conditioning techniques such as those shown above, complex behaviours can be created. For example, in our example of the rat in the Skinner box, we might train the rat to 'dance'. Having trained the rat to press the lever when the buzzer sounds, we now decide that we want it to turn around in a circle once before pressing the lever. It is unlikely that the rat will do this spontaneously, so at first the rat is rewarded for actions which, although accidental, are in the desired direction. For example, when the buzzer sounds, food is not released until the rat makes a movement of the head to the right. After a while, the rat will reliably make a right head movement when the buzzer sounds. Then, we do not release food until there has been a right movement not only of the head but the shoulders, then a movement of head shoulders and front part of body, etc, etc. Using this technique, the rat can be trained to turn in a circle before being given the food. With sufficient patience, the rat could, for example, be trained to turn round clockwise, then anticlockwise, then clockwise again before being rewarded. Using such techniques, animals can be conditioned to perform a wide variety of 'tricks'. Indeed, two psychologists turned animal trainers adopted such techniques to train animals to do 'cute' things for American television commercials (Breland and Breland, 1966). However, the important point is that any behaviour, no matter how complex, is made up of simpler elements of pairings of stimulus and response.

## Associationism and behaviourism

To this extent, the theory of operant conditioning is uncontroversial, and frankly, rather dull. It tells us nothing which animal trainers have not known since antiquity. 'Animals will do things if they are rewarded' is hardly surprising. However, Skinner went further with the theory and made it rather more interesting. In this, he was following earlier work, not only by Tolman, but also by John Watson (1878–1958) an earnest and rather overbearing advocate of conditioning theories, whose own academic career was cut short by sexual scandal[2] (he subsequently earned a living as a pundit on child rearing[3]).

At its most basic, Skinner's argument has a certain appeal. When we observe behaviour, we cannot tell what is going on in the brain of the person concerned. Even if we opened up the brain, we could not physically see the thought processes taking place. In order to judge what the person is doing, we can only observe two things – the stimulus he or she receives and the response he or she makes to it. This is all we can be certain about. Thus, when we train a dog to sit, we know that the stimulus (the command to sit) is met with a response (the dog sitting down). This connection between the stimulus and response can be strengthened or weakened by conditioning. If the dog is rewarded for sitting down on command, then the link is strengthened, and the dog is more likely to sit down on command in the future. On the other hand, if we decided to punish the dog for sitting down when told to 'sit', then the link between stimulus and response would be weakened, and in the future, the dog would be less likely to sit on command. Note that we do not have to infer anything about what is going on in the dog's mind – everything is purely in terms of the stimulus, the response and the strengthening or weakening of the link between them. Hence, the general field of study is often known as *Stimulus-Response* or *S-R Learning.*

---

2   By today's standards, rather boring: he had an adulterous affair, which in the early years of this century was not looked upon as lightly as it would be now.

3   This stuck to dictatorial principles of conditioning. Amongst his charming advice was no kissing or cuddling of your own young children – a handshake in the morning was felt to be sufficient (and character-building into the bargain).

The argument is reinforced by the following argument drawn from philosophy. If we accept that learning can be seen in terms of linking stimulus and response, then the next leap of faith is to argue that we cannot 'know' the cause of anything – all we can do is learn an association between items. This is not as strange as it first sounds. Suppose that one throws a piece of paper on a fire. It will burn. How does one know this? Because in the past, one has seen that when paper is exposed to a naked flame, it ignites. However, one does not know that the flame *causes* the paper to burn – what one has actually witnessed is that there is an association between the exposure of the paper to the flames and its burning. Similarly, if one drops something out of one's hand, it will fall to the ground. One cannot know that gravity causes this – all one can judge is that from experience, one has associated dropping things with them falling downwards. This argument is not a new one, and was first elaborated by the British philosopher David Hume (1711–1777). His work gave rise to a school of philosophers called the *Associationists*, who were active throughout the nineteenth century, and whose work Skinner used to justify his work. If, argued Skinner, one cannot know that one thing is caused by another, then all one has is the connection between items. Hence, it is futile to talk of what is going on inside the mind – all that matters is the association made between the stimulus and the response.

Skinner rose to prominence in the 1930s, when his ideas were enthusiastically met by many in Psychology. The rigorous rejection of anything but stimulus and response excluded discussion of what was occurring in the mind. This was a killing blow to many other areas of study popular at the time, which relied upon *introspection* (examining one's own thoughts to try to discern the processes which caused them). The new study of *behaviourism*, as it came to be called, remained 'top dog' in academic psychology for the next three decades. Research and teaching was dominated by a need to prove that any behaviour, no matter how complex, could be reduced to stimulus and response, strengthened or weakened as appropriate by reward or punishment. Not everyone appreciated this. Clive James, the UK television presenter and literary critic, as a student at Sydney University in the 1950s, enrolled for a psychology course fairly typical of the period:

'Psychology was taught by a faculty composed of mechanists, behaviour-
ists and logical positivists. They would have made Pavlov sound like a
mystic had he been foolish enough to show up. He must have heard how
boring they were, since he never appeared, but it was not for want of having his name invoked. The whole faculty salivated *en masse* at the mere
mention of him. As so often happens, dogmatic contempt for the very idea
of the human soul was accompanied by the limitless belief in the
quantifiability of human personality.' (James, 1980, p.134).

It must be acknowledged that there is something intuitively irksome about
behaviourism in that by attempting to analyse purely in terms of stimulus and
response, much of the complexity and wonder at thought and behaviour is
lost. However, this cannot be taken as a valid critique – the fact that a theory
is not aesthetically pleasing does not make it wrong. A more damning
condemnation of behaviourism came from experimental evidence which
demonstrated that in some instances, there was more to behaviour than
stimulus and response.

## Criticisms of behaviourism

If we accept that learning takes place by the association of stimulus and
response, then we need to demonstrate that the association can be
strengthened without inferring that something is taking place in the mind.
The only feasible solution is, as we have seen, to infer that rewards and
punishments can alter the strength of the link. One researcher, Tolman (e.g.
Tolman, 1932) demonstrated that, in some instances, this explanation was
inadequate. In one study, he gave rats the task of finding their way out of a
maze. When they got out, some of the rats were rewarded, whilst the other
rats were not. When the experiment was repeated on subsequent days, the
rewarded rats got progressively faster at finding their way through the maze,
whilst the non-rewarded rats went through at roughly the same speed each
time (they tended not to take the most direct route, but wandered around the
maze, apparently aimlessly). This is exactly what behaviourist theory would
predict. The rewarded rats are having the behaviour of getting out of the
maze strengthened, so they learn the way through the maze. The
unrewarded rats are not having their behaviour strengthened, so they do not

get any faster. In fact, the theory continues, the unrewarded rats will not be learning anything about the maze, because there is no incentive for them to do this. The problem for behaviourism is this. If Tolman began to reward the previously unrewarded rats, then, once rewarded, they began to perform as well as the rats who had been rewarded all along. So, if a rat was not rewarded until the sixth day of testing, then by the eighth or ninth day, it was going through the maze as quickly as a rat which had been rewarded from day one. This creates a problem for the behaviourist model. How can the previously unrewarded rats suddenly catch up with the 'always rewarded' rats so quickly? The only feasible explanation is that in the days prior to being rewarded, the unrewarded rats were forming a 'mental map' of the maze as they wandered round it (a process sometimes called *latent learning*). However, according to a rigid behaviourist model, this cannot be so, because mental maps are not reducible to a stimulus-response concept.

A further critique of behaviourism came from Albert Bandura's theory of *social learning*. Bandura observed that, often, we are reasonably good at performing certain tasks from the first time we try them. For example, the first time we try to kick a ball or drive a car, we do not have to learn very basic movements and gradually build them up into a set of more complex actions – we simply have a go, and usually make a pretty good attempt at it. This can only occur if we have formed an idea of the behaviour in our minds before we try it. The way in which we form such an idea is by observing others do the same thing. In this, we are aided by *vicarious reinforcement*. If we see others rewarded for performing certain acts, then we are more likely to copy them. If they are punished, we are more likely to avoid them. Bandura showed an example of this is a series of experiments known as the *Bobo doll studies* (e.g. Bandura *et al.*, 1963). Bobo the Clown was a popular children's TV character in the USA in the late 1950s and early 1960s. In one of the key experiments, children were shown a film of a woman dressed like a school teacher playing with some toys, including a large inflatable model of Bobo. In one version of the film, the woman plays sensibly with the toys. In the other, she attacks the Bobo doll and 'beats him up'. The children, having seen one or other version of the film, are shown into another room containing toys, including the Bobo doll. If the children had seen the 'responsible play' film, then they similarly tended to play responsibly. On the other hand, if they had seen the 'beat up Bobo' film, they tended to behave in a similar manner, imitating what they had seen the woman do. Note that at no time in instances of social learning are we directly being rewarded or punished – it is a model of the behaviour in our minds which we are adjusting. However, if we have a model in our minds, then this flatly contradicts a rigidly-enforced model of behaviourism.

The findings of such studies sounded a death knell for the more extreme forms of behaviourism. Clearly, there are instances where learning must necessarily involve mental models, and cannot just be seen in terms of a simple association between stimulus and response. Some of behaviourism's more ingenious and vociferous supporters endeavoured to show that these mental model explanations were either wrong or could be reduced to simpler stimulus-response pairings, but they were in the main fighting a rearguard action. It would be wrong, however, to think that because in its extreme form behaviourism received a critical drubbing, the theory is totally without worth. A 'milder' form of behaviourism – *neobehaviourism* – acknowledges a role for mental models, but argues that a principal driving force is association learning. This is an argument which seems intuitively reasonable, and is one, for instance, which is currently receiving support from some workers in *artificial intelligence* which, amongst other things, attempts to model the workings of the mind using computer programmes. A more backhanded compliment to behaviourism is that it spurred psychologists into realising that models of mental processing have to be more rigorous than simply trying to codify the products of introspecting one's own thoughts. When models of mental processing did make a comeback in the 1950s they were, as can be seen in other chapters, more sensible and robust.

A more troublesome issue concerns the ethics of testing animals. Most people would agree that the dignity and well-being of any animal should be respected even if ultimately one is going to eat it. The decision on whether conditioning animals by rewarding them contravenes this dignity is perhaps a matter of personal choice. The case against animal experimentation becomes stronger when one considers experiments in which the animals are punished. For example, training an animal to perform a particular act in order to avoid receiving an electric shock or other forms of pain (an experimental method used frequently in the past) is less easy to countenance than sending a rat down a maze and giving it a titbit of food at the end.

It should also be remembered that behaviourism was not just a theoretical stance. The basic tenets guided approaches in areas of applied psychology as well. One of behaviourism's biggest influences has been on the treatment of mental illness. *Behaviour therapy* attempts to treat patients by altering their associations with events and situations so that they learn new and 'better' behaviours whilst casting off the old and maladaptive ones. In keeping with the tradition of behaviourism, no analysis of the underlying mental state of the patient is allowed (cf. Chapter 12). Another, more controversial, use of behaviourism was in educational theory. Skinner, like Watson before him, believed that children's (and indeed adults') behaviour and learning could be shaped by conditioning techniques. He advocated *programmed instruction* – the pupil reviews a piece of information, answers questions about it, and proceeds to a more advanced task if he or she is correct. Learning is thus incremental, with the child acquiring knowledge in comfortable 'bites'. The work has been criticised for being too harsh and mechanistic, though it can be argued that the basic principles of conditioning are used in all forms of education – only the thickness of the sugar coating differs. A problem with such developing models of education is that in some instances it creates a messianic will to change society as a whole. Skinner obeyed this rule, and a novel – *Walden Two* (Skinner, 1948) describes how an ideal community can be created by his conditioning methods. A further book – *Beyond Freedom and Dignity* (Skinner, 1971) – argued that the concept of 'freedom' was erroneous, and that people are (and should be) controlled by conditioning. It takes little imagination to guess who Skinner felt should be doing the conditioning. *Sed quis custodiet ipsos Custodes?* – but who is to guard the guards themselves?

FURTHER READING

Skinner (1948) and Skinner (1971) make interesting reading for those who have a taste for such things. A good overview is provided by Mackintosh (1983). For those interested in what animals might be capable of learning beyond basic conditioning, Pearce (1987) is strongly recommended.

# CHAPTER 8

# Memory

## Functions of memory

Memory is most often thought of in terms of its role as our record of what we have encountered in the past, be it personal events, or facts which we have had to rote learn at school or at work. It is very much our store of knowledge, and without it we lack not only information about the world about us, but also a sense of who we are. Because such issues are central to our lives, it is tempting to see memory solely in these terms and examine the issue no further. However, memory is also an essential component of our present and future lives. Without it, we could not remember to do things in the future, nor could we comprehend the here and now (e.g., without a memory store, how could we recognise the words spoken to us?). It is no exaggeration to state that we are defined and controlled by our memories. Therefore, in considering memory, we have to consider the various roles which memory takes in our lives, and this is a rich field for psychologists.

## The three store model

One of the simplest ways of investigating memory is to consider the lengths of time over which different memory stores operate. The current 'industry standard' model is the *three store model* which argues that our memories can be divided into (surprisingly enough) three components – *sensory memory, short term memory* and *long term memory*. Several commentators have proposed this model, but most acknowledge that its origins lie in an influential paper by Atkinson and Shiffrin (1968). The model begins with the common sense notion that whatever we learn has to be encountered through the senses (and principally through sight and sound).

*Sensory memory*

When we see or hear something, a sensory memory is formed. This is a *very* short-lasting recording which disappears in under one second. We know that it exists because of some very elegant experimental work by, amongst others, Sperling (1960). Sperling showed his subjects a visual image of an array of letters arranged in three horizontal rows. The image was presented very briefly, using a machine called a *tachistoscope*, which is designed to display images for fractions of a second. The participant was then asked to report what he or she saw, but with an added proviso. After the display was shown, a musical tone was played to the subjects, who were instructed that if they heard a high pitched tone, they were to report what they saw on the top line; a middle-pitched note, the middle line; and a low-pitched note, the bottom line. The subjects could do this with a fair degree of accuracy, provided they heard the tone within a second of seeing the display – if they were kept waiting longer than this, then they could not remember what they had seen. Therefore, the subjects could 'see' the image for under a second before it faded. It was established that this was not a simple afterimage (e.g., as occurs when one stares at a light bulb and then looks away), which leads to the conclusion that there is a very brief visual memory formed when we seen things. Other work has established that there is a similar sensory memory for acoustic information (known as *echoic memory*). This is experienced by many people when asking someone to repeat what they have just said because they did not quite hear it, and then realising what was said before the person repeats the message. What has happened is that the listener has referred back to his or her echoic memory of the message and re-analysed it, this time correctly.

The role of sensory memory is an interesting one, but its role in the total 'memory machine' is probably rather peripheral. In many ways the linchpin of the process is short term memory which is where information is sent to once it has been identified by the senses.

*Short term memory*

Definitions of 'short term memory' vary between researchers. In essence, it is one's memory for what has just taken place. Typically, this means memory for what has happened in about the last twenty seconds or less. Short term memory is notoriously frail. To take the standard example of this, the reader should look at the list of numbers printed below, then look away and try to remember them in sequence:

5   1   9   7   8   2   6

Most readers should be able to remember all or most of the sequence. However, if one were now to put down this book and do something else for a couple of minutes, then it is doubtful if one could remember the sequence, unless during that time one had consciously tried to remember it. This is the key feature of short term memory – unless a conscious attempt is made to retain information, it is quickly lost. One of the things which people often ask is why short term memory is so unreliable – why do we forget the overwhelming majority of what we encounter? The simple answer is that if we did not forget, then memory would be so clogged up with irrelevant information that the mind could not function. For example, the majority of what we hear and see is only of transitory importance (e.g. we do not need to remember every shopping list we have ever used). Short term memory is in many respects like a sieve – it sorts through what we need to retain for future use and discards the rubbish. This does not always work perfectly – we can all recall instances where we wish we could remember more of what happened. However, this is the price we often have to pay for keeping a streamlined memory store.

Short term memory has a fairly small capacity. The figure normally quoted is that if we are given a list of words or numbers, then most people can remember somewhere between five and nine items (generally, the more intelligent you are, the larger your memory). The late George Miller, a very articulate writer on the subject, coined the phrase *the magical number seven, plus or minus two* to denote what people typically remember (Miller, 1956).[1] There are ways of increasing how much can be remembered, and Miller argued that each 'item' a person could remember consisted of a *chunk* of information. The composition of a chunk varies according to the prior knowledge of the sub-

---

1   Generally, people have longer memory spans the higher their IQ.

ject. For example, consider the list '2014266977'. If one were attempting to remember this list simply as a set of individual numbers, then it would probably be beyond one's memory span. However, suppose one recognised the numbers as forming a recognised sequence. such as the 'phone numbers of friends (e.g. '20142' was one such number, and '66977' the other). In this instance, one would see the numbers not as ten separate items to be remembered, but as two items. This is an example of forming chunks – grouping items to be remembered into a smaller set of bigger items which one finds easy to remember. This capacity for remembering can be taken to impressive lengths. For example, a study by Ericsson and Chase (1982) showed that, with training, a volunteer could remember sequences of eighty or more numbers. The volunteer was a keen runner, and recoded the numbers he was presented with into sets of running times typical of different lengths of races. In other words, he was not remembering eighty or more *separate numbers*, but a smaller set of *groups of numbers*. Thus, by chunking, the amount which can be held in memory (also known as *span*) can be increased.

Another feature of short term memory is the *serial position effect*. If we are given a list of items to remember, then we tend to remember best those presented at the beginning of the list (the *primacy effect*) and at the end of the list (the *recency effect*). Items in the middle are generally less well remembered. This reveals a key characteristic of short term memory. Namely, that it is acting as a 'relay station' and passing on information to a more permanent memory store. Researchers argue that if we are given a list of words to remember, we begin to process them as soon as we hear or see the first word. Words which come early in the list are accordingly processed first and these, it is argued, will have been dealt with and passed on to another, more lasting memory store by the time the person has to recall as much as they can of the list. Because the words have been passed on to a more permanent store, they should be reasonably well remembered. The final few items on the list will still be fresh in the short term memory, and they too will be well remembered. The items which will be relatively badly recalled will be those in the middle of the list, lying 'in limbo' between the recently-encountered and the passed-to-storage items.

*Long term memory*

The final component of the three store model is long term memory, which refers to a more-or-less permanent store of information. This is in essence 'fed' by the earlier stages of Atkinson and Shiffrin's model, and whatever is learnt has first been processed by the short term memory store. The total capacity of long term memory has never been accurately calculated. Also, it is reasonably impervious to many physical changes. For example, unless a person suffers from a very severe illness such as dementia, then ageing has little or no effect on memory for facts, such as definitions of words (cf. Stuart-Hamilton, 1994). Long term memory thus differs from short term memory in terms of capacity. The two stores also tend to find different features salient. For example, in most instances, people find similar-sounding words harder to store in short term memory (e.g. 'cat, beg, day' would be easier to remember than 'cat, rat, bat') – a phenomenon called the *phonemic similarity effect*. Again, the ease with which short term memory can remember a list depends upon how long it takes to say it – the longer it takes to pronounce, the less likely it is to be remembered (the *word length effect*). Memory span is not so much determined by the number of words as their length (e.g. 'cat, boy, man' would be easier to remember than 'cabbage, chocolate, establishment'). Long term memory is less affected by these factors. However, it is more prone to errors if words of similar meaning are being recalled (*semantic similarity effect*).

## Working memory

The three store model was hugely influential on cognitive psychologists and is still accepted as a general description of the manner in which memory functions. However, the detailed description of short term memory was felt to be unsatisfactory, since it described only a limited portion of what short term memory must do. A common method of testing short term memory is to give someone a list of numbers or words and ask them to repeat them back. The longer the list which can be repeated, the bigger the memory span. Variants of this technique require the person to repeat the items on the list back in any order (*free recall*); or in the order presented (*ordered recall*); or more sadistically, in reverse order (*reverse recall*). To make the task more difficult, subjects might be asked to perform an unrelated task between being told the list and being asked to repeat it. This *distractor task* is intended to interfere with the formation of a memory trace.[2] Such tasks can tell one a great deal about how people can memorise lists in the laboratory, but relatively little about how short term memory is used in everyday life. For example, it is very rare for a person to be asked to remember a list of words without any purpose. Much commoner uses are, for example, holding information in short term memory whilst performing another task. Examples include: remembering a phone number whilst dialling it; carrying over numbers in one's head whilst doing a piece of arithmetic; or, whilst speaking, remembering a piece of information which must be imparted later in the conversation. Using short term memory in this manner (remembering something whilst performing another task) is often called *working memory*, and a highly influential model, which recast short term memory in these terms was devised by Baddeley and Hitch (1974) and subsequently revised (see Baddeley, 1995). In Atkinson and Shiffrin's model, short term memory had been seen as a *unitary store* – i.e. everything to be remembered was stored in a single 'mental compartment'. Baddeley and Hitch argued that short term memory consisted of several stores. The *central executive* controlled the short term memory process. It could store a very limited amount of information, but its chief function was to control the running of the two main memory stores. The first of these is the *articulatory loop* (later renamed the *phonological loop*) which is responsible for storing verbal information (e.g. words, numbers, etc). The second is the *visuo-spatial sketchpad*, which stores visual and spatial information.

The working memory model is now very widely accepted and forms the basis for many assumptions about how memory works. There is neurological evidence (see Baddeley, 1995) that particular sections of the brain perform the functions of segments of the model (e.g. some areas of the frontal lobes appear to be involved in central executive functions). Again, a great attraction

---

2     A common variant is the *Brown-Peterson task*, in which people must count backwards (typically, in threes).

of the model is that it helps explain how memory works in the 'real world', as opposed to artificial laboratory settings.

## Types of long term memory

The sentiment that memory studies were rather artificial began to stir researchers into action about twenty years ago, when they began to examine memory not as an ability to be studied in isolation in the laboratory, but as a facet of everyday intellectual life. The concept of 'memory in the real world' (see Cohen, 1989) acknowledged the practical role of memory, and in particular led to a radical revision of concepts of long term memory. Instead of being regarded as a worthy but dull store of accumulated knowledge, researchers began to categorise it according to the functions it performed. It should be noted, however, that different categorisation systems often overlap, and it is difficult to see how they *all* can be correct – often the divisions are useful for practical purposes, but may not reflect reality in terms of differences in the anatomical areas of the brain involved in storage.

## Memories of one's own life

An intuitively obvious division, first proposed by Tulving (1972), is to consider memories for facts and information which are not concerned with one's own life (*semantic memory*) and contrast this with *episodic memory*, which is memory for events directly concerned with one's own life (e.g. personal details, day-to-day occurrences, etc). Often memories of facts are disconnected from memories of personal experiences (e.g. although most people know that Beethoven's Ninth Symphony is called 'The Choral', few people will remember where, when and how they learnt this information). The issue of personal involvement in memories has been addressed in other manners. For example, *autobiographical memory* (which is subtly different from episodic memory) refers to memory for events which are specific to an individual person's life, rather than a shared experience with others of the same general background and age. A curious feature of this type of memory is the *reminiscence peak*, which is the phenomenon that the bulk of autobiographical memories stem from when people were aged 10–30 years. The reason for this is probably that this is the period of life when most interesting and memorable things happen to a person. Curiously, nothing is usually remembered from the first months or even years of life (*childhood amnesia*). Freud, who examined the phenomenon, not surprisingly argued that this was because of suppression of emotionally-fraught memories. Later researchers have taken the more prosaic view that it is because very young children do not have the necessary intellectual powers to store memories effectively so that they can later be retrieved.

A special feature of autobiographical memory is *flashbulb memory*. This is the memory of highly significant and emotionally-charged events in one's life. These can be very personal (e.g. first sexual experience, learning that Santa Claus does not exist, etc) or can be reactions to very newsworthy events which practically everybody alive at the time will also have (e.g. memories of 'what were you doing when you heard that Princess Diana had died?' or, for people over a certain age, 'what were you doing when you heard that Kennedy had been shot?'). The memory is unusual in that the person remembers (often in some detail) their own situation when they heard the news, which is the sort of information which is missing from conventional recollections. It has been argued that flashbulb memories are stored differently, use different neurotransmitters, etc. However, a more prosaic, but plausible, argument is that because such events are meaningful, they tend to be replayed in the mind very frequently, so that they become unusually well stored. It should not be supposed, however, that flashbulb memories are necessarily any more accurate than other forms of memory. For example, there is a famous[3] anecdote about a famous psychologist (Ulric Neisser) recalling his flashbulb memory of hearing of the bombing of Pearl Harbor. He 'remembered' the news interrupting a radio report of a baseball match – this was impossible, since this took place in December, when baseball is not played. Similarly, there is the case of Piaget's recollection of being kidnapped. He had a distinct memory of a kidnap attempt on himself when he was two years old, which his nurse successfully prevented. As an adolescent, Piaget discovered that the nurse had made up the whole episode, and accordingly, his memory was an elaboration of her story, rather than of a real event.

3    Famous in cognitive psychology, anyway.

A less dramatic version of autobiographical memory is the division of memories into *specific* and *generic*. The former are memories of specific single events, whilst the latter are memories of events which occurred many times, but which coalesce into a single memory. For example, memories of eating meals in a school canteen are likely to be of the general experience of eating there – there will not be a specific memory of each occasion when one ate there.

In contrast to autobiographical memory is *remote memory*. This is memory for non-autobiographical events which have occurred during a person's lifetime, and which are part of their memory of the past, rather than part of general semantic memory. For example, remembering that George Bush was elected President of the USA would not count as part of remote memory because the information that George Bush was once US President is part of general knowledge (i.e. it is not solely tied to events in the past). Tests of remote memory typically present people with names or events from the past which were well-publicised at the time, but quickly disappeared from public view thereafter. One such test – the *Famous Names Test* (Stevens, 1979) asks people to consider a list of names and decide which are of people who were famous in the past, and which are names invented by the experimenter. Some names are very famous indeed (e.g. Cliff Richard), and are identified by anyone not suffering from dementia, whilst others were famous for only brief periods at certain times in the past (e.g. John Conteh or Reggie Whitcombe[4]). Remote memory tests are unusual in that almost always older people perform better on them than younger adults. Curiously, however, individual names on the Famous Names Test are as relatively famous within a young age group as they are within an old age group. For example, if 'Mr X' is the ninth-most recognised name amongst seventy-year-olds, then he is likely to be about ninth-most recognised by twenty-year-olds (Stuart-Hamilton, Perfect and Rabbitt, 1988). This indicates that the mechanisms for maintaining awareness of names work in a similar manner for all age groups.

4    For younger and overseas readers – Sir Cliff Richard is a very popular singer in the UK; John Conteh was a famous boxer in the 1970s, and Reggie Whitcombe a champion golfer pre-World War II.

## Using memories

Aside from considerations of one's personal involvement, a key function of memory, as argued above, is to help to make sense of the world. One method of approaching this is to divide long term memory into memory for basic facts (*declarative memory*) and contrast this with memory for how to do things (*procedural memory*). This is not as trite a division as might first appear. For example, there is evidence that patients with some forms of brain damage can be taught to perform complex physical tasks (e.g. solving the Tower of Hanoi problem), which they will then complete very rapidly, whilst claiming that they have no knowledge of how to do the task. Therefore, declarative and procedural memories need not be based upon the same neurological mechanisms.

Another consideration in using memories in problem-solving is that the full memory of how a problem might be solved may not be stored – instead it is extrapolated from more basic pieces of information. For example, consider the statement 'there is usually heavy demand for wool from shops in July and August as birds start knitting pullovers for the winter'. This is nonsense, of course, because memory informs one that birds do not use shops, knit, or wear clothes. However, there is not an explicit single memory covering the issues raised in the statement – nobody has a memory that birds do not visit woolshops in the summer months. Instead, the interpretation is based upon a logical interpretation of a basic set of memories, such as birds are animals; animals do not do human 'civilised' things; knitting and shopping are civilised things. Ergo, animals and hence birds do not do these things. The basic facts which are worked upon form *explicit memory*, whilst the extrapolation of information from these facts is called *implicit memory*.

Implicit memory is very useful because it enables the mind to be flexible. If recognition could only take place if a question or problem exactly matched up with a memory, then memory would be very poor indeed. However, there is a price to be paid for this flexibility. Because memories have a component of interpretation, errors can creep in, sometimes with serious results. This is elegantly demonstrated by the work of Bartlett.

## Schema theory

In his classic book on memory called, appropriately enough, *Remembering*, Bartlett (1932) demonstrated how memory was prone to misinterpretation, and in particular, how memories might be shaped to fit what the person expected to be there. A key facet of this argument is the concept of the *schema*. A schema is a mental representation of a particular event or situation, and is essentially a set of expectations about what it will be like. A schema can be about something known (e.g. a school class room schema will contain expectations of chairs, desks, teacher, children, imparting of information by the teacher to the pupils, assessment of the pupils' performance, etc). Or, it can be of something unknown. For example, although there is no definite proof of visits from other planets, people have expectations about what visiting extraterrestrials might be. To a large extent these are shaped by existing biases. For example, it has been noted that the spate of 'bug eyed monster' films of the 1950s (notably such classics as *Invasion of the Body Snatchers*), in which the aliens were very hostile, coincided with the USA's preoccupation with the danger of a Russian invasion. In general, nothing is more fixed to its period of origin than a science fiction film.[5]

Bartlett demonstrated that schemas[6] do more than distort visions of the future, however. In one of his best-known experiments, he gave people a native American story to read, called *War of the Ghosts*. This is a folk tale which is told in a narrative style completely different from the European tradition. If a (British) person read this tale and then recalled it some time later, the details of the story subtly changed, so that remembered incidents became more akin to a familiar narrative pattern. Furthermore, the longer the interval between encountering the story and retelling it, the greater these changes. A similar pattern was observed if people were asked to draw pictures from memory. In one study, Bartlett performed a version of 'Chinese Whispers', in which the first person tried to reproduce an unfamiliar drawing from memory. The second person tried to draw the first person's drawing from memory, the third

5    E.g. *2001: A Space Odyssey* is a magnificent film, but consider the costumes and decor of the space station sequences, which are pure 1960s.

6    Or *schemata* – either is acceptable.

person tried to draw the second person's drawing, etc, etc. In this manner, a complex Ancient Egyptian hieroglyph of an owl, for example, over progressive drawings became a simple drawing of a sitting cat. In short, schemas can distort memory of what was there to a memory of what the person felt ought to be there.

The distortions of memory introduced by a schema can have serious consequences. In a series of classic studies, Loftus and colleagues (see Loftus, 1979) demonstrated that eyewitness reports of events could be seriously distorted by the schema used. For example, if people saw a film of a car crash, they were likely to estimate a higher speed for the cars if asked what happened when the cars 'smashed' into each other, rather than 'bumped'. Again, police detectives are more likely to continue questioning a suspect when he or she fits a stereotypical profile of a 'villain' than if they do not, in spite of objective contradictory evidence (see Gudjonsson, 1992).

A related issue is *false memory*. The process of subjectively judging memories involves *reality monitoring*, which is a self-assessment of how true one believes a memory to be. As has just been seen, the danger is that a statement or suggestion about an event which never occurred can become memorised as a true memory of a real event. This is especially contentious when considering issues such as child sexual abuse. Sexual abuse can and does create lasting psychological damage. Therefore, a therapist treating a patient may have sound grounds for questioning whether that patient suffered abuse in early life. A negative answer to a direct question such as 'were you abused as a child?' may not mean that the person was not abused, since many victims of such attacks repress their memories of these events (e.g. Williams, 1992). In trying to break through a psychological defence, the therapist may resort to methods such as hypnotism. The grave danger with such methods is that the therapist may, by questioning about abuse, create the impression in the patient's mind that abuse took place when in reality there was none. Over time, this suggestion may create a false memory of abuse, and innocent memories (e.g. of bathtime, being read a bedtime story) may adopt far more sinister connotations. False accusations such as these divide families and may lead to the alleged perpetrator losing his (usually it is a male who is accused) job and facing prosecution.

Based on such evidence, one may ask why schemas are used, if they are so unreliable. Again, the matter becomes one of pragmatics. Although they do introduce errors, in the main schemas are very useful in lightening the intellectual load. For example, suppose that one did not have a 'stairs schema' providing one with a general memory of how to walk up stairs. If every set of stairs had to be treated as a completely new entity, then life would be unnecessarily labourious.[7] Again, schemas protect one from over-learning unnecessary information. There is little purpose, for example, in learning every trip to a restaurant or a lavatory as a specific event. It is far more efficient to let them all blend into generic memories. In short, the schema is a necessary fudge.

The general concept of the schema is now widely accepted. Research subsequent to Bartlett has established that schemas have several key features. First, an individual schema will contain a set of expectations about what will be found. These vary in importance. Some are absolutely expected (e.g. a 'room schema' will carry an expectation of walls, a floor and a ceiling). Others will be expected but are not necessary (e.g. furniture), whilst in other instances one of a set of options will be expected (e.g. manner in which the walls are decorated – wallpaper, paint, etc). If an item is not present which is strongly expected then often people will falsely remember it being there. For example, Brewer and Treyens (1981) gave people the task of recalling everything they could remember seeing in a postgraduate's office which they had visited for about half a minute. People correctly recalled some items, but falsely recalled seeing 'typical' student items such as books and pens (in fact, none had been there). Why should this happen? It would appear that if a key item is not remembered, then the schema will often provide a false memory of the most obvious alternative which would be expected to be present (what is called the *default value*). Hence, if a person expects pens and books to be in a postgraduate room, then he or she will often falsely imagine they were there when they are not. Inter alia, this provides a serious problem for interpreting eyewitness accounts – how much did a witness actually see and how much are false additions by their schema? Again, it may be questioned why schemas should contain such an obvious flaw. The reason is that for the ma-

---

7    And the absence of a 'going to the lavatory' schema does not bear contemplating.

jority of the time, filling in missing details with default values greatly speeds up understanding. Suppose a friend says that he went to a football match the other night – without a schema for attending sports events, one would then have to ask questions such as 'were other people there?', 'how does one watch a football match?', 'what are the physical arrangements for accommodating spectators?', etc, etc. Even the simplest conversation would take a very long time. Schemas exist to make life simple: their primary purpose is to make sense of situations (what Bartlett called 'effort after meaning'). The proportion of occasions when they are helpful far outweigh the times when they distort information seriously enough for it to be of practical importance.

Another key feature of schemas is the concept of the *schema plus tag* (Graesser and Nakamura, 1982). This states that repetitions of similar events tend to get melded into a single generic memory. Individual events will stand out and be remembered only if something out of the ordinary occurred (i.e. the event has a tag attached to it). Also, within a particular event, an item will be remembered if it is atypical for the schema. For example, in the Brewer and Treyens study cited above, people were more likely to remember items not normally associated with a postgraduate's office (e.g. a pair of pliers) than many mundane and more predictable items.

A final consideration is that schemas apply to various levels of processing. For example, schemas might deal with relatively mundane practical events such as how to get a tight lid off a jar, but they can also be concerned with abstract concepts, such as recognising rational behaviour. Furthermore, many commentators argue that these schemas can be arranged hierarchically, so that different combinations of schemas can be employed for different situations. For example, driving into town will involve many of the same schemas ('driving the car' schema, 'finding a parking place' schema, etc) whether the end destination is the dentist or a restaurant.

One of the key proponents of this argument is Schank (e.g. Schank, 1981). He originally devised a concept of *scripts* (essentially, schemas for performing sequences of actions) but refined his model into the *memory organisation packet (MOP)*. This is a collection of several scripts, which together enable a person to cope with a specific situation. MOPs may have scripts in common (e.g. like the going to the dentist or restaurant example just cited). Rather than waste *memory space* with storing an identical script in each MOP, it makes intuitive sense to keep a 'mental library' of scripts, which can be drawn upon for different situations. This may explain why people tend to confuse events whose MOPs have a lot of scripts in common (e.g. visits to a zoo and to a park). MOPs can be joined together to form *metaMOPs*, which are a conglomeration of several smaller MOPs (e.g. a 'day out' metaMOP may call upon a driving MOP, a shopping MOP, a visiting an ancestral house MOP, a bad weather MOP, etc). Schank also proposed the model of a *thematic organisation packet (TOP)*, which is a mechanism for abstracting conceptual links between different situations (e.g. being jilted by a girlfriend/boyfriend and losing a business contract).

Schema theory can thus be seen as enormously useful in describing memory and how it shapes one's understanding of the world. However, a problem with it is that it is very vague and prone to teleological reasoning.[8] Thus, if a person makes a memory error, then this can be attributed to the workings of the schema. Because schema theory can describe practically any type of error, this makes the whole matter rather tedious. This may strike the reader as being an unreasonable complaint – if a theory accurately describes what happens, why should this be a matter of discontent? The reason is that schema theory only generally describes what happens – it does not offer a particularly deep insight into *why* an event occurs.

## Awareness of memory

So far, discussion about memory has concentrated upon how it works, with little regard for a person's own awareness of memory. Self-awareness and, by extension, knowledge of mnemonic strengths and weaknesses is known as *metamemory*. Often people use metamemory in gauging the accuracy of their recall. For example, in judging the validity of a statement, most people use *metamemory inference*, which is the belief that something cannot be true because one would have heard about it if it was. For example, consider the statement 'extraterrestrials disrupted the 1995 Superbowl by landing a

---

8   A logical flaw in which a person argues that because something is the way it is, other things have evolved to suit it (e.g. because shoes are the shape they are, feet are shoe-shaped).

spaceship on the pitch'. This, one can argue, cannot be true because such a major event would be remembered. Other aspects of metamemory are concerned with knowledge of the extent of one's memory store (*epistemic awareness*) and how items can be retrieved from memory or made easier to remember (*systemic awareness*). Humans' abilities at tasks such as these are often astonishingly good, but usually pass unnoticed. For example, consider the following words – how many can the reader define?

ribible, antidisestablishmentariansm, manumit, adumbrate[9]

Before readers feel too disappointed about not knowing some of the definitions, it is worth considering the mental process which has taken place to decide that an answer is not known. Consider all the information which is accrued in the mind – not only all the words, but all the definitions and pieces of knowledge attached to them. That vast data base has been searched through in a fraction of a second to determine that the word being looked for is not there. Imagine trying to find whether the word 'carpet' appeared in Chapter 2.[10] This is a matter of sorting through a few thousand words, rather than several hundred thousand pieces of information – how long would this take?

## Enhancing memory

A variety of ways exist to enhance memory. A type of memory not so far discussed is *prospective memory*, which is remembering to do something in the future. A variety of methods can be devised to help this, which can be divided into *internal cues* (i.e. producing a prompt from within the mind) and *external cues* (putting something in the surroundings which, when perceived, will remind one to do something, such as an alarm clock or the proverbial knot in the handkerchief). Generally, external cues are more effective, but surprisingly, getting older seems to have relatively little effect on re-membering appointments and similar actions (see Maylor, 1990).

---

9   Answers: a mediaeval musical instrument; being opposed to the church being separated from the state; liberate; foreshadow.

10   Please don't try looking – it doesn't.

Other methods of improving memory have tended to concentrate on improving recall of lists of items. It can be readily established that if one is shown a list of numbers or words, and one makes no attempt to remember them, they will be quickly forgotten. One of the most straightforward ways of improving memory of lists is to repeat the items on the list in one's head – a process known as *rehearsal*. This can be further categorised into two kinds – *maintenance rehearsal* simply rehearses the information without attempting to transform it, or add properties to it which will make it more memorable. Thus, trying to remember the words 'cat, dog, bag', a person would simply repeat the words to him- or herself over and over again. *Elaborative rehearsal* is more sophisticated. The person attempts to enhance the memorability of a set of items by 'enriching' their mental image. There are several ways in which this might be done. For example, in the *keyword technique*, the person associates the *to-be-remembered* or *TBR* items by forming a striking visual image which links them. For example, the list 'cat, dog, bag' might be formed into an image of a cat chasing a dog with a bag in its mouth. The image would be a striking one, and hence is more likely to be remembered.

Another method, devised by the Ancient Greeks, is the *method of loci technique*. This requires some preparation prior to trying to memorise a list. First, the person forms a mental image of a room with which they are familiar. Then, the TBR items are mentally placed at different locations in this mental image. For example, suppose one had to remember the digit list '1, 4, 5, 3'. One might imagine one's living room – the 1 is sitting in an armchair, the 4 is closing the curtains, etc, etc. The legend of Simonides of Ceos is sometimes cited as an exponent of this technique. Simonides, an Ancient Greek poet, was a guest at a banquet. For reasons too lengthy to explain here,[11] the banqueting room collapsed just after Simonides had been called outside. The guests were too squashed to be accurately identified, but Simonides was able to identify which body was which by remembering the mental image of the seating arrangements. Another method of elaborative rehearsal is the *peg-word system*. The person first learns a simple rhyming system (e.g. '1 is a bun; 2 is a shoe', etc). The information can then be used in two principal

11   Basically, the host of the banquet had offended the Olympian gods, but Simondes hadn't.

ways. When given a list of numbers to remember, the subject can associate the numbers with their associated images. This enriches the images, and should make them easier to recall. The system can also be used to encode a short series of words. The first word in the list is made into a visual image with the image representing the first number. The same process is repeated for the other words. (e.g. if the first two words in the list of to-be-remembered items are 'clock' and 'car', the subject might form an image of a clock sandwich and a shoe driving a car).

Another consideration is the context in which the TBR items are encountered and that in which they are recalled. Generally, the *encoding specificity principle* applies. This states that the probability of recalling an item is dependent on the degree of similarity between the contexts of the learning and recall sessions – the more similar the two situations, the higher the recall. A version of this is *state-dependency*, which refers to the degree to which recall is dependent upon the subject's internal state. For example, several studies (cf. Baddeley, 1995) showed that subjects remembered information which they had learnt when drunk better when they were drunk again than when they were sober (and similarly, soberly-learnt material was better recalled when sober than when drunk).[12]

Another influence on memorability is the degree to which a 'good quality' memory trace can be created. First, the creation of memory traces (often called *encoding*) can be done at varying levels of 'intensity'. The more a TBR item can be scrutinised, generally the better it can be remembered. This is not simply a matter of the person having longer to look at the item. The general principle of *levels of processing* assumes that if an item has been analysed for 'deeper' qualities, such as its meaning, then it will be remembered better than an item which has only been studied for more 'surface' qualities, such as what it sounds like (cf. Baddeley, 1995; Eysenck and Keane, 1995). Again, if an item is encoded without distractions of extraneous noise, etc, then this too will obviously improve memorability.

---

12    In case any enterprising reader thinks they have hit upon a novel exam revision strategy – the overwhelming evidence is that intellectual performance is better in a sober than in an even mildly inebriated person.

A final consideration on memorability is the quantity of assistance available to the person when trying to recall items. Retrieving information from memory can be by either *recall* or *recognition*. Recall is the process of retrieving a memory without any cues or other aids, whilst in recognition, the person is presented with an item and must decide if it is one of the TBR items. Typically, recall is harder than recognition, because the former requires a person to search their memory store, whilst the latter 'only' requires the person to match an item against items in the memory store. A variety of methods are available for testing these processes. Ordered recall and free recall have been described earlier in this chapter. In *cued recall*, the person is helped by being provided with partial features of the TBR item(s), such as the first letter, words which sound like it, etc. This can provide a useful insight into how items are stored in memory, since by varying the cue, we can see which are the most salient (e.g. if the first letter is better at retrieving a memory than giving a word which means the same, then this may indicate that the person stores memories of words in terms of their constituent letters rather than meaning). In a recognition task, several options are available. For example, a person may be shown items in sequence and he or she must decide if each in turn is a member of the TBR list. Recognition tasks almost invariably include some items which were not on the TBR list (the *distractor items*). A variant of the recognition task is the *forced choice recognition task*, in which the person is presented with a TBR item and one or more distractor items at the same time, and must choose between them. Distractor items may be chosen for particular characteristics. For example, they may be similar to the TBR items in some manner, since this can reveal information about how the information is stored. For example, if the person erroneously chooses distractor items which sound similar to the TBR items, but correctly rejects distractor items which have similar meanings, then this may be evidence that the person has stored the TBR items in terms of what they sound like.

## Summary

It is clear that memory can be regarded in several different manners depending upon the needs of the situation. One common method of describing memory is to divide it up according to the length of time the memory is stored, as is the case with the three store model. However, memory cannot just be regarded as an entity to be studied in isolation in a laboratory – its principal use is not in remembering word lists, but in helping people cope with everyday intellectual problems. This can be seen in the important revision of the short term memory component of the three store model known as working memory. Long term memory has been categorised in many ways. Amongst the most discussed are: the divisions of memory into stores concerned with personal matters and those with more 'impersonal' facts; and the use of schemas to assist comprehension of items and events. It is important to note that memory is fallible. Much is forgotten to make room for only the most important information, and in the case of schemas, memories may be simplified and stereotyped. This is usually the price to be paid for convenience and efficient day-to-day functioning. Memory can be aided, both by a person's own strategies and also depending upon the way in which memories must be retrieved. The neurological basis of memory is discussed in Chapter 10.

FURTHER READING

Alan Baddeley's *Memory* (Baddeley, 1995) is an excellent and comprehensive introduction to the topic. For readers looking for a somewhat shorter piece of reading, then Best (1995) or Sternberg (1996) may be of especial interest. Gillian Cohen's (1995) *Memory in the Real World* is a more specialised text (though very readable), dealing, as the title implies, with uses of memory in real life.

# CHAPTER 9

# Perception

## Introduction – The specious present

Perception is the study of how the mind interprets information provided by the senses. In a broad sense, this is the concern of much of Psychology, so the term is usually confined to the processing of specifically sensory information, rather than including the thoughts and behaviours which result from detecting a stimulus. Hence, perception is concerned with how one might detect, for example, a charging bull – the subsequent mental operations involved in running away are not of relevance. Perception is therefore concerned with the senses – sight, hearing, smell, taste, and touch being the most often cited. However, the majority of interest has centred on sight (*visual perception*) with some attention being paid to hearing (*auditory perception*) and relatively little on the other senses. This arguably reflects the relative importance of the senses. Whilst touch, smell and taste are of relevance to one's existence, they are not as vital for survival as sight or hearing.

At its most basic, perception occurs because the mind interprets information sent to it by the senses. This takes time (albeit a fraction of a second), because the information from the sense organs must travel along nerves before it reaches the brain. Therefore, what the mind detects and interprets in fact occurred a fraction of a second earlier – in other words, the world which one perceives is not the present world, but the world as it appeared a fraction of a second earlier. Hence, it may be said that we live in the *specious present*.[1] This is just one of many distortions of reality which occur during perception, as shall be seen. What people suppose to be a true impression of the world is in fact the product of a great deal of neurological

---

1    The term has also been used to describe short term memory, for similar reasons.

and psychological fudging. In this chapter, some of the key topics surrounding perception research will be examined, concentrating upon sight and hearing. A brief discussion of taste and smell will be made, because these topics neatly illustrate the manner in which one's perceptions are rarely the product of a simple sensory input alone.

Before doing this, it is important to state two caveats. The first is that the majority of research in perception assumes that perceiving the world involves an active manipulation of what the senses receive, so that what one is aware of seeing, hearing, etc, is a product of interpretation, rather than an unmanipulated view of the world. This point will be repeated many times in this chapter, because it is so central to perception research. However, it must not be supposed that it is the sole view. The most consistently-voiced argument against it is provided by J.J. Gibson's *direct perception* theory. This is enormously complicated, not least because Gibson devised a new and difficult terminology to describe it (see Best, 1995, for an excellent overview). However, the essence of the theory is fairly simple. It is obvious that the perception of the world must involve a certain amount of mental interpretation. For example, as many commentators have noted, although the world is in three dimensions, the receptive surface of the eye has only two dimensions. How can the third dimension of depth be perceived without a mental interpretation? 'Traditional' commentators have argued for rather complex mental mechanisms which manipulate the limited visual information which enters the eyeball. Gibson argued that the image entering the eye is far from limited and contains all the information which is needed. For example, he argued that much of depth perception relies upon attending to such phenomena as *optic flow* (as one moves along, items move towards one, and as they get closer, they appear to accelerate) and *texture gradient* (items further away are closer together and less detailed). The point is that these pieces of visual information do not have to be interpreted – they are *there*, all ready to be perceived. It must be stated that Gibson's theory is far from universally accepted – at the very least, it can be demonstrated that even if the mechanisms he described *could* be used, there is no proof that they *will* be used, and plenty of proof that other, more interpretive methods *are* used (see Best, 1995). However, it is important for readers to be aware that in addition to the mainstream, 'interpretive' view of perception, another (though less widely accepted) viewpoint also exists.

The second caveat is that much of the work described is based upon experiments upon animals. It is impossible to know about the anatomical structure of the sense organs and the nervous pathways to and from the brain, and how these operate, without such experimental work (see Chapter 1 for further discussion of this issue, and Dawkins, 1990). Readers who have ethical concerns about such work have been accordingly advised.

## Vision

In very simplistic terms, visual perception consists of the following principal components. The eye essentially consists of a ball of clear jelly. Light comes into the eye via a lens, which is elastic and, by means of subtle muscular movements, can be stretched or squashed. These actions alter the focusing of the eye, so that objects at different distances can all be focused sharply. The focused image passes through the jelly and projects onto the *retina*, which is the inner coating of the eyeball. The surface of the retina is coated with light-sensitive cells, which detect the image being projected on to them, and send information on what they have detected to the brain (chiefly an area of the brain called the *visual cortex*) which interprets the information and presents a mental image of what the eye has detected which is subjectively perceived as 'vision'.

Each of the above stages, is, as might be expected, rather more complicated than the above may suggest, and each stage alters and manipulates the visual image so that by the time a person is consciously aware of it, it has been considerably altered from the image which entered the eye. For example, there is inevitably some distortion of the image from the physical limitations of the eye itself. The most obvious example of this is a defect in vision such as long- or short-sightedness, which can be attributed to such factors as a slightly misshapen eyeball or imperfect lens (one problem which many older people face is that the lens becomes less elastic, making focusing on nearby objects difficult). However, even with supposedly 'perfect' vision, there will be some distortions. For example, the lens is not completely clear, nor is the jelly-like fluid which fills the eye (hence the curious 'floaters' – worm-like shapes which one is sometimes aware of, which are nothing more than dead cells). Therefore, there will be some loss of clarity of image because of this. Again, the optics of the lens are such that the image which is projected onto the retina is upside down (subsequent processing compensates for this).

Once the image is focused onto the retina, it cannot be guaranteed that every bit of it will be detected. The clearest example of this is the *blind spot* – the area in each eye where the neurons which have collected information from the retina group together into the *optic nerve* and form a pathway leading into the brain. Light falling on this (small) area is not detected (one is not aware of a black hole in one's vision because of compensatory mechanisms).

The retina contains two kinds of receptors called *rods* and *cones*. These are named after their supposed appearance (though some imagination is required). Cones (of which there are about 7 million in the human eye) are concentrated towards the centre of the retina, particularly the area where the sharpest image is focused, called the *fovea*. Moving away from the fovea, the number of cones diminishes, and there is an increase in the number of rods (about 120 million per eye). The retina can therefore be imagined like a screen, with the central, most sharply focused image being projected onto the cones, whilst the peripheral (i.e. more than about 20 degrees from the fovea), and less sharply focused area, is covered with rods. From this it may be supposed that cones are concerned with scrutinising objects, whilst rods deal with peripheral vision, where the need is less on focusing than being aware of items coming into view. To a certain extent, this is true. For example, if an image falls on rods at the periphery of vision, then this creates a response to move the eye so that the image now falls on the centre of the retina: the image is not identified by the peripheral vision itself (Gregory, 1966). Again, receptors are far more densely packed at the centre of the retina, indicating that this is where the principal processing of information will take place.

Since cones are apparently doing the most important task of analysing images, why are rods, 'stuck' on the periphery, needed at all? The answer is chiefly that cones are relatively ineffective in low lighting conditions, such as night time, which is where rods excel. Humans are not principally nocturnal creatures, but nonetheless need to be able to find their way in the dark without blundering into obstacles, predators, or other dangerous situations. Therefore, in low lighting conditions, vision is principally by means of rods. Since rods do not receive the most focused part of the image, vision tends to be less accurate, but it is adequate for 'getting around'. In purely nocturnal species, rods are used more extensively or even exclusively (Bruce and Green, 1985). During day time vision, rods are of less use – because they are more sensitive to light, they are easily 'blinded'.[2] Furthermore, rods can only detect in shades of grey – only cones are capable of colour vision.

When receptors[3] are stimulated, they send a signal along the optic nerve indicating that they have detected light. Receptors send a stronger signal the brighter the light detected. Because light gets stronger or weaker does not mean that this change will automatically be detected. Generally, *Weber's Law* applies (named after Ernst Weber, a 19th century physiologist, who discovered it). This states that the smallest change in stimulus required for a change to be noticed, divided by the strength of the stimulation, is a constant. Placed in more prosaic terms – the stronger the initial stimulus, the bigger the change has to be before it is noticed. This makes intuitive sense. If a room is lit by one candle, then adding another candle will make a lot of difference. One the other hand, if a room is lit by 50 candles, then adding one more is unlikely to be noticed – instead a lot more will have to be added. By extension, *Fechner's Law* states that the subjective impression of an increase will be large when the stimulus is originally quite small, whereas the increase will be perceived as relatively small when the stimulus is already quite strong. It should be noted that neither law is totally accurate, particularly for extremely strong or weak signals, but both are very useful rules of thumb.

Therefore, the eye is introducing inaccuracies into the perceived image before it has even reached the brain. Not only are optical errors created by physical flaws in the eyeball, and accuracy of vision compromised by where

2    When a receptor is hit by a light particle, a chemical inside changes and this causes a signal to be sent along the optic nerve. After this, the chemical needs time to recover before it becomes active again, during which period the receptor cannot be stimulated. For various reasons, this recovery process is much longer for rods than for cones.

3    For reasons of simplicity, rods and cones will be treated together as 'receptors'.

on the retina the image falls (i.e. whether on to rods or cones) but the operation of Weber's law means that humans do not perceive all the nuances of changes in light and shade. Some of these flaws are the products of necessary compromises in the design of the eye. For example, a balance has to be made between rods and cones because humans have a need to see in both day and night-time (see Bruce and Green, 1985, for further discussion). Again, the primary reason why Weber's Law applies is because the nervous system is incapable of signalling all the different levels of lighting possible. In any case, there is no particular need to be aware of every nuance of changing light levels. Keeping note of relatively broad changes is enough, and a system which (roughly) follows Weber's Law is adequate in this regard.

The retina performs several more acts of 'biasing' signals before information is sent to the brain. One of these is *lateral inhibition*. When a receptor is stimulated, it sends a signal along the optic nerve to the brain, but at the same time, sends signals to the surrounding receptors, trying to *suppress* their level of activity. This suppression is in proportion to the strength of stimulation. Thus, if a receptor is strongly stimulated, it will likewise try to suppress its neighbouring receptors strongly; if it is weakly stimulated, then it will only attempt to suppress its neighbours weakly. It at first seems bizarre that having detected a light source, the first act of a receptor is to try to suppress its neighbours, but in fact there is a sound reason for this. Namely, lateral inhibition enhances points of contrast between light and dark areas in an image. This is best explained by an example. It is important to remember that the brightness of an image is signalled by the strength of the signal from the receptor; thus, the stronger the signal, the brighter the image.

Suppose that part of the retina is 'looking' at the boundary between a white and a black area (e.g. the border between two squares on a chess board). The receptors 'looking' at the black area will be less stimulated, because less light is hitting them. In contrast, the neighbouring receptors 'looking' at the white area will be relatively strongly stimulated. Using lateral inhibition, the 'black' and 'white' receptors will try to suppress each other. However, the white receptors, because they are sending out a stronger signal, will suppress the black receptors more than the black receptors can suppress them. What this means is that the black and white sections will have their relative brightnesses exaggerated – the black area will appear blacker (because the black receptors have had their signals depressed by the activity of the adjoining white receptors) whilst the white area will appear relatively bright (because the black receptors' attempts at suppressing the white receptors have been relatively weak).

Why should exaggerating the contrast where lighter and darker images meet be important? The most straightforward answer is that in general, where lighter and darker images meet often indicates the boundary between two objects. This can be very important, if, for example, this is the boundary between the edge of a cliff and a sudden drop, or the contrast between a tripwire and the ground underneath. By exaggerating the contrast between light and dark, lateral inhibition makes the detection of the physical boundaries between different objects very much easier.

Some receptors in the retina, called *ganglion cells*, 'collect' signals from several adjacent rods or cones. Ganglion cells thus have a bigger *receptive field* (i.e. the size of the image they can 'see') than an individual rod or cone. Work on the ganglion cells of cats established that they have a specialised pattern of response. Kuffler (e.g. Kuffler, 1953) looked at the response of single ganglion cells in a cat's eye to a spot of light shone on a screen in front of the (anaesthetised) animal. The ganglion cell did not respond unless the light fell in a very specific area. Furthermore, response within this area was curious. In some cases, if the light fell in the centre of this area, then activity was increased. However, if the light appeared in the periphery of the area, than activity was decreased. This is an example of a *centre on cell*. in contrast, other cells displayed the opposite pattern – a light at the centre of the area decreased activity, whilst a light at the periphery increased activity. This is an example of a *centre off cell*. The full explanation of the purpose of such cells is complex (see e.g. Bruce and Green, 1985), but suffice it to say that such cells will be useful in detecting contrasts in dark and light and detecting movement. The most important point to note here is that even before leaving the retina, the process of codifying an image, and in the process, distorting it (though for sound reasons of easing identification, as has been seen) is already under way before the message even reaches the brain.

Signals from the retina are sent via the optic nerve to the brain. The majority of the signal goes to the visual cortex, located at the 'back' of the head. This explains the apparently contradictory phenomenon that some people go blind after receiving an injury to the back of the skull – the eyes still work perfectly, but the brain is too damaged to interpret the information being sent to it. How the brain interprets the information provided by the retina is complex and is still not fully resolved. However, at a general level, it can be stated that the visual cortex is divided into more specialist areas, each dealing with a particular type of vision. Thus, one area may deal with processing information about the relative lightness and darkness of parts of the image, another with movement, another with the colour of the image, etc. This information is then combined in a manner not yet fully understood, so that the final mental image which is subjectively called 'sight' is created. Vision is therefore not just a matter of the retina sending a set of nervous impulses to the brain which are simply and immediately converted into a mental image.

If different areas of the cortex specialise in analysing different aspects of the image, what of the individual brain cells? Hubel and Wiesel (1959) demonstrated that the cells in the visual cortex are similarly specialised. The simplest examples of this are (appropriately enough) *simple cells*. Hubel and Wiesel inserted a microscopically small recording probe into a cell in part of a cat's visual cortex. What they found was that the cell would only respond when the cat saw a line in a particular orientation (e.g. slanted at 10 degrees from true vertical). If a neighbouring cell was tested, then this would also respond to a line, but this time it had to be in a slightly different orientation (e.g. 12 degrees from vertical) for it to respond. Hubel and Wiesel determined that these cells are arranged in columns, with each cell responding to a line at a slightly different angle from the one above or below it. Other cells are more sophisticated in their tastes (and, not surprisingly, are called *complex cells*). These respond if more stringent criteria are met (e.g. line in a particular orientation and of a particular length), and again, are arranged in columns. The result of this organisation is that the cells of the visual cortex are arranged in groups of feature detectors, each pre-set to analyse an image for a particular set of features.

If this information is combined with the knowledge that different sections of the visual cortex specialise in different aspects of the visual image (colour, movement, etc), then it becomes apparent how the visual cortex operates. An image is sent through sets of cells, each of which examines it to judge if it possesses the attributes that set of cells is designed to detect. Thus, if a person is shown a red wall with no distinguishing features, then the visual cortex's cells will have rather a dull time. For example, areas designed to detect lines, angles and movement will not find anything to report. Only the detectors which respond to the colour red will have anything to report. Thus, the visual image will be of a monotonous red. On the other hand, if a person is shown a black line on a white background, then many more areas of the visual cortex will have something to report.

## Pattern recognition

The above issue raises the large and vexed topic of how patterns and shapes are recognised. The neurophysiological evidence just presented demonstrates that visual images can be recognised by means of *feature detectors*, each of which analyses one small part of the image, and which in combination form a picture. Each feature detector in itself copes with too small an area to form a coherent picture – it is the mass action of all of the feature detectors which is important, rather like the tiny dots of a newspaper picture or the picture on a television screen. Such processing, where the image is created by building up from simple components is known as *bottom up processing*. It is important to remember that each component in a bottom up model does not 'know' what it is processing – it is simply a component of a larger mechanism, in the same manner that an individual nerve cell does not 'know' that it is part of the brain.

An influential model using the bottom up method was the *Pandemonium model* by Selfridge (1959), which was subsequently developed by Lindsay and Norman (1972). This attempted to explain how printed letters are recognised, using sets of feature detectors which were nicknamed *demons* (there are some charming cartoons illustrating the model). Suppose that a person is asked to identify the letter 'A'. Because letter recognition happens so quickly, it is difficult to appreciate that when one first sees a letter on the page, one does not know what it is, beyond being a black pattern on a white background. One of the under-appreciated wonders of psychology is the speed with which this type of shape is recognised. The Pandemonium model argues that the first thing which happens is that a set of detectors called *line demons* analyse the shape and identify the lines with which it is composed. In essence, what happens is that there is a line demon for each line and curve which can be found in a letter. Each line demon 'looks' at the letter and decides if the line it represents is present. In the case of 'A', line demons representing curves will not be excited, but line demons representing straight horizontals and diagonal verticals will be. The excited line demons in turn pass information to the *angle demons*. These take the information provided by the line demons and judge the angles at which the lines meet. In the case of 'A', line demons 'looking' for lines which cross over each other (e.g. as in 'X') will not find anything, but angle demons looking for lines meeting at an acute angle will find features. The angle demons pass their findings on to *letter demons*. These take the information provided by the previous two stages of processing and 'look' for letters which best fit the features identified. No letter is completely unique, in that it will share some features with other printed letters. In the case of 'A', several other letters have a horizontal line meeting a vertical (B, E, F, H, P, R) or have long vertical lines (M, N, V, W, Z). Therefore, these letter demons will find something to excite them in the available information. However, although the B, E, F, H, P, R and M, N, V, W, Z letter demons will be excited, they will only be weakly excited compared with the A letter demon which possesses not only a horizontal line meeting a vertical, but also sloping vertical lines. Therefore, of all the letter demons, the A demon is the most excited. This information is passed on to the *decision demon*, which decides which letter demon is providing the correct interpretation. This is the strongest excited one, which in this case is 'A'. Therefore, the decision demon decides that the printed shape on the page is the letter 'A'.

The Pandemonium model provided a very useful and influential model of how letters can be recognised by a series of processes each of which in themselves is simply blindly making a single simple decision – namely, is the particular feature they have been set to identify actually there? This of course mimics what is known to take place in the visual system – Hubel and Wiesel's work demonstrates that the visual cortex is composed of just such sets of simple feature detectors. The Pandemonium model is the precursor of more complex models, but an enormous debt of gratitude is owed to it because it effectively set the basic framework which many other models of feature processing would follow. However, in itself, bottom up processing cannot provide a complete answer.

A 'pure' bottom up model assumes that when processing begins, the person has no idea at all what the the object to be identified is. Therefore, he or she begins by looking for the most basic features, and works up from there. However, this is rarely the case. Usually, people have some preconception of what they will see, and so tend to look for evidence to confirm this hunch rather than paying very deep attention to the features. This is an example of *top down processing* – namely, where perception consists of looking at features to determine whether an hypothesis is correct, rather than looking at features with no pre-determined idea. This at first may seem paradoxical – how can one look for something before one knows what one is looking for? However, there are many instances where just such perceptions take place. In reading, some words are *filler words* – words like 'the', 'of' and 'and' must be there for grammatical purposes, but they are so predictable that scant attention is paid to them when reading. This can be demonstrated by recording eye movements of readers – filler words are looked at very briefly, if at all (many readers will have not noticed that the word 'the' is repeated in a sentence in this paragraph). What probably happens is that people use top down processing – from what they have read, they expect filler words at certain points in a sentence. These are not analysed very deeply – provided the features of a filler word look roughly correct, they will be accepted at a cursory glance (see e.g. Ellis, 1993). This also explains many proof readers' errors. Given the task of checking a book, newspaper or similar article before it goes to the presses, an author or editor will almost invariably miss some printing errors, simply because they are 'skipped over'. The reader thinks he or she knows what is there, and does not bother to check very deeply. This can prove disastrous. Take the case of the 'Wicked Bible', the 1632 edition of the Good Book in which the word 'not' was omitted from the Seventh

Commandment.[4] With bottom up processing, such errors would not occur, because every word would be analysed in its own right, without any prior hypotheses of what it must be. Thus, the reader would not skip over words, or think that words 'must' be there when they are not.

This begs the obvious question – why use top down analysis at all, given that it will make errors where bottom up analysis will not? The simplest explanation is that bottom up processing is in most cases too slow. If everything has to be worked out from first principles, then this takes longer than making a guess. Although errors will be made, these will be relatively few (this is obvious from everyday experience – if top down processing was totally inaccurate, then reading would be practically impossible). In fact, analysis probably is a mixture of both top down and bottom up processes. This is persuasively argued by Neisser (1976) in his *cyclic model of perception* (also known as *analysis by synthesis*). In this, he states that in analysing an object, people simultaneously will test hypotheses whilst beginning an analysis of basic features. Because analysis is being conducted from 'both ends' simultaneously, this should speed up identification. To take a simplistic example – if a person expects to see a zebra, then a zebra will be identified faster if whilst the person is looking for confirmatory features (four legs, looks like a horse, etc) the bottom up processes are supplying information that there are stripes, ears, eyes, etc. If only the bottom up processes or only the top down processes were working, then identification would take longer.

It must be borne in mind that in describing these processes, it may sound as if the perceptual system searches for clues at a leisurely pace, like a determined but sluggardly bloodhound. Of course, in reality, such processes take but a fraction of a second, in the same manner that a computer programme can take hours to describe but only an instant of time to operate. Models of pattern recognition are moving apace. More recent theories (see e.g. Ellis, 1993) have moved on from the models of Selfridge and Neisser, but at their heart retain many of their main features. It is worth repeating that, in nearly all instances, the aim of a pattern recognition model is to demonstrate how a complex pattern can be identified by the combined action of a large

4    The one about *not* committing adultery.

number of simple feature detectors. It must also be remembered that pattern recognition provides yet further evidence that perception is a matter of twisting visual information to make it fit – people do not simply perceive what is there unaffected by interpretative processes. In the most basic bottom up processing, recognition is not of what is actually there as much as how features of what are seen concur with pre-wired feature detectors. With top down processing, features are treated in a more cavalier attitude still – only those which suit the observer's expectations are looked for. These are, it must be stressed, largely unconscious acts – more deliberate biasing, such as that witnessed in many social psychology experiments (see Chapter 4) is in effect a lie performed on an economy with the truth. Humans never act on a truly accurate view of the world.

## Some other curiosities of vision

Pattern recognition is not the only manner in which what is there is subsumed to the need to see what is expected. A good example of this is *shape constancy*. Consider a conventional table, with four legs and a rectangular surface. Unless one looks at a table from directly above its top, then one does not see a rectangular surface. The image which strikes the eye is of a rectangle viewed from an angle, which is nearly always some form of diamond shape. However, if asked what shape the table is, one will unhesitatingly reply 'it's a rectangle'. By a similar token, a round coin will be described as a circle, even though, except when viewed straight on, the exact visual image is an ellipse. Again, there is the case of *size constancy*. It is intuitively obvious that the further away an object is from an observer, the smaller it becomes (thus, watching a friend walking into the distance, we do not become concerned that he or she is shrinking). However, although an object decreases in size the further away it gets, the subjective impression may be that the object is larger than it actually appears in the visual image. A useful demonstration of this point is to close one eye and look at a distant object (e.g. a tree or house). Keeping one eye shut, 'measure' the object with the thumb and forefinger, so that the image just fits in the gap between these two digits. Keeping thumb and forefinger rigidly in position, now focus on a nearby object and look at the size of the gap between thumb and forefinger. It will appear very small indeed – far smaller than the object in the distance subjectively appears to be.

There are sound reasons why such 'distortions' of vision are useful aids. For example, it is obvious that one wishes to recognise objects from many angles, and not constantly to have to think that 'although the image is an ellipse, if seen in its 'correct' orientation, it is a circle'. Shape constancy enables one to do this. Again, size constancy keeps one aware of objects in the distance so that they do not get completely ignored (very useful if such objects are e.g. predators or rain clouds). The issue of seeing objects for what they represent rather than in terms of their literal visual image ultimately addresses the issue of *Platonic Forms*. The Ancient Greek philosopher Plato argued that it was impossible ever to see an absolutely pure example of any object. This is not as bizarre as it may first sound. Think of a dog – what is a 'pure' form of a dog? The simple answer is that there is no such thing: different breeds of dog vary so much in appearance that it is impossible to think of a single dog which represents all varieties. For this reason, we may assume that, in recognising a dog, we have an internal checklist of the features which we would expect a dog to possess, and if what we see before us matches this, then we recognise it as a dog. Plato argued that this internal checklist is a pure concept[5] which will never match anything in reality. In his honour, this concept is usually called a Platonic form. The validity of Plato's arguments has been debated at inordinate length (see Hospers, 1990), but of interest here is the more mundane concept that recognition of items is often less a matter of seeing what is there than of assessing the degree to which they match with what is expected. This can be seen further in the example of the *Gestalt* school of perception.

'Gestalt' is a German word meaning 'whole', and describes a psychological movement which became especially active in the 1920s and 1930s (see Schultz and Schultz, 1987). The theory has many permutations, but at its heart lies the concept that what matters is the total image, rather than its individual parts. This is best explained by example. Consider the following dots:

5    He thought it was provided by the gods, but this part of the argument need not be accepted.

•　　•　　•　　•　　•　　•

Try as one might, it is impossible not to see these dots as forming a line. There is an organising 'force' (the *law of Pragnanz*) which compels the person to organise what is seen into the simplest convenient pattern. The Gestalt view was a refreshing change from some earlier models of perception, which had emphasised the need to examine how a complex image could be broken down into its most basic constituents, and reminded people that a prime objective of perception is to make sense of what is seen. The law of Pragnanz does just this, by demonstrating that there is a drive to infer patterns from images. Ultimately, Gestalt theories of perception became ossified. Although they are useful descriptions of what occurs, the explanations of why they occur proved unsatisfactory. Again, the debate about 'which is more important – the parts or the whole?' ultimately is rather tedious, and can be overcome by models such as Neisser's cyclical model mentioned above.

A final curious feature of vision to be considered is the case of *visual illusions*. These are instances where the mind perceives a visual image which is at variance with the objective reality. The most famous example of this is the *Muller-Lyer illusion*. Basically, if two lines of equal length are shown side by side, they will appear to the same. However, if outward pointing arrows are put on one ( ⟷ ) and inward ones on the other ( ⟩———⟨ ), the latter will appear longer. Clearly this is wrong – the lines are the same length, as can be demonstrated by measuring them, and yet the illusion remains, even when armed with this knowledge. Why should this be? The specific answer is hard to establish. Perhaps the most plausible explanation is one which is also labyrinthine. It begins with the supposition that one is accustomed to seeing lines bounded by inward pointing arrows in the corner of an object going away from one (e.g. two walls of a room meeting in a corner form a straight line bounded by angled lines formed by the boundaries between the walls and the ceiling and floor). Similarly, a line bounded by outward pointing arrows is seen in a pointed object coming towards one. If two lines are the same length on the retina, but one is apparently pointing away and one is pointing towards one, then it follows that the one pointing away is 'in reality' bigger (in the same way that a tall and short person can be made to appear the same size on the retina by the tall person standing further away). Therefore, the brain interprets this line to be bigger. This is an interesting explanation, and it is a pity that the experimental evidence for it is only equivocal (see Best, 1995).

Visual illusions often reveal idiosyncrasies with specific parts of the visual system. Their importance is therefore often rather specific and out of place in a general textbook (see e.g. Gregory, 1966, for more detailed discussion). However, at a general level, they are of considerable importance. This is simply because they illustrate the shortcomings of the visual system. When a perception does not match with reality, then this can provide an illustration of how the perceptual process works in a method which would otherwise be hidden, simply because the process usually produces what is expected of it (see the example of complementary afterimages below). They also provide further evidence that the perceptual system interprets sensory input, rather than passively reporting what is there.

## Colour vision

Colour vision is a sound example of how different parts of the visual system combine in their actions to produce a perception. At first sight (no pun intended), it may seem obvious how colour vision works. In the 19th century, independent research by Young (in Britain) and Helmholtz (in Germany) separately produced the *trichromatic colour vision theory*, also known as the *Young-Helmholtz theory*. This argued that there are three types of colour receptors in the eye, which respond to either red, green, or blue light. Thus, if only a blue light is shone on the eye, then only those receptors responsive to blue light will be activated, creating the perception of the colour blue. By the same token, if only a red light is shone, then only the red receptors will be stimulated, and if only a green light is shone, then only the green receptors will be stimulated. Other colours are made up of different combinations of green, red and blue light. For example, yellow is produced by combining red and green. A yellow light shone on the eye will stimulate green and red receptors, and this combination of activity will produce the perception of yellow. Neurophysiological evidence for this theory was produced by Wald and Brown (1965) who demonstrated that cones in the retina could be divided into three categories – namely, those which were particularly responsive[6] to either red, green, or blue light.

The Young-Helmholtz theory has the virtue of being simple – colour can be perceived by the action of three simple colour detectors. Unfortunately, it is not completely accurate, and further processes are now known also to play a role. One of the these is described by the *opponent-process theory*, first proposed by Hering in the late 19th century. Hering argued that colour perception occurs because pairs of colour receptors in effect act against each other. He began by arguing that although many colour combinations can be perceived, it is impossible to perceive a colour which is reddish-green or yellowish-blue. This led him to argue that there are two basic colour receptors – one which responds to either yellow or blue and the other which responds to either red or green. Perception of single colours is easily explained. If, for example a red light is shone on the eye, then only the red 'half' of the red–green pair will be stimulated (ditto yellow with the yellow–blue pair). A colour other than the ones in the pairs will simply be a combination of the more 'activated' members of the pairs. When a colour is perceived, only one detector in each pair can be in operation. Thus, the colour violet will be detected by the combined actions of the blue detector from the yellow–blue pair and the red detector from the red–green pair. Different shades will be signalled by relative levels of activity. Thus, a reddish-violet will have a relatively highly activated red receptor, and a bluish-violet a relatively activated blue receptor. The only colour combinations which cannot be seen are the aforementioned blueish-yellows and greenish-reds (because members of the same pair cannot act in conjunction with each other). The opponent process theory provides perhaps the simplest explanation for *complementary afterimages*. If a person looks at a single colour for a minute or so and then looks at a white surface,

6    NB – Although the cones were *most* responsive to one colour, they would also respond (though with less vigour) to colours nearby in the spectrum.

then an 'afterimage' of the opponent colours will appear (e.g. if a person looks at a red cross, then the after image will be of a green cross). This is because the colour receptor is temporarily exhausted, leaving the opponent colour to display itself (e.g. in the red cross example, the red receptors can no longer respond, so the only receptors which can be active will create a perception of green).

It may be wondered how the Young-Helmholtz and opponent process theories can be reconciled. In fact, it now seems likely that the two theories are both valid, and describe the workings of different parts of the visual system. The Young-Helmholtz theory, as has been seen, appears to concur with the workings of the retina. The opponent process model appears to describe the operation of some cells in the brain responsible for co-ordinating information passing along the optic nerve (e.g. DeValois and Jacobs, 1984).

The two models of colour vision described so far describe how colour is perceived when just one colour is being viewed. When a person can only see one colour and nothing else, then some strange tricks can be played upon that person's colour perception. For example, a piece of red paper seen under a 'normal' white light will appear red. This is because the light reflected off the paper is red. However, it is possible to manipulate the wavelengths of light shining onto the paper, so that now the wavelengths reflected off the paper are those which would normally come off a green piece of paper. In these conditions, the person perceives the red piece of paper to be green. The same procedure can be repeated with any other colour paper, and the same phenomenon will occur. If only one colour can be seen, then the piece of paper will not be seen in its true colour, but in whatever colour the light has been manipulated to reflect off the paper. Neither the Young-Helmholtz nor the opponent process theories have any problem in explaining this phenomenon. The receptors can only process the information which enters into the eye – because a clever lighting trick has made a red piece of paper look green, they cannot judge that the paper is 'really' red and so create a perception of red. They simply process the light waves and report a perception of green.

However, as soon as more than one colour is present, the perceived colour change does not happen. For example, suppose that the same lighting 'trick' is done on a piece of red paper which is surrounded by other pieces of paper of different colours. A person shown the piece of red paper will not see it turn green, but will still see it as remaining red, provided he or she can see the other colours in the display. If the other colours are covered up, so only the red square can be seen, then it will appear green once more. If the colours are once again shown, then the square becomes red once more. This is the phenomenon of *colour constancy* – namely, an item will be perceived as the same colour under a range of very different lighting conditions provided other colours can be seen at the same time.

The mechanism of colour constancy is not fully understood, but involves the visual cortex making some very sophisticated computations of the relative lightness and darkness of parts of the visual image. Although colours may change their 'colour' under different lighting conditions, they tend to remain relatively lighter or darker than each other (this can be appreciated by considering black and white photographs of scenes whose coloured appearance one knows – yellow, for example, is always lighter than red). It would appear that the 'true' colour of an item is perceived by how light or dark it is relative to other objects in the visual field (see Land, 1977).

Colour constancy provides further proof (if proof were needed) about how the visual system manipulates 'true' images. However, like other fudging of information, this is for a sound reason. Without colour constancy, the world would change alarmingly in appearance as one moved through it. Anyone who has used a camera (and especially a video camera) will know the peril of moving from outdoors to indoors without altering a colour filter. Left to its own devices, a camera will record indoor scenes as appearing rather jaundiced or a dirty brown. This is because indoor lighting usually produces a fairly yellow light. Similarly, outdoors lighting can appear very harsh and blue-tinged, because 'in reality', that is the colour of the great outdoors. Humans are usually unaware of these lighting changes (e.g. stepping out of the front door does not cause everything to appear blue) because of colour constancy. This is not just a matter of aesthetics, however. There are obvious survival advantages in ensuring that the appearance of an item learnt under one light condition can be recognised accurately when encountered again under other lighting conditions (the colour of poisonous mushrooms, for example).

## Hearing

Just as the eye converts light energy into nervous impulses, so the ear converts sound waves into nervous impulses which can be interpreted by the brain. The physical composition of the ear is relatively simple. The ear lobe serves the function of helping to 'catch' sound waves and funnel them into the *external auditory canal* (the 'ear hole'). Sound takes the form of minute fluctuations in air pressure. These waves pass along the auditory canal until they (literally) hit the *tympanic membrane* (eardrum). This in turn vibrates, and these vibrations are transmitted along a sequence of tiny bones called the *ossicles* (comprising the *malleus, incus* and *stapes*), which connect the ear drum to the *cochlea* (loosely, the 'inner ear'). The cochlea is in essence a spiral shaped hollow bone containing fluid and a structure called the *organ of corti*. When the vibrations reach the cochlea, the fluid vibrates, causing waves to be passed along it. These waves are detected by the organ of corti (by means of tiny hairs which line its surface). The organ of corti converts the movement of the hairs into nervous impulses which are transmitted along the *auditory nerve* to be interpreted by the brain. Therefore, the ear essentially consists of a series of mechanisms for converting air vibrations into first vibrations of bones then fluid before being converted into nervous impulses.

One of the most important tasks of the ear is to identify the frequency of sounds (i.e. how 'low' or 'high' they are). Two methods are used. For relatively low frequency[7] sounds (up to 4000 Hz), it is likely that the *frequency theory* (also known as *temporal theory*) applies. In other words, the auditory nerve sends a signal which matches the frequency of the sound (i.e. a 1000

---

7    Frequency is measured in Hertz (Hz), which is the number of times per second something vibrates. Thus, a tone of 500 Hz sends a vibrating pattern which repeats itself 500 times per second. Typically, a young adult should be able to hear sounds from circa 20 Hz to at least 16,000 Hz.

Hz tone is responded to by a neuron firing at 1000 times per second, etc[8]). For higher frequency sounds, the auditory nerve cannot send signals at a rate which can 'keep up' with the frequency of the sound, so instead the *place theory* (Von Békésy, 1960) applies. The organ of corti is so constructed that different parts of it are maximally responsive to different frequencies. The area nearest the junction with the ossicles is most responsive to low frequency sounds, whilst the area furthest away is maximally responsive to the highest frequencies. The frequency of a sound is indicated by the section of the organ which vibrates most (i.e. if a section far away from the ossicles vibrates most, this indicates a high frequency, etc).

Damage to the ear can cause deafness. A common form of this is *conduction deafness*, which is physical damage to the eardrum or ossicles caused by disease, or environmental factors, such as working in a noisy environment without adequate hearing protection. Often such deafness is selective, and loss of ability specifically to hear high frequencies is common, largely because the organ of corti is physically most delicate in the section responsible for hearing high pitched sounds. Another form of deafness is *nerve deafness*, which as might be supposed, affects the ability of the auditory nerve to conduct information to the brain. It is a chilling thought that most people can expect to have some form of hearing loss by the time they reach old age (Corso, 1981, 1987).

## Selective attention

One of the perennial problems with Psychology is that in many instances it deals with mental processes which are so commonplace that they have probably never or only rarely attracted the curiosity of a layperson. If one were to ask someone to introspect about what makes humans or animals intelligent, then one would probably get answers along the lines of 'ability to solve problems', 'ability to remember' etc. However, without selective attention, few (if any) 'higher' mental acts would be possible. Why?

---

8    Since neurons can fire at a maximum circa 1000 times per second, how can they represent a 4,000 Hz sound? The answer is by ingenious group firing of several neurons working together (see Rose *et al.*, 1967).

Selective attention might be defined as 'the ability to concentrate on one aspect of a sensory input to the exclusion of other aspects of it and other inputs' (Stuart-Hamilton, 1995b). In other words, being able to concentrate on the task at hand. The alternative to this would literally being unable to distinguish between different items in one's consciousness and to act on one to the exclusion of others. Quite simply, everything would have the same level of importance. So, in reading this page, one could not 'shut out' any background noise (indeed, it would not be background noise – it would be seen as 'important' as everything else). The book would not stand out from everything else one could see – they would all be seen as equally demanding of one's visual processes. Even if one could look at the book, one would not be able to concentrate on just the words one wanted to read, because the other words on the page would also be demanding simultaneous processing. People sometimes complain that they cannot concentrate on everything at once. In fact, this is one of the great glories of human perception – the ability to shut out some things to concentrate on others is a cardinal feature of a sophisticated mental life.

Selective attention has arguably been known about and manipulated for centuries. Consideration of such items as paintings and, more recently, advertisements and machine operating panels, shows that artists and designers can exploit the tendency of people to view selectively. Apparently background objects in a painting can, by falling on the same plane of view, direct the viewer towards the focal point of the picture. By using different sized and coloured print, or placing the slogan against an attractive picture, an advertiser can direct a potential customer towards reading the advertiser's message (and away from compulsory but potentially off-putting statements, such as the price or potential health hazards). A control panel can be designed so that the eyes fall 'naturally' on the most important pieces of information, whilst keeping less important data on the periphery of vision. However, such approaches, whilst tacitly recognising selective attention, are not a rigorous examination of the phenomenon.

The modern approach to selective attention began in the 1950s, with a series of experiments investigating the *cocktail party phenomenon*. This describes the situation one encounters at parties where one can concentrate upon a conversation, and 'shut out' the many other conversations taking place in the room at the same time. Work by Cherry in the 1950s (e.g. Cherry, 1953) examined this problem systematically. He gave people a *shadowing task*. In a basic version of this experiment, the person hears two spoken messages played over stereo headphones, with one message going to the left ear and one to the right ear. The person is told to repeat back the message played to one particular ear, and to ignore what they hear in the other ear. For example, if a person has been told to repeat back what they hear in the left ear, and he or she hears '1, 2, 3, 4' played to the right ear and 'a, b, c, d' to the left ear, then the person must repeat back 'a, b, c, d' and not, for example, '1, 2, 3, 4' or 'a, 2, b, 4'. Cherry found that the task was difficult or even impossible if the messages to the two ears were spoken by same voice, but was far easier if the messages were in separate voices (e.g. the left channel spoken by a female voice, the right channel by a male voice). In a variant of the experiment, Cherry played the two messages to both ears simultaneously. Again, this made shadowing the intended message almost impossible. In other words, Cherry demonstrated that selectively attending to one message requires the message to sound different from the surrounding messages and to come from a different direction from the other sounds.

Broadbent (1958) provided a *bottleneck theory of attention* to account for Cherry's findings. To explain this, one can begin with a common sense observation that the mind is limited in the amount of information it can process at any one time. Furthermore, only a limited amount of information is likely to be of any value or interest. Thus, sitting in a familiar room reading a book, one wants to concentrate on the book, not constantly to be distracted by wanting closely to scrutinise everything in the room – this would be a waste of effort and time. However, how does one 'shut out' unwanted information without first processing it to find out whether one wants to know it or not? The problem is rather like a senior government official who needs only to see the most important information. Routine matters, such as re-ordering paper clips or calling the photocopier engineer are the tasks of underlings – he or she is paid too high a salary for it to be wasted on trivial matters. However, how does one decide what is important enough for him or her to see? In a well-regulated office, there will be set procedures for deciding this. In Broadbent's model, information is shut out if it is not physically similar to the message to which the person is trying to attend. In this, the model therefore accords with what Cherry found – namely, messages appear to be followed on the basis of their physical appearance. Broadbent's model assumes that unattended messages are rejected because they are not physically similar to the attended message. This means that they are not processed very 'deeply'. The concept of *processing depth* argues that items can be examined at different levels of comprehension, which are arranged hierarchically. The most superficial level is to examine an item just on its surface appearance (e.g. what it looks or sounds like). Deeper levels of processing will examine the item for what it means (see e.g. Eysenck and Keane, 1995). It follows from this that by Broadbent's model, people should have little idea of the content of the unattended message – all they have done is analyse it for its superficial appearance; what it means should not be known.

There is another feature of cocktail (or indeed other) parties which is hard to explain by this aspect of Broadbent's model. At a party, one can be having a conversation with someone, and suddenly be aware that somebody else is talking about one (indeed, this is another – and contrary – meaning of 'the cocktail party phenomenon'). The only way in which one can do this is if one is attending to conversations other than the one one is currently having. However, by a strict interpretation of Broadbent's model, this is impossible – the unattended messages are rejected on the basis of their physical characteristics. 'Deeper' levels of interpretation (such as recognising one's name) should not take place. However, following Broadbent's initial work, experimental evidence began to accumulate demonstrating that people could indeed attend to more of the supposedly 'unattended' message than Broadbent had argued. For example, Underwood (1977) made use of what is known as the *semantic facilitation effect*. Essentially, this is the phenomenon that a word will be read faster if it is preceded by another word drawn from the same semantic category (e.g. one will recognise 'bread' faster if it is preceded by 'butter' than if it is preceded by 'rhino'). Underwood demonstrated that in a shadowing task, performance was facilitated if words which were semantically related to the attended words were played on the 'unattended' channel. In other words, people were processing the information on the supposedly unattended channel to a greater depth than had previously been supposed. Had they just treated the unattended channel at a superficial level, then they would not have known what the words meant, and hence could not have used the information so obtained to facilitate performance.

Although there is evidence that information is processed to a deeper level than Broadbent's model proposed, the fact remains that one is not *consciously* aware of the content of the unattended message. For example, at a cocktail party one might become aware that someone is talking about one, but most conversation will not be detected beyond being part of a background noise. What this means is that although unattended information is being processed in some depth, it will not usually become available for conscious inspection. This gives rise to the theory that unattended information is processed to a greater depth than Broadbent proposed and only then is excluded. There are therefore two theories. One (Broadbent's) argues for early removal of unattended stimuli, and is therefore called the *early bottleneck model*, whilst the other argues for relatively late removal, and is therefore known as the *late bottleneck model* (the authors most associated with this are Deutsch and Deutsch, 1963).

The debate as to which model is better has been debated at some length, but a sensible compromise between the two extremes was provided by Treisman (1964), who argued for the *attenuated filter* or *attenuated bottleneck*. This argues that the unattended information is processed, but not to the same depth as the attended information, and that the depth of processing could be adjusted according to the circumstances. In effect, the bottleneck could be moved up or down depending upon the situation the subject finds him- or herself in. This neatly explains both aspects of the cocktail party syndrome – if the conversation one is having is not very cognitively demanding (or interesting), then one may have spare mental capacity to allow one to process other conversations in the room, hence allowing one to eavesdrop on other conversations. Experimental proof of this assertion is provided by Treisman and Geffen (1967) and Treisman and Riley (1969). They gave people the task of shadowing a message but making a response (pressing a button) when they heard a particular word, which could be contained in either the attended or the unattended message. The researchers found that people could detect the word when it appeared on either the attended or unattended message (thereby refuting the early bottleneck theory), but they were far more likely to detect the word when it appeared in the attended message (thereby refuting a rigid interpretation of the late bottleneck theory, which would argue that 'unattended' messages are processed in sufficient depth that most of the target words should have been recognised).

To summarise: selective attention works by filtering out information. This filter was first thought to be early in the process, and filtering out on the basis of physical characteristics of the message ('the early bottleneck'), but later work argued that the filter happened after the unattended messages had been processed rather more deeply ('the late bottleneck'). The compromise (and now generally agreed-upon) argument is that the filter is attenuated, and can be applied early, late, or in the middle, depending upon the needs of the task. Generally, people will try to filter out unwanted messages as early as possible, to save processing time and space (i.e. 'mental effort').

## Taste and smell

### Taste

Taste is detected by receptors on the tongue, principally located on or surrounding the *papillae* (the tiny 'lumps' on the tongue's surface). The term 'taste bud' is in fact something of a misnomer, since the receptors are contained within microscopic pits in the tongue's surface. An individual taste receptor is likely to be responsive to more than one kind of taste, but will probably be maximally responsive to just one. The perception of taste occurs because a group of receptors simultaneously detect the same taste and this combined signal 'tells' the brain about the taste (cf. Logue, 1991). It often surprises people to learn how relatively insensitive the tongue is to different tastes. It is generally agreed that the human tongue can only detect four 'flavours' – salt, sour, sweet, and bitter (though some commentators add 'metallic' to this list). The sensation of different tastes is created by the combined action of these *taste primaries*. For example, sugar will only stimulate sweet receptors, whilst a Chinese sweet and sour dish is likely simultaneously to stimulate sweet, sour and salt receptors. It is also worth noting that the intensity of taste is relatively low. When asked to assess foods for the strength of the four taste primaries, most foods and drinks get fairly modest ratings (Beebe-Center, 1949). Readers may sensibly query how this can be so since, subjectively, one is aware of enormous differences in taste (e.g. contrast the taste of very ripe Stilton cheese with a bland Bechemel sauce). The answer is that much of what is subjectively thought to be 'taste' is in fact smell. This explains why when one has a heavy cold, food is tasteless – it is not that the cold has destroyed the taste buds, but that with a blocked nose, the food cannot be smelt.

*Smell*

Smell receptors in the nose are responsive to *odour primaries*, but the exact number of these is disputed (Logue, 1991). Researchers have devised some colourful names for the hypothesised basic scents, such as 'camphoraceous', 'ethereal' and (more prosaically) 'putrid'. It is known that smell receptors send signals to an areas of the brain called the *olfactory bulb*, and that different scents are represented by different patterns of activity within the bulb.

## Food preferences

It should be remembered that the primary reason why animals possess the ability to taste and smell is not so that they can distinguish between different types of cuisine – it is because these senses are necessary for survival. Many predators, for example, rely upon smell to detect the scent of prey (they cannot rely upon it being within sight when they feel hungry) and so they have a heightened sense of smell. Animals may also use scent as a marker of territory. Many species of deer, for example, have special glands which secrete a powerfully-smelling substance over trees and rocks marking the boundaries of their territory. Since they cannot keep the whole of their territory in view at the same time, this serves as a 'keep out' sign if another deer strays too near the territory when the owner is elsewhere. Dogs mark out their territory by urinating against convenient objects within it (hence explaining their penchant whilst being taken for a walk for urinating a small amount against every lamp post, instead of letting it all go against the first one encountered).

In humans, the sense of smell is less pronounced than in some animals, and it is not used as a territorial marker. This is because use of other senses and a superior intellectual ability mean that capturing prey and conversely, avoiding being preyed upon, can be attained by other, more effective means. However, taste and smell are still important in feeding. Their prime importance is in: (a) avoiding poisoning and (b) detecting foods which will give the most nutrition for the least effort. In tasting and smelling food, one of the first purposes is to identify if it has caused illness in the past. Animals will almost always avoid foodstuffs which have made them sick in the past, even if they were only ill on one occasion (a phenomenon known as *one trial learning*), and humans share this characteristic. Again, taste and smell also can identify if a 'safe' foodstuff has decayed to a point where it is no longer edible. As people age, sense and taste deteriorate, so older adults run a higher risk of contracting food poisoning because they cannot as easily detect signs that food may be 'off'. The role of taste and smell in detecting highly nutritious food returns one to the concept of taste primaries. These identify some of the most salient nutritional features of food. For example, a sweet food usually indicates that it is ripe and will provide a high concentration of calories, whilst sour indicates unripe and not only fewer calories but a higher risk of indigestion. Salt is necessary for maintaining the correct balance in the body's chemistry (shortage of salt creates an increased liking for the taste), and bitter can indicate an inedible substance.

Accordingly, smell and taste are primarily survival mechanisms. They were not designed with wine tasting or gourmandising in mind. Nonetheless, with increased prosperity, and new farming and transportation methods providing a wider choice of foodstuffs in shops and restaurants, the issue of food preferences becomes salient. One of the most striking characteristics is the overwhelming preference (usually separately) for sweet-tasting and salty substances. In survival terms, this is understandable, but even presented with an adequate and seemingly inexhaustible range of foodstuffs, people gravitate towards such things (Logue, 1991). Food manufacturers have exploited this by adding more sugar and salt into some products than is nutritionally or aesthetically necessary. This is for sound economic if not health reasons – sugar is usually the cheapest ingredient, and the 'tang' from salt can compensate for paucity of other flavourings.

Other preferences are more complex. Some are genetically determined. For example, adults from different races have varying levels of tolerance to milk and dairy products. The majority of Europeans, for example, are *lactose tolerant*, but many oriental people cannot digest such substances once they are past infancy. Other preferences are cultural. For example, coffee and chilli are both aversive when first encountered, yet if a culture has acquired the habit of consuming such things, then people will persevere until they too can tolerate them. Again, different cultures may treat the same food in different ways. For example, Mexicans tend to regard cocoa as a flavouring in savoury dishes, whereas in most of the rest of the world, it is primarily an ingredient of confectionary. On a slightly less extreme scale, the French in particular find the British taste in chocolate (relatively low percentage of cocoa and a higher concentration of milk) peculiar – a feeling which is entirely reciprocated.

Cultural preferences do not stop at the foods themselves – the manner in which food is packaged may also be influential. For example, meat and meat products are rarely sold in green packaging (presumably because of associations with rotting flesh). Again, lamb or beef are rarely offered in packages showing frisking lambs or large-eyed cattle (though curiously, chicken products can show a picture of a chicken without creating feelings of carnivorous remorse). Overall, human consumers are remarkably susceptible to the image of the product, often electing food on the basis of 'the sizzle rather than the meat' (Packard, 1981, p.95). At issue once again is the fact that, as with hearing and sight, perceptions of taste and smell are not simply a matter of the senses telling the mind what is there, but of an active combinatorial effect of basic sensory information interacting with intellectual expectations.

FURTHER READING

There is a very useful summary of perception and attention issues, with some excellent illustrations, in Roth (1990). Gregory (1966) is (rightly) considered a classic on the topic of visual perception and his comments, more than thirty years after publication, are still pertinent. Ellis (1993) provides a useful guide to the processes of letter perception and reading. Logue (1991) is excellent not only for her review of the psychology of eating and drinking, but also for providing a sound guide to the physiological mechanisms of taste and smell.

# CHAPTER 10

# Biopsychology

## Introduction

As the term suggests, *biopsychology* is the study of the interaction between biological and psychological processes. Not surprisingly, this is a huge field of study, much of which draws upon fields more properly considered as part of one of the biological sciences, such as neurophysiology and physiology. Nonetheless, since it is vital to know not just how the mind works, but how it enacts its decisions and is governed by bodily processes, consideration must be given to at least some of the key topics.

## The brain and nervous system

The study of the physical basis of mental activity is one of the key areas of psychology, and one which perhaps exhibits the greatest interchange of ideas and techniques with other academic disciplines, including such unlikely bedfellows as neurophysiology and philosophy. To understand the nature of the issues involved, it is necessary first to understand something about the anatomy of the nervous system and how it works.

### The neuron

The technical term for an individual 'nerve cell' is a *neuron* (or *neurone* in some books). Neurons vary in size (from several centimetres in length to a fraction of a millimetre) and shape, but most have essentially the same structure – they have a cell body (containing the genetic information about the cell and assorted mechanisms for keeping the cell alive) and some branch-like projections. These projections are of two types: some *receive* signals from other neurons, and are called *dendrites*; others *send* signals to other neurons, and are called *axons*.

Neurons can be divided into two types – *excitatory* and *inhibitory*. When an excitatory neuron is active, it sends a signal to the other neurons to which is connected, making them in turn active. Thus, if the neurons are arranged in a chain, when the first neuron is active, each neuron in turn become 'switched on' so that a nervous impulse is sent along the chain. As might be expected, an inhibitory neuron does the opposite. When it is active, it *stops* the neurons to which it sends signals from becoming active.

The mechanism by which a neuron sends a signal (whether excitatory or inhibitory) to another neuron is known as the *synapse*. Although it has been said that neurons are 'connected' to each other, in reality, there is a microscopic gap between the end of an axon and the surface of the neuron with which it is communicating: this is called the *synaptic gap*. When a neuron communicates with another neuron, a signal travels along the axon and when it reaches its end, it causes the axon to in effect 'spit' some chemical across the gap, striking the surface of the adjoining neuron. This in turn makes the neuron active or stops the neuron being active (depending upon whether it is an excitatory or inhibitory neuron which has made the signal). The chemical used in the 'spitting' is called a *neurotransmitter*.

Although the communication between neurons is by means of a chemical, the signal within a neuron is an electrical pulse. It is *very* unwise to push this analogy too far, but in essence, the signal within a neuron is like a pulse of current travelling along a wire in an electrical circuit.

Nervous pathways are formed throughout the body and the brain by means of sequences of neurons 'connected' to each other. For a signal to be transmitted along a pathway, the first neuron in the chain is activated, which causes the subsequent neurons in the pathway to be activated one after another. For example, if a man stands on a drawing pin, this will cause a pain receptor (which in itself is a type of specialised neuron) in his foot to be activated. This in turn activates the neuron to which it is connected, which in turn activates the neuron to which *it* is connected, and so on, with the message being sent along neurons which progress up the body, until the signal reaches the brain where it can be interpreted. Note that each neuron in the chain does not 'know' what message it is carrying – it is up to the brain to interpret what the signal means (how this might take place is discussed later in this chapter). A simplistic analogy is of a message being passed along a line of illiterate relay runners before it reaches a person who can read – only the final recipient can understand the message. Another important point is that the transmission of the signal along the nerves, although fast, obviously takes time. We know this because it has been found that the physically more distant a part of the body is from the brain, the longer it takes for a person to be aware that the part of the body has been touched. Hence, we are aware more quickly that our hand has been touched than we are of our foot. Following from this is a further consideration that because the nervous system always takes some time (no matter how brief) to 'tell' the brain about what it has detected, what we think is 'the present moment' is in fact what existed several milliseconds ago – we can never be aware of the present time exactly simultaneously with its occurrence (a phenomenon which has been called 'the specious present' – a phrase first coined by William James).

The above description indicates the basis of how signals are sent in the nervous system, but there are several caveats. The first is that so far we have considered neurons in terms of a single neuron acting on another single neuron. In fact, it is very rare for one neuron to be connected to just one other neuron. Usually a neuron is connected to many other neurons (there may literally be thousands of connections), and usually a neuron is not activated or suppressed by just one other neuron communicating with it – instead, lots of neurons have to signal to the neuron at the same time if it is to become active.

A second point concerns neurotransmitters. Different parts of the nervous system use different neurotransmitters. For example, quite a sizeable section of the brain uses a neurotransmitter called *acetyl choline*, and the neurons concerned are known collectively as the *cholinergic system*. By similar reasoning, the *dopaminergic system* is the collection of neurons using the neurotransmitter *dopamine*. The different neurotransmitters have different effects, which are more properly the preserve of *neurophysiology* (the study of the structure and function of neurons and related matters). However, it is important to remember that neurons can be classified by the type of neurotransmitter they use. Inter alia, this explains why certain drugs can have an effect upon behaviour and perception. The opiate drugs, such as heroin, specifically affect the uptake of only some types of neurotransmitter sites, causing the neurons involved in pleasurable feelings to be activated, whilst other neurons (using different neurotransmitters and involved in other thought and emotional processes) remain unaffected.

A further point to note is how the intensity of a signal is transmitted. Let us return to the case of the man standing on the drawing pin. If he treads hard onto the pin, then this will hurt more than if he treads lightly. How does the nervous system indicate the level of pain? One way of doing this would be by an *analogue* method – the stronger the pain, the bigger the electrical pulse within the neuron and the bigger the dose of neurotransmitter released. However, for various reasons, this would be inefficient (principally because the *range* of strengths of sensation would be too narrow and the system is error-prone). The alternative method is to convey the strength of a stimulus by varying the frequency with which a signal is sent. In other words, if a mild sensation is being signalled, then the neurons concerned might send a signal at a rate of a few per second. However, if a strong signal is being sent, then the same neurons will fire (i.e. send a signal) at a faster rate (e.g. several hundred times a second). In other words, the strength of the signal is indicated by the frequency with which the signal is sent, not by its physical strength.

A final point concerns the physical structure of the neurons. Some neurons are wrapped in an insulating roll of fat, called the *myelin sheath*. This has the same effect as insulating plastic surrounding an electrical wire – namely, a signal passes along it faster and there is less 'leakage' of signal. Generally, the thicker the sheath, the faster and 'cleaner' the signal which is sent along it. Some neurons do not have a myelin sheath (they are not *myelinated*), and these tend to be slower and less efficient.

To summarise so far:

(1) neurons transmit signals electronically within themselves and with other neurons by 'spitting' neurotransmitters via the synapse

(2) the synapse can be excitatory or inhibitory

(3) the signal intensity is by frequency, not magnitude

(4) some neurons are myelinated.

Mainstream psychology does not spend a great deal of time considering the workings of the neuron, and the reader may be excused for wondering why *any* attention needs to be paid to it. The reason is that although the neuron is not central to psychological theory, a basic understanding of its workings is necessary in order to appreciate several key models of mental functioning. One of these – *connectionism* – will be mentioned later in this chapter. First, however, it is necessary to consider the anatomy of the nervous system at a broader level.

### General anatomy of the central nervous system

The nervous system is composed of neurons (responsible for transmitting nervous impulses) and a variety of other types of cells (notably the *glial cells*) whose responsibility is essentially to provide the neurons with nutrients and generally act in a supporting role. For the purposes of this discussion, we will confine ourselves to discussing the role of the neurons. The conventional way to subdivide the nervous system is into the *central nervous system*, composed of the *spinal cord* (contained within the backbone) and the *brain*. The central nervous system (or *CNS*) has three basic tasks – to receive information from the body's senses: to interpret this information; and to send signals to the body in response to this information. Information is carried to and from the CNS by means of the neurons of the *peripheral nervous system (PNS)*. A major difference between the neurons of the central and peripheral nervous systems is that if a neuron in the latter is damaged, it can rebuild itself, whereas a damaged neuron in the CNS cannot be replaced. This is an important point which will be returned to later in this chapter. An important terminological distinction is that a collection of neurons forming a single pathway in the peripheral nervous system is called a *nerve*, whilst a similar arrangement in the CNS is called a *tract*. In many instances, psychologists forget this distinction and tend to use 'nerve' to refer to *any* nervous pathway.

#### PERIPHERAL NERVOUS SYSTEM

The anatomy of the peripheral nervous system can, for most situations, be adequately classified according to the type of message it carries. The principal distinction is between *afferent* neurones (carrying information *to* the CNS) and *efferent* neurones (carrying information *from* the CNS). Of the efferent neurons, *motor* neurons carry signals to the skeletal muscle (i.e. the muscles used for movement) and *autonomic* neurons carry signals to glands, smooth muscle, cardiac muscle, etc. (i.e. bodily functions over which there is little conscious control). To confuse matters, it should be noted that some commentators use a different system, calling afferent neurons 'sensory neurons' and efferent neurons 'motor neurons'.

The peripheral nervous system represents different parts of the body un-equally. For example, there are far more nerves servicing the hands and face than, say, the back. The obvious reason for this is that we need to touch and feel things more often with our hands and mouths than with our backs, so more neurons are simply being placed where they are most needed. By the same token, whilst we receive reasonably reliable information from the skin and skeletal muscles, far less information on the intestines and other internal organs is available for conscious inspection. For example, the intestines are kept busy processing food and pushing it along a lengthy tube of guts ready for excretion, but we are blissfully unaware of this. Similarly, the workings of the gall bladder and pancreas are usually autonomous. A sound reason for this is that it is arguably difficult enough to concentrate on moving and thinking without being distracted by the state of yesterday's lunch.

In other instances, the peripheral nervous system is distributed in a man-ner which may seem counter-intuitive. For example, the neurons serving the hands and arms are arranged so that for either hand, one nerve serves the outer two fingers and outer section of forearm and another represents the in-ner two fingers, thumb and inner forearm. It might be intuitively supposed that the arrangement would be the forearm represented by one nerve and the hand by another. However, this state of affairs has at least a useful diagnostic function. If a patient goes to a doctor complaining that their whole hand feels numb, but not the arm (a condition known as *glove anaesthesia*), then the doc-tor knows that the problem probably will be psychological and not physical. Because the nerves function in the manner just described, it is very difficult for the hand alone to be numb (temporary numbness just of the hand can be induced by different means such as sitting on it for a while, but not long-term numbness) – if a patient complains of glove anaesthesia, then the roots proba-bly lie in the imagination.[1]

---

1    Some relatively rare forms of physical injury *can* give glove anaesthesia, but probabilistically, a
     psychological explanation is more likely.

CENTRAL NERVOUS SYSTEM

In psychological terms, the spinal cord is in itself fairly unsophisticated, but serves the vital function of relaying signals between the brain and body. Pathways to and from the lower part of the body tend to leave and enter the spinal cord near the 'bottom' of the spine, and to and from the upper body parts at a higher level. A serious spinal injury thus severs many of the links between brain and body, and the higher up the spine the damage occurs, the greater the loss of bodily control. Because neurons in the CNS cannot repair themselves once damaged, this loss is permanent. Not all nervous contact between brain and body is via the spinal cord, however. For example, an important set of twelve nerves called collectively the *cranial nerves* connect the brain to, inter alia, face and eyes without the intermediary of the spinal cord. This in part explains why even patients with very severe spinal injuries maintain their sight, speech, etc.

Although the spinal cord, as said, plays little part in processing of information, it possesses the important function of the *reflex arc* (a simple connection between afferent and efferent neurons). This can make the body respond to some forms of stimulation. Many reflexes (such as the well-known knee jerk reflex) are produced in this manner.

The spinal cord projects into the brain, or more accurately, the section of the brain called the *brain stem*. Many lay persons think of the brain as being a homogeneous mass of 'grey matter', but in fact the brain is a collection of distinct though interconnecting structures. For anatomical and functional reasons, the brain is often divided into four principal divisions. The first is the brain stem. Located behind this at the base of the skull is the *cerebellum*. Located above the brain stem is the *diencephalon*, or *interbrain*. Seated above and overlapping the other three segments is the *cerebral cortex* (often simply called the 'cortex'), the wrinkled 'top' of the brain. Generally, the further a structure is away from the spinal cord, the more sophisticated its functions.

The functions of the different areas of the brain could in themselves fill several textbooks. Many of the brain's workings, whilst vital for everyday functioning, are of relatively little interest within mainstream psychology, because they are concerned with purely bodily rather than psychological functions. For example, the brain stem is not heavily involved in 'intellectual' processing. It is chiefly concerned with the maintenance of 'life support' mechanisms, such as control of blood pressure, digestion, respiration, etc. It also receives the inputs from some of the senses, and channels them through to other systems in the brain. The cerebellum is concerned with maintaining balance and movement, and receives input from, inter alia, muscles and the semi-circular canals of the inner ear (although the rare congenital *Arnold-Chiari malformation* of the cerebellum may in severe cases cause mental retardation).

Rising 'up' the brain, the diencephalon is composed of several components, which have more noticeably 'psychological' functions. Amongst these, the *thalamus* co-ordinates and channels sensory information and the execution of motor movements. Damage to this region gives rise to Parkinsonism (see Chapter 12). The *hypothalamus* might be loosely said to control bodily needs – hunger and satiety (see below), sexual drive, anger, etc. The *hippocampus* is, in evolutionary terms, the oldest section of the brain. It is involved in emotional control, but of principal interest to psychologists is its role in memory. Some unfortunate individuals who have had this area of the brain destroyed (by disease or accident) cannot retain any new information in their memories for more than about two minutes. Therefore, the hippocampus is in some manner involved in putting information to be remembered into a long term memory store.

The cortex is responsible for the execution of most higher intellectual functions. It is divided into two *hemispheres*. The divide runs vertically from front to back, along the centre of the head. The hemispheres are linked by several pathways which bridge this divide, of which the most important is the *corpus callosum*. For most individuals, the right hemisphere controls visuo-spatial skills, and the left hemisphere controls verbal skills.

The cortex can also be divided into *lobes*, which have distinct psychological functions. The *frontal lobes* extend from the front of the skull back to the temples (i.e. they lie, roughly speaking, behind the forehead). They are mainly involved, inter alia, in the control and planning of actions, such as producing sequences of movements, getting words and letters in the right order in speech and spelling, and producing socially appropriate behaviour. The frontal lobes are also involved in memory – principally in identifying which events in memory occurred in the recent past and which in the distant past. The *temporal lobes* are situated (not surprisingly) in the positions of the right and left temples. One of their principal roles is in interpreting information, and in particular the left temporal lobe is vital in comprehending speech and print (see Chapter 5). The temporal lobes are also strongly involved in memory, particularly the long term retention of information. Because of the specialisation of the left and right hemispheres, the left temporal lobe tends to store verbal memories and the right temporal lobe tends to store spatial information. The *occipital lobes* are at the rear of the brain. They are involved in reading, but their principal function is in vision. Virtually all processing of visual information takes place in the occipital lobes. The *parietal lobes* are located on the top of the brain, surrounded by the other three lobes. In part they are responsible for maintaining awareness of the body's state and location. Their principal intellectual role might be said to be symbol interpretation, and they are involved in object recognition and reading.

A sensible question is how we know what each bit of the brain is responsible for, since we cannot open up the brain and 'see' the neurons working. Equally, we cannot introspect and ask ourselves which bit of the brain is working when we are doing a particular task, because self-awareness simply does not work like this. Indeed, perversely enough, the brain cannot physically feel anything. Were one to touch an exposed brain, then the person concerned would be unaware of being touched. For this reason, headaches cannot be the brain 'hurting' – more typically they are due to head muscles tightening and causing pain on the head's surface.

Knowledge of brain function instead comes from other sources. The principal of these is damage to the brain. This can occur by many means: head injuries due to car crashes and bullet wounds are two obvious examples, but there are others, such as strokes and brain tumours. It must be stressed that many people who receive brain injuries make a full recovery (e.g. other neurons in the brain take over the same tasks – there is some duplication of resources in the brain – or a leakage of blood which has put pressure on neurons and stopped them working drains away). In other, less happier, cases, the effects of brain injury are fairly widespread. Stroke patients who lose some or all ability to move parts of their body are a case in point. From a psychological viewpoint, this is interesting, because it demonstrates quite clearly that the brain must be controlling the body, since damage to the brain has resulted in loss of control over the body.

Some instances of brain injury have subtler and indeed sometimes bizarre effects. For example, one patient could no longer distinguish between artificial and natural objects. Another (a farmer) could recognise his sheep by their faces but not other humans. In one of the most intensively-studied cases, a patient known as *H.M.* (patients in case studies are traditionally called by their initials) suffered damage to his hippocampus whilst having a brain operation to treat a particularly severe case of epilepsy.[2] The operation took place in the 1950s. H.M. could not retain any information which he had learnt since this time. Thus, years later, he could be told that men had walked on the Moon, and would be astonished. Within a couple of minutes, he had forgotten what he had been told, and would be astonished over and over again every time he was told the same piece of information.

As can be seen, damage to sections of the brain leads in turn to damage to particular aspects of behaviour or thought. By this means, it is possible to map out what different areas of the brain 'do'. Readers may wonder how reliable such studies are. Several criticisms can be made. The first is that the studies are based on the evidence of single or small groups of patients. It might be the case that they are unusual in that damage to Area X in one person's brain may result in a radically different change in behaviour than if the damage occurs in Area X of another person. In other words, the anatomical location of different psychological functions may be located differently between individuals. This is implausible, because it is unlikely that such a huge amount of variability would be permitted by the genetic blueprint which makes up our bodies (e.g. if sections of the brain can have various locations, then so should arms and legs).

A second criticism is less easily dealt with. This concerns the question of *dissociation*. Suppose that damage to 'Area X' of the brain is shown to affect language. Can we conclude that Area X is involved in language processing? It

2    Some forms of epilepsy can be corrected by severing the links between a part of the cortex which is sending 'defective' signals and the rest of the brain. In some cases, other tissue is also accidentally severed. It must be stressed, however, that cases such as H.M.'s are *extremely rare.*

is possible that this is true, but not logically watertight. Language is a fairly sophisticated skill. It is possible, for example, that 'all' the damage to Area X has done is lowered the general intelligence of the patient, so that he or she can no longer use language. However, Area X might have nothing at all to do with language *per se*. By analogy, deflating the tyres on a car will stop it moving, but it would be erroneous to conclude that the tyres controlled movement. Therefore, to show that Area X is concerned with language, *double dissociation* is required. In essence, this requires demonstrating that patients with one kind of brain damage can perform tasks of type A but not type B, whilst another group of brain damaged patients can do tasks of type A but not type B. This is reasonable proof that damage to a particular part of the brain is associated with a specific skill rather than a more general form of functioning. Thus, in our example, a patient with damage to Area X will be expected to demonstrate 'normal' abilities at other tasks, including those which patients with damage to another area of the brain cannot do. However, the latter patients should be able to do the tasks which the Area X patients cannot do.

The above is a rather convoluted but necessary procedure if the functioning of an area of the brain is to be established. Human patients with brain damage are not the sole source of such material, however. It should also be noted that much of our knowledge of brain functioning is derived from animal experimentation, where brain damage has been deliberately created. The ethical considerations are for the reader to decide, but in terms of accuracy of findings, there is little doubt that the precision with which brain areas can be removed (damage due to accident or stroke is by definition rather less accurate) means that more certainty can be placed on the findings that a particular brain area is responsible for a particular function.

Another method of gaining insight into brain functioning is the brain scan. It is possible, using methods such as *positron emission tomography* (the *PET scan*) to demonstrate which areas of the brain are particularly active during which types of mental activity. Typically, a volunteer is given an injection of (very mildly) radioactive glucose solution. Cells use glucose for energy, and when cells increase their activity, their uptake of glucose rises as well. In a PET scan, monitors can calculate which cells are particularly active by detecting the rate at which the radioactive glucose is being consumed. It is thus possible to follow the activity of brain cells whilst various kinds of thinking take place. If particular areas of the brain become especially active during some kinds of thinking (e.g. about verbal problems) but are relatively quiet during others (e.g. mathematical problems) then this indicates which areas of mental activity they are most directly involved in. The accuracy of PET scans and similar is still relatively crude – general areas of activity can be detected, but finer details cannot. However, as technology improves, so should the resolution of the images and hence the level of information which they can provide.

*For discussion of how mental processes manipulate information received by the brain, see Chapter 9 on perception.*

## The mind–body problem

So far we have discussed the brain, the central nervous system and the mind very much as synonyms. However, philosophically speaking, this link between mind and brain is far from clear-cut and constitutes the *mind–body problem*. This issue has bedevilled philosophy for centuries, and there is little hope of resolving it in a few paragraphs. Nonetheless, it is an important issue, and one about which a psychologist should have some awareness.

The essence of the problem is this. There is nothing one can truly be aware of other than one's own existence. Suppose I tell you that I am a mad scientist, and whilst you think you are reading this book, you are not: in reality, you are nothing more than a brain which I have wired up to electrodes in my laboratory, and by stimulating your brain I have created these illusory thoughts. Were I to alter the type of stimulation to your brain tissue, then I could instantly make you believe you were, for example, walking or riding a bike. There is no watertight reasoning which can refute this argument: it may be highly *unlikely*, but it is not *impossible*. Ultimately, one has no way of knowing beyond any logical doubt if the world around one exists or is an illusion. The only thing about which one can be certain is that one is aware of thinking and of existing (it is literally impossible to be awake and not be aware of oneself). Thus, whether you are a brain on a petri dish, or a human being with a body, you are still aware of thinking about yourself, no matter what else may be illusory. Therefore, because one is [literally] self-conscious of being able to think, one can be certain that one has *some* form of existence, even if the true state of the physical world cannot be decisively determined.

All this sounds like the sort of activity which gets philosophy a bad name. It sounds like a clever playing with words, since is perfectly obvious that in daily living, people do not spend their time pondering about the true existence of the physical world. Nor in daily living do philosophers or psychologists. Since the argument revolves around a logical rather than pragmatic argument, it would be foolish to treat daily living in anything other than a 'common sense' way. However, that is not the point of the argument. If, the reasoning continues, we cannot be certain that the *mind* of a person is the same as the *body* of a person, how can we be certain that the mind and the body are connected? In other words, how do we *know* that the brain is responsible for producing the mind? Or, put another way, how do we know that what we are self-consciously aware of as being our 'mind' is a product of our brain? This is the essence of the *mind–body problem*, and was first explored by Rene Descartes (1591–1650), arguably the most important of modern philosophers. He summarised the dilemma in the famous Latin phrase *cogito ergo sum* ('I think, therefore I am').

At first sight, the answer seems to be very simple. We saw above that brain damage can produce changes in mental activity, and that damage to specific areas of the brain produces changes in specific aspects of thought and behaviour. Therefore, surely we have clear evidence that the mind is a product of the brain? Alas, the problem is not as simple as that. Although undoubtedly brain damage can influence the mind, it can be argued that 'all' that is happening is that the mind can no longer adequately express itself through the medium of the brain because the brain is damaged. A loose analogy is that if a television set becomes damaged in such a way that channel 2 can no longer be received, but other channels can, this does not mean that channel 2 has ceased to exist. However, this argument cannot be pushed too far as there must be *some* point at which the mental and ethereal world of the mind makes contact with physical world of the brain, otherwise the mind could not operate at all. Descartes himself thought that the meeting point was the pineal gland, though later commentators have easily disproved this (e.g. damage to the pineal gland does not cause loss of mind). Many (too many) later philosophers and psychologists have attempted to explain this dilemma, but no truly satisfactory solution has been found.

At this point, some commentators have concluded in effect that any psychology based upon linking mind and brain is therefore 'disproved'. This, however, is not the case. What has been shown is that the link between mind and brain cannot be proven but nor can it be satisfactorily *disproved*. As alluded to above, the problem joins many other philosophical conundrums which cannot be solved. However, logically messy as it may be, the best working hypothesis, based upon empirical evidence, is that there is a link between mind and body, and so it is prudent to conduct research on the *assumption* that thought and brain processes are inextricably linked.

## Artificial intelligence

The mind–body problem is not yet over, however, because it raises itself in another format in considerations of *artificial intelligence (AI)*. This is a relatively loose term referring to attempts to replicate mental functioning using computer programmes.

We know that the brain is composed of neurons interlinked together and that each neuron has a simple function – it either excites, inhibits, or is inactive. The brain's functioning is simply(!) composed of billions of such neurons doing these three actions, and their combined activity results in mental processes. It is easy to write a very basic computer programme which will simulate the three actions of an individual neuron. Suppose that instead of just simulating one neuron, a programme tries to simulate the actions of a large network of such neurons. In essence, one will have a network of computer replications of neurons which will *function* in the same way as 'real' neurons. In principal, if one could work out the entire network of neurons in a real brain and replicate them exactly in a computer, then one would have a computer model of a real brain. This is not yet possible, but suppose for a moment that it were feasible. Furthermore, suppose that this 'computer brain' could be put into an artificial body which again was an exact replica of the 'real thing'. We would now in effect have a fully functioning machine which *functioned* exactly the same as a real person.

However, note that the word 'functioned' has been stressed. Although the android would look and act like a real person, would it have self-awareness? In other words, would it, like humans, be *aware* that it was thinking? This is a difficult, if not impossible, question to answer. On the one hand, it can be argued that if the android had bodily components and functions which in every way corresponded to a real human's, then surely all its physical actions and mental processes will also be the same. On the other hand, this presupposes that a conscious awareness of oneself is simply a product of activity of the brain, which brings one back to the mind–body problem. It would be fair to say that many people who can accept that a machine might be created which exactly resembles a human would draw short of ascribing consciousness to it, if for no other reason than a belief that consciousness is a unique gift bestowed on the living. In turn this veers dangerously towards the theological concept of the soul, at which point the debate becomes one of religious belief, and faith in the incorporeal is not a prerequisite of studying psychology. There is no simple answer to the problem and since we are still some years from creating such a perfect android, the debate is still largely an armchair debate.

Current attempts to replicate mental functioning using computers have met with patchy success. This in part is due to the enormous obstacles which have to be overcome before even a rudimentary simulation can be achieved. Let us take a simple example. Suppose that we wish to create a programme to recognise red apples. A computer is attached to a video camera, and it must interpret the camera's images to determine if a red apple is in view or not. This is a task which a human, unless severely visually handicapped, can do effortlessly. However, how might a computer programme do this?

First, we would need to ensure that the computer is programmed to recognise the colour red and distinguish it from other colours. Since red light is only emitted within a certain waveband of light, we might create a visual filter which only will respond when those wavelengths are in view. How do we then distinguish between red apples and other red objects? Since apples do not have straight lines, then one might programme the computer to exclude from consideration any objects with straight lines. This *sounds* easy, but how does one programme a computer to find the outline of an object and then calculate how straight the boundary is? Again, what if there are several red objects within view, some of which partially hide the others – how does one make a guess at the outline of an object when only part of it can be seen? These are easy tasks for a human, but the programming required to get a computer to do these same tasks is immense. This, however, is only the start of the problem. How do we now get a computer to distinguish between an apple and similarly-sized round objects (e.g. a red billiard ball)? The computer has to be programmed to recognise the curves and indentations of a 'typical' apple. However, there are many shapes of apples – how do we programme the computer to recognise not just one apple variety but lots of different varieties? Again, what if the apple is not a pure red, but has speckles of brown or green? Or yet again, what if the angle of viewing is changed, so that, for example instead of looking at the side of the apple, the view is changed to over the apple? How will this affect shape recognition?

The above are *some* of the problems facing a researcher trying to programme a very simple recognition skill into a computer. Such barriers can and have been overcome, but it explains why computer simulations to date have tended to be replications of relatively simple skills. This is not being disrespectful to experts in the field, but complex replications at the present time simply require too much programming time to be feasible. However, given the numbers of people now working in the field and the growth of knowledge, inevitably more and more complex skills will eventually be replicated (though the question of the degree to which they imitate the *mind* will of course still need to be resolved).

Allowing for their limitations, early models of artificial intelligence performed remarkably well. However, researchers began to question how realistically they imitated genuine brain functions. A central problem concerned the question of the *homunculus*. Suppose that a model of word recognition is created, in which a computer attached to a video camera must scan a page of text put in front of the camera, and then produce on the VDU screen what it has 'read' from the page. There are several ways in which this might be done, but one might hypothesise a simple model in which in successive stages, the computer identifies which black shapes on a piece of white paper are letters and which are not, then identifies the words formed by the letters. How does the computer 'know' when it has got the correct answer? The simple answer is that by itself the programme cannot – it has to be 'tweaked' by the human programmer until it produces acceptably accurate answers. In effect, there has to be a little person (an homunculus) overseeing the operations to make sure they work correctly. This is of course unlike human mental activity, where there is no homunculus in the brain monitoring what is done. Real mental activities have to be capable of correcting and improving themselves without an external agency adjusting them.[3] Early computer models had great difficulty in working without tacitly or explicitly assuming an homunculus.

Another problem with early models was that their very basic operations were unlike those of the nervous system. In essence, the early models tended to work by doing one tiny part of the process, then another, then another, in sequence (albeit very quickly) – what is called *serial processing*. This gave the impression of intelligent thought, but it is not how the brain manipulates information. Instead, the brain can be seen as being composed of sets of *neural networks*, in which thousands or millions of neurons are joined together in vast 'webs'. Thought probably takes place by neurons in these webs acting simultaneously and in tandem (what is called *parallel processing*), rather than one neuron firing, then another, then another, in sequence. The process by which these webs work is also known as *connectionism*.

An illustration of how a web might work may be useful here. Suppose that one wishes to store memories of words using the brain's neurons. One method might be to have different groups of neurons, each of which contains the memory of one word. This would be inefficient and liable to damage. Suppose that a some of the neurons in the group die – it will be recalled that neurons in the brain cannot be replaced. So if the neurons in the group die, then so does memory for the word. In a web, memories are stored differently. A memory is created by a pattern of activation across the whole web. By 'pattern' we mean that some neurons will be activated and others inactive, so

---

3   If one does not accept this argument, then one has to explain how the homunculus's mind can correct and improve the mental operation it is overseeing, which in turn leads to the ridiculous argument that the homunculus has an homunculus in its head, and that homunculus has an homunculus in its head, etc, etc.

there is a characteristic pattern of 'on' and 'off' neurons which together represent a word. Different words are created by different patterns of activation. Unless there is a catastrophic loss of nerve cells, then the web can cope with neuronal loss. Space prevents a full explanation, but essentially, it can be demonstrated that if members of a web are lost, the remaining members of the web are sufficient to replicate any stored patterns. Furthermore, this can be done entirely by self-regulating mechanisms – there is no need for an homunculus to 'fill in the gaps'.

Using modern computers, it is a relatively simple matter to create artificial neural webs, and at least for the foreseeable future, connectionist models in one guise or anther will form the backbone of artificial intelligence research.

### Awareness

The above discussion touches on one aspect of awareness – namely, how one can be aware of one's own state. As has been seen, this apparently simple process bedevils artificial intelligence research, whilst providing humans with perhaps the only guaranteed proof of their existence. However, 'awareness' has a rather more mundane, though equally interesting, role to play in the discussion of a person's level of awareness of their surroundings; in more prosaic terms, how wakeful they are.

A person's level of consciousness fluctuates throughout the day. The most obvious manifestation of this is that for most people, they are asleep at night (i.e. have a low level of consciousness) and are awake during the day. However, even during periods of consciousness the actual level of wakefulness varies (typically, we increase in wakefulness from rising to about midday, and then this gently declines until bedtime). Similarly, the depth of sleep varies through the night, as shall be seen. It should be stressed that even when deeply 'asleep', people are still monitoring the world around them, albeit at a very low level (e.g. how could alarm clocks work unless this was the case?). Even if very heavily sedated (e.g. for an operation) some people are still capable of recognising and remembering things said by those around them whilst they were unconscious. Therefore, although people may say that they are 'dead to the world' when asleep, this is far from being the case.

It should be noted, however, that these cycles of wakefulness and sleepiness (*circadian rhythms*) vary between individuals and also across the lifespan. For example, one obvious difference is that not everyone needs the same amount of sleep. This appears to be 'natural' – people who sleep longer are not necessarily lazy, and trying to reduce the amount of time they spend asleep usually is doomed to failure. Also, there appear to be no health differences between people who need a lot and a little sleep (see Kolb and Whishaw, 1990). There are also individual differences in the hour at which a person likes to commence sleeping given a completely free choice (although most will still choose some time within the hours of darkness); again, this appears to be a 'natural' phenomenon, not just a personal whim. As we grow, the sleep pattern also alters. Young babies, as parents discover to their cost, have a different sleep cycle, and alternate between sleep and wakefulness several times per day. Gradually, as they grow older, the sleep becomes concentrated into fewer episodes, until the sleep is contained in a single night time 'block'.

There is little doubt that we need sleep. Studies of sleep deprivation (i.e. where a person is deliberately kept awake) have found that most people can comfortably manage to stay awake for about three days without any particularly major ill-effects.[4] Longer than this, and mental and physical performance deteriorates, though the effects of this vary between individuals, and the degree to which the person feels stressed by the experience. Why sleep should have evolved as such a necessary part of life is open to debate. The most logical explanation is threefold. First, when animals are sleeping, their calorific demands are less than when awake and moving around. Thus, if one sleeps, proportionately less food has to be gathered. Second, by sleeping, one keeps still, and, provided a safe place is found, this may keep one safe from predators. Third, most animals are maximally suited to being active either at night or during the day. Therefore, sleep may be a way of rendering the animal immobile during the part of the 24 hour cycle for which it is not adapted.

---

4    Typically, performance of very taxing intellectual problems gets worse, but 'daily living skills' remain largely unaffected.

Keeping quiet and doing nothing may thus be an evolutionarily sound principle.

Sleep, once entered into, is composed of a repeating cycle of stages. Measurements of the brain's electrical activity (an *electroencephalogram*, or *EEG*) demonstrate that each stage is characterised by a predominance of a particular form of electrical activity. When awake, this consists of patterns of activation known as *alpha activity* and *beta activity*. When a person enters the first stage of sleep (known, not unsurprisingly, as *Stage 1 sleep*), this pattern of activity becomes less 'intense', and becomes *theta activity*. *Stage 2* follows, in which there are occasional bursts of activity (*spindles*), before the deeper levels of *Stages 3 and 4*. At this point, a sleeping person is hardest to wake up. The EEG activity is characterised by *delta activity*, in which the pattern of activity resembles (appropriately enough) slow, deep waves (as compared with the short but comparatively frenetic pattern of alpha activity). Stages 3 and 4 are distinguished by the percentage of delta activity (in Stage 4 it is in the majority, in Stage 3, it is present, but is under 50 per cent of all activity).

Thus, as the sleeper progresses from Stage 1 to Stage 4, he or she becomes progressively more unconscious. This typically takes about a 1–1.25 hours. Then, the level of consciousness suddenly rises, and the sleeper enters into *rapid eye movement (REM)* sleep. The EEG pattern shows an increase in theta and beta wave activity (i.e. those associated with wakefulness or light sleep); metabolism increases to near-wakeful levels; and, though the eyelids remain shut, the eyes move in rapid bursts of movement (hence the name). However, the rest of the body does not respond to this upsurge in activity – simultaneously, the voluntary muscles are paralysed. After some ten minutes or so, REM sleep subsides, and the cycle begins again (not surprisingly, the rest of the sleep cycle is called *non-REM* or *NREM sleep*). This cycle continues throughout the period of sleeping. Typically, each cycle becomes 'shallower' until the person wakes up. Later cycles spend proportionately longer in REM sleep and skimp on, or even do not enter, Stages 3 and 4. This pattern is true for most adults. There is, however, variability between individuals and across ages. For example, children spend longer in REM sleep, whilst older adults have a lowered level of Stage 3 and 4 sleep.

Most dreaming tends to take place during REM sleep (some dreams are reported during NREM sleep, but they tend be rather more vague).[5] Why people dream is still open to debate. Freud and his followers (see Chapters 3 and 12) believed that dreams enable the subconscious to play out repressed desires, thoughts and memories, which could be interpreted and thus assist in therapy. Freud greatly valued dream interpretation, calling it the 'royal road to the unconscious'. Psychologists have tended to reject dream interpretation along with much of Freudian theory, as being *post hoc* and 'unscientific' (see Chapters 3 and 12). Various modern theories play down the role of the 'subconscious' and instead emphasise, in one form or another, the idea of the brain as a machine, using the period of relative inactivity to perform self-repairs or diagnostic checks. For example, one suggestion voiced in several permutations is that dreams are simply a by-product of some areas of the brain associated with the senses 'limbering up'. This produces sensory images which are 'made' into a narrative by other sections of the brain trying to interpret them and joining them together into a narrative. Another, and not unrelated, theory by Crick and Mitchison (1983) is that dreams are a by-product of the brain acting like a computer purging files and 'debugging' its neural nets and, in effect, deleting unwanted information. Whatever the precise explanation offered, modern theories usually do their best to debunk any idea of a mystical subconscious.

Because of the necessity of sleep, disruptions to it can cause appreciable problems. Anyone who has experienced jet lag will immediately appreciate the problems inherent in wanting to follow a sleep cycle out of phase with everyone else. The deleterious effects of sleep deprivation have already been briefly mentioned. Hallucinations and delusions are common if the process continues after about three days, with reports, *inter alia*, of irrational fears of persecution and of seeing frightening creatures. These are typically resolved when the person is allowed to sleep (surprisingly, the person usually only sleeps for the normal length of time – there is little evidence of sleeping lon-

---

5    Researchers know when people dream because of experiments, the simplest of which is to wake volunteers at various stages of the sleep cycle and ask if they were dreaming. Almost everyone has dreams – those who claim they do not probably simply cannot *remember* dreaming.

ger 'to catch up'). *Insomnia*, or self-perceived lack of sufficient sleep, is obviously less easily dealt with. Occasional bouts of insomnia are experienced by nearly everybody, and are often related to physical illness or temporary stress. When the underlying cause has been removed, the normal sleep pattern returns. In other cases, the insomnia appears to be the sole problem. It should be noted that in some cases the person affected may in fact be getting a perfectly reasonable amount of sleep (there is considerable 'normal' variability in the amount of sleep a person needs). Five hours a night may be all some people need, but if they have heard that everybody 'should' sleep for eight hours or more per night, then this can make them apprehensive about what is for them the right thing. In other cases, the lack of sleep does appear to give genuine cause for concern. A variety of therapies are available, many of which emphasise sensible common sense remedies, such as avoiding caffeine, not reading or even trying to think once in bed, etc.[6] American textbooks (particularly general introductory texts) often list selections of drug treatments for insomnia which may be bought without prescription; typically they are not licensed in other parts of the world.

Other individuals suffer the opposite of insomnia – namely, *hypersomnia* or *narcolepsy*, in which the person seems to need 'too much' sleep. As noted before, in part people may have an unrealistic expectation of what the 'right' amount of sleep is, and what is too much for one person is too little for someone else. However, in cases of hypersomnia, the afflicted person may fall asleep during the day,[7] often unwillingly and unwittingly; in addition, he or she may have a relatively disturbed sleep pattern at night. Drug therapies can often tackle at least the worst excesses of the condition.

As can be seen from the above review, it is apparent that the circadian rhythm is not simply a case of being either awake or asleep, but instead is a process of cyclical change between levels of awareness, which for conve-

---

6   The traditional idea of a tot of alcohol as a 'nightcap' is wrong – if anything it will cause a
    person to be *more* wakeful later in the night. However, the other traditional remedy of warm
    milk is supposed to work (for those – unlike the author – who can stomach such a vile
    concoction), as is a regular routine.

7   *Not* to be confused with a tendency to fall asleep after a big midday meal – the so-called
    *post-prandial dip* is more to do with the effects of digestion and the natural tendency most people
    have (big meal or not) to feel sleepy in the early afternoon as part of their circadian rhythm.

nience, we label as 'awake' and 'asleep'. Furthermore, disorders can disrupt this flow so that people spend too much time in one state rather than another. There are other ways in which this balance can be changed, for both legal and illicit reasons. These are covered in the study of changing levels of consciousness.

Perhaps the oldest method of changing consciousness is through *meditation*. This is an all-embracing term for a variety of techniques. All have as a basic purpose the intention of creating a different level of awareness. This may simply take the form of feeling more relaxed, and less aware of earthly considerations. More extreme methods can make some individuals, for want of a better term, feel as if they have escaped their everyday existence and have reached a radically different level of awareness. Meditative methods obviously require as a first step that the person stops monitoring the here and now. Some techniques involve a 'cleansing' by mental exercises designed to free the mind of thoughts, to create an impression of a clear space, ready to receive new and different experiences. Other methods encourage the person to concentrate onto a single repetitive phrase or thought, which is consistently repeated, so that it loses all meaning,[8] and becomes mesmeric in its own right.

This striving for a changed consciousness through meditation has been practised by most of the world's major religions for millennia. The aim of attaining an awareness of the world removed from physical concerns has obvious an obvious religious appeal, and the technique, allied to a spiritual awareness, can be a powerful one. However, meditation can also be an entirely secular process, as the plethora of self-help books on the subject illustrate. There is certainly nothing 'magical' about meditation. Practically anyone who makes a regular habit of sitting in a quiet room, relaxing, and then spending half an hour quietly repeating a mantra may, when they stop, feel more relaxed and in a slightly different state, within a few sessions. Note that this altered state may not be as 'mind expanding' as many might hope. Persistent practice may repay dividends for some, but it is worth noting that the very deep states of meditation reported by, for example, some Eastern di-

8    Try repeating 'rhubarb' for a few minutes.

vines, are only obtained after years, and often decades, of practice and a rigorous lifestyle of self-denial and piety.

Another method of changing consciousness is *hypnosis*. Again, the technique is of some antiquity, though most western interest was first aroused by the activities of Anton Mesmer (1734–1815), a fraudulent character who used the technique as part of what was in effect a faith healing racket (hence the synonym for hypnotism – *mesmerism*). It is important to escape the idea induced by countless movies that people can: (a) be persuaded to do anything whilst hypnotised and that (b) hypnotism can be achieved by nothing more than gently swinging an old fashioned pocket watch backwards and forwards. The truth is rather more complex. First, hypnosis can be induced in several ways. All have an underlying motive of relaxing the person and (rather like meditation) making them dissociate from the present reality. Commonly-used techniques include getting a person to close their eyes and then concentrate on a mental image created by the hypnotist. This image encourages further relaxation and shutting off of extraneous thoughts and sensations (e.g. imagining a stone slowly sinking into a deep, deep pool of water). Other methods require the person to concentrate on a repetitive act, such as having their arm gently stroked or (for once the cliché is valid) a gently swinging object. Again, in spite of the cliché, the hypnotic state induced by such techniques is not one of a completely compliant zombie. A hypnotised person has in effect switched off some of their perceptions of reality, but not all of them. Thus, they are more able to attend to the hypnotist's voice (others in the room will usually be ignored), and will be more receptive to suggestions and images presented by the said hypnotist. However, there are limits to this. For example, a hypnotist who directly suggested that the person takes off their clothes is likely to be met by a (rightly) aggrieved individual snapping out of the hypnotic state. However, if a person is hypnotised to a sufficient depth, the hypnotist might be able to persuade him or her that it is very very hot, they are in the bedroom, and they might like to take off their very hot and heavy clothes. Persuasion need not just be effective during the hypnotic state. The hypnotist can also persuade a hypnotised person to do something after they come out of the trance, and even to forget what was said during the hypnosis (although still act on any instructions given without remembering why).

Given the power of hypnotism to persuade, there are clearly a number of uses to which it may be put. Hypnotism has been used in a variety of legitimate medical and dental procedures to, for example, ease sensations of pain. Again, hypnosis has been used by a variety of practitioners to tackle a wide range of problems, from dieting to stopping smoking. Claims for the efficacy of these techniques are mixed (see Sternberg, 1998), but results are generally positive for at least some patients. However, it is important to note that the person must be compliant and amenable to these methods. It is very difficult or even impossible to hypnotise a person unless they want to succumb, and many others cannot be hypnotised to a sufficient depth for therapy to be very effective.

Of greater concern is that hypnotism can also be used for rather more dubious ends. For example, the use of the technique in stage shows has been very heavily criticised. Occasional stories surface in the media of people who have died in accidents following participating in a hypnotism show, which may or may not be linked to hypnotic suggestions made on stage. Whether people are genuinely hypnotised when they participate is open to debate. Trying to enter a trance whilst being watched by several hundred people is not exactly conducive to relaxation. A more likely explanation is that participants are prepared to use the event as an excuse to make fools of themselves, and that any 'hypnotic state' is at best very shallow.

Another misuse of hypnosis is that it can implant false and potentially damaging ideas into the minds of some particularly impressionable people. For example, there is currently a heated debate about the extent to which hypnosis in therapeutic situations may have led to false memories of child abuse (see Chapter 8). Since it is very easy to make suggestions during hypnosis which can be incorporated into true memories (e.g. Dywan and Bowers, 1983), it is conceivable that whilst under hypnosis a person could be easily persuaded that an innocent childhood memory has more sinister overtones.

How hypnotism works is open to debate. It would certainly appear that physiologically, hypnotised people have a similar but nonetheless significantly different pattern of responses (e.g. as measured by EEG) from people who are merely in a light doze or awake but deeply relaxed. Whether one accepts hypnotism as a genuine phenomenon rather depends upon whether one attends to the similarities or the differences between these states. Many psychologists believe that hypnotism is in effect no different from other forms of relaxation and that if people are more compliant, this is because they are in effect role playing[9] the part of a hypnotised person. In other words, they want to believe in the process and so will go along with whatever the hypnotist requests. Subjectively, hypnotised people report that a hypnotic state feels radically different (in particular, more 'involving') than just relaxing, but this might be part of the role play. An opposing theory argues that hypnotism works by allowing the person to in effect 'shut off' some mental processes and concentrate solely on others (e.g. to suppress aversive pain sensations). Whichever theory is correct does not necessarily 'disprove' hypnotism. For example, if a person stops smoking because of hypnotherapy, does it matter if he or she was deep down only role playing? To use the old phrase, 'if it ain't broke, don't fix it'. In other words, *legitimate* hypnotic techniques may be valid regardless of what is 'really' happening. However, some of the more excessive claims that a hypnotised person enters a new realm of consciousness are probably best given a wide berth.

A final method of changing consciousness to be mentioned in this chapter is the use of *psychoactive drugs*. In other words, drugs which alter psychological functioning.[10] The range of these is considerable, but they broadly fall into four groups.

*Stimulants* (or *uppers*) work by, not surprisingly, stimulating the body into higher levels of activity. Some of these, such as cocaine and amphetamines, have legitimate medical uses, but the overwhelming use is illegal. The sensation from such drugs is of an intense 'high' in which the user gains (temporary) feelings of overwhelming power and control. This is followed by a depression and, with many drugs, a craving for more. Over time, a bigger dose of the drug is required to attain the same results. In many cases, the user

9    NB: this does not imply conscious deception; the person may enter into the spirit of the act without any realisation that they are pretending.

10    Note that this is not often a psychoactive drug's sole purpose. For example, opiate drugs also have a legitimate use as painkillers.

becomes addicted (i.e. there is an overwhelming physical and/or psychological drive to keep using the drug), resulting in almost inevitable social, economic, physical and mental decay. Before non-drug using readers begin tut-tutting piously about this, it should be borne in mind that the two most frequently used stimulants have not been mentioned yet – namely, caffeine and nicotine. The addiction to cigarettes is well-known, but it is also possible to be addicted to coffee. Most regular coffee-drinkers can feel down if deprived of coffee for a few days, but some rare individuals can suffer from *caffeinism*, or severe addiction to coffee and caffeine-containing products (e.g. chocolate) which can be every bit as difficult to cure as an addiction to illegal drugs.

In contrast to stimulants, *depressants (downers)* operate by depressing the workings of the body. These include *barbiturates* and alcohol. Both create feelings of relaxation and, by depressing some control mechanisms, release inhibitions (hence the popular misconception that alcohol acts as a stimulant). As with many other psychoactive drugs, they can create addiction – certainly alcoholism is by far the biggest form of drug addiction after smoking.

A third group of psychoactive drugs is labelled the *narcotics* (though the term is often also used for all illegal drugs). These began life as legitimate drugs used in pain relief. Best known of these are the *opiates* derived, in one form or another, from the opium poppy – *opium, morphine, heroin* and *codeine*. As might be anticipated from this description, they are drugs which create a feeling of numbness. With this comes a sensation of utterly pleasurable relaxation which surpasses the cessation of pain (for this reason, opiates are used considerably in treating terminal cancer patients). However, the drugs are also highly addictive, and their high price creates a market for crime, since addicts need extremely large sums to finance their habit.

The fourth and final drug group comprises the *hallucinogenic drugs*, whose principal function is to distort and manipulate perception.[11] The best known members of the group are *LSD* and *cannabis*. Reactions to hallucinogens (particularly LSD) vary enormously between occasions and individuals. Al-

---

11    Many of them act as stimulants as well.

though the distortions of reality can at times be entertaining and non-threatening as espoused by some of the more florid rock bands of the late 1960s, the effects can also take on the qualities of a long nightmare. *Flashbacks* (the recurrence of hallucinations years after they were first experienced) are also not unknown.

It should be stressed that all the illegal drugs described above are illegal for good reason – namely, that they seriously impair judgement and many have serious long term health risks (notably death). Not all illicit drugs are as dangerous to health as others (e.g. cannabis is relatively benign in many respects), but given the range of legal pleasurable outlets available to even the least enquiring mind, the use of illicit drugs cannot be countenanced.

Awareness can thus be seen to be a rather nebulous concept. Although it is easy to group states as either 'awake' or 'asleep' the variability in levels of consciousness and the ways in which these can be manipulated indicate a rich field of study.

## Motivation

Before concluding this chapter, mention will be made of a further area of biopsychological research – namely, motivation and emotion. This is a complex topic which draws not only upon biopsychological concepts, but also, to some extent, upon theories derived from social psychology. *Motivation* in essence refers to the factor or factors which lead an individual to act in a particular way. People do not act randomly: there is a reason why they act as they do. An *emotion* is the person's total physical and mental state in response to a particular situation. The two factors have clear links with each other. For example, a person's emotional state may change their motivation, whilst the results of being motivated to act in a particular way may in turn affect a person's emotions.

Theories of motivation have a long history, and certainly several of the early psychologists, including William James, made it a central topic of study. Many of the early theories attempted to attribute motivation to instinctive reactions. They essentially argued that individuals have a drive to do something because they are obeying an instinct (i.e. a drive which we are born with). The problem with the theory is that it was taken too far, and every behaviour was seen as acting out an instinctive drive. However, this was often a circular argument (e.g. because a person did X, this was because there was an instinct to do X; however, the proof of an instinct to do X was that the person was doing X). However, the theory is not unreasonable in some situations. For example, many animals will *always* display a particular behaviour in a certain situation (e.g. a mating ritual during breeding season to a potential mate; a newborn baby will suck anything placed in the mouth). Most notable of these perhaps is *imprinting*. Some species of ducks form an emotional bond with the first object/entity they see after hatching.[12] This bond will remain nigh-on unbreakable thereafter. Conveniently for the duck, this object is usually the mother duck. However, if the mother is replaced with a human, then they will bond with the human. This is an extreme case of how an instinctive act can very firmly shape motivation, but it is only one of many in which a response is 'pre-wired'. However, it is not true for *all* occasions.

More recent theories of motivation are rather more complex, and no single explanation will suffice for all eventualities. Many theories use to a greater or lesser extent the concept of the *hedonic continuum*, devised by the early psychologists to describe that fact that every action must create to some extent a feeling of either reward or punishment. An individual is obviously motivated to attain positive feelings, so primarily motivation must be geared towards performing rewarding deeds. Physiologically, there is justification for this argument. It has been known since work by Olds and Milner (1954) that if stimulating electrodes are inserted into some sections of a rat brain, that the rat will, given the opportunity, spend most of its time stimulating these areas. Clearly these areas of the brain produce a rewarding sensation. In humans, the *mesolimbic system* of the brain is strongly involved in creating sensations of reward, and is also stimulated by many psychoactive drugs. Therefore, the brain is capable of producing rewarding sensations which could provide the physiological basis for motivation.

However, motivation to perform certain acts is not a simple, uncontrolled desire. We do not, for example, have a motivation to eat or drink which never

---

12    More accurately, the item which is most present in the first few hours; this is called the *critical period*, when bonding must occur if it is to happen at all.

stops. Equally, the level of motivation can change under different circumstances. Therefore, motivation is mediated by other mechanisms. One of these is the *inverted-U function*, also known as the *Yerkes-Dodson law*.[13] This simply states that the level of arousal shapes how well and how arduously we perform a task. If arousal increases, then so does performance *up to a point* – if arousal increases past a certain point, then performance actually declines. There is therefore a fine balance in motivation – simply increasing arousal may actually be counter-productive in some cases.

In other instances, motivation is controlled by *homeostasis*. This simply refers to bodily mechanisms designed to keep a balance. For example, in eating, it is obviously necessary that we should feel a motivation to eat, otherwise we would starve to death. However, it is unwise to make this motivation too strong, or people will overeat and become obese. Therefore, homeostatic mechanisms seek to motivate eating and then de-motivate when the person has eaten the right quantity of food.

The hypothalamus is heavily involved in maintaining feeding balance. For example, the section of it called the *lateral hypothalamus* is involved in initiating feeding, whilst the *ventromedial hypothalamus* is involved in stopping feeding by creating feelings of satiety (in rats, destroying the appropriate sections of the hypothalamus results in either very very fat animals or animals which will never eat and thus starve to death). The hypothalamus is triggered into initiating hunger signals by the level of blood glucose. The individual cells in the body require glucose carried to them in the blood to live. Except under special circumstances, blood glucose is obtained by either digesting food or breaking down body fat. Too low a blood glucose level therefore indicates the need for more food. The brain also receives information from the body. For example, the liver is extremely sensitive to the level of blood glucose and will signal the need to initiate or cease feeding. The stomach and intestine will also signal when they receive food. A principal signalling mechanism is the hormone *cholecystokinin (CCK)*; its release into the blood stream will cause feelings of satiety. It is the combination of all these mecha-

---

13    See also Chapter 3.

nisms which determines the degree to which a person feels hungry.[14]

However, very important as homeostasis is, animals are not necessarily complete slaves to it. For example, homeostatic signals for hunger can be ignored if, say, a person is on a reducing diet (and is sufficiently strong-willed!). Again, laboratory rats will grow fat if instead of just being fed a consistent diet of food pellets, they are allowed a wider choice of tasty foods (*supermarket rats*). The same phenomenon can be observed in many humans who go on expensive holidays. Conversely, taste aversions may deter people eating some foods even if very very hungry. For example, how hungry would the reader have to be before they would consider eating boiled maggots? As with food perception (see Chapter 9), personal and cultural preferences can override or control more 'basic' mechanisms.

Another motivational theory is concerned with the fact that nearly all acts which we feel motivated to perform are cyclical. Thus, once we have done a particular act, there is a period of pleasure, and there often follows a feeling of wanting to do it again. Solomon's *opponent process theory* (e.g. Solomon, 1980) argues that we seek a neutral level of emotions. When an action creates a move away from neutral (e.g. a positive feeling of pleasure about an act) this will be met by a feeling in the opposite direction (e.g. a negative feeling or 'winding down'). Solomon adds to this that a positive emotion may begin as a large move above the neutral baseline. However, if the act is repeated, the increase in positive feelings will *decrease*. However, the negative feelings following this rise will *increase*. This means that the act now gives little pleasure, but the aftermath is much worse. Clearly this does not apply to every act we feel motivated to perform, but it does describe some forms of addiction very well. For example, alcoholics or drug addicts may feel little satisfaction from drinking or taking drugs *per se*, but the negative sensations which are created by abstinence are far far worse. Therefore, once in a state of dependence, they continue to use the alcohol/drug not to create a high as much as to avoid a low.

---

14    Curiously, an empty rumbling stomach in itself is not an effective signaller of hunger (though when full, stretch receptors in the stomach are an important component in signalling satiety). For example, people who have had their stomachs surgically removed still subjectively feel hunger in much the same way as before.

Not all theories of motivation are quite so physiologically-based as the ones described above. For example, it is apparent that although levels of motivation may in themselves be physiologically mediated, they can, as seen in the case of hunger, be overridden by psychological factors. *Maslow's hierarchy of needs* (e.g. Maslow, 1954)[15] conceptualised that we prioritise our motivations in the symbolic form of a pyramid, with higher level needs not being addressed until the lower levels have been dealt with. The levels, in order of ascension, are: physiological needs, safety and security needs, belongingness and love needs, esteem needs, and need for self-actualisation. Clearly these move from the basic needs of living and survival to the more rarified.[16] A rather similar view divides motivation into *intrinsic motivation* (being motivated to do something for its own sake) and *extrinsic motivation* (being motivated because of an external reward, such as wages). However, it must also be borne in mind that motivational levels will not be the same for everyone. One commonly-use measure is the *need for achievement (NAch)* which assesses the degree to which a person is motivated to succeed at a particular task. The level of NAch differs considerably between individuals.

## Emotion

As already defined, an emotion is the person's total physical and mental state in response to a particular situation. Again, as has already been stated, this has an obvious interaction with motivational forces.

A feeling of emotion may often subjectively feel as if it is all in the mind, but almost always emotions are a complex interaction between the body and brain. As stated earlier, people with spinal injuries lose the ability to feel and control parts of their body, and the higher up the spinal cord the injury occurs, the greater this loss. It has also been found that the greater the loss, the less 'emotional' a spinally-injured person feels in an emotion-provoking situation. Thus, they have a mental feeling of the particular emotion (sadness, rage, etc), but it feels less intense and 'complete' than before the injury. This finding supports William James's argument that emotion is largely a product

15    See Chapter 3.
16    Self-realisation is a fine thing, but it does not usually pay the bills.

of the body's response rather than the mind's. A contemporary, Carl Lange separately devised the same concept, and the theory is hence known as the *James-Lange theory*. If a raging bull chases you across a field, the argument goes, you run and *then* feel afraid because you are running. This can at times seem counter-intuitive (surely it is because you *feel* afraid that you run?). A more 'scientific' criticism is that the body's physiological processes are too slow for physical changes (e.g. in hormonal levels, heart rate, etc) to take place and be detected before a mental feeling of emotion is felt. *Inter alia*, this argument led, about forty years later (in the 1920s), to the *Cannon-Bard theory*. This argues that, essentially, after the recognition of the event, the response and the emotional feeling arise simultaneously. However, this does not explain all instances of feeling emotion. The *Schachter-Singer theory* (e.g. Schachter and Singer, 1962) argues that several different causes can create the same basic physiological response – how we label the emotion depends upon our cognitive interpretation. The idea is not a new one. In *Three Men in a Boat*, Jerome K. Jerome spins out a lengthy comic discussion about how we can commit appalling acts on our friends (e.g. ducking them under water, playing malicious practical jokes) which will be seen as amusing, whereas the same acts committed on a stranger would rightly be perceived as criminal assault. Similarly, being hit in the face with a custard pie would be seen as funny if done by a friend during horseplay but would be perceived as an attack if done by a stranger, with concomitantly different emotional responses.

Schachter and Singer's theory has a certain appeal, but subsequent research has generally found that the experimental support for it is less clear-cut than first appeared. Current theories, often labelled under the general heading of *appraisal theories*, argue that emotions are created by an ongoing dynamic process, in which physiological and cognitive process feed off each other. Thus, when entering a new situation, the mind evaluates it for potentially emotionally-arousing factors; the situation is then re-evaluated once or more when entered into, and the feedback from physiological mechanisms shapes the interpretation of the event, whilst the interpretation also manipulates the physiological response. The theory thus emphasises emotion as a constantly interacting system of emotions and thoughts, rather than a simpler 'first this, then that' process (see e.g. Sternberg, 1998).

FURTHER READING

As can be seen, biopsychology covers a lot of ground, from the basic anatomy and function of the nervous system through to the complex world of emotion and motivation. What has been described here is just the tip of the iceberg; hardly surprisingly, since the field of study covers not only psychological issues but also draws heavily upon related fields, such as physiology. Reading materials on the topic are legion. Several larger overviews are available in many of the basic introductory texts (Sternberg, 1998 is recommended). Carlson's *Physiology of Behavior* (e.g. Carlson, 1986) is often-recommended as a more specialist text, and this and several similar titles are likely to be found on the shelves of any university or college book store. Logue (1991) is very informative (and entertaining) on the subjects of hunger and thirst. A novel and useful guide to brain anatomy is provided by Diamond *et al.*'s (1984) *The Human Brain Coloring Book.*

# CHAPTER II

# Comparative Psychology

## Introduction

Comparative psychology is the study of differences and similarities of behaviour across species. This can be done for its own sake (i.e. through interest in how other animals behave and think) and also to try to determine if common behaviours govern all or most animal behaviour (including human). This area of study is at an intersection of work by not only psychologists, but also members of other professions, such as biologists and ethologists (people who study animal behaviour in its natural context). Underlining a lot of the research is an acceptance of the theory of evolution. This, whilst widely accepted by many religious people, is not universally accepted. It is not the intention to offend any readers, but of necessity, this chapter is built upon the basic tenets of evolutionary theory.

## Darwinian theory

Charles Darwin's theory of evolution (Darwin, 1859) basically states that different species have evolved by chance. In most situations 'in the wild' there are more offspring born than there is food to feed all of them. Therefore, those offspring which are best equipped for their environment will tend to survive, whilst the rest will die. Thus, the fastest and strongest predators and the best camouflaged prey will survive and reproduce, whilst their slower or more conspicuous brethren will not. What makes the fastest, strongest or best camouflaged is the chance result of breeding: parents cannot 'select' their children to be a particular type. Thus, for example, some offspring will be born stronger, faster or better camouflaged than others. This is the result of the chance variation inherent in sexual reproduction (e.g. this explains why siblings do not look identical). However, parents of a particular physical type will *tend* to have offspring which are similar (e.g. tall

240

parents tend to have tall children; and siblings may look different, but have *some* features in common). Over time, a species may evolve because advantageous changes gradually alter it, by 'pushing' it in a particular direction. Thus, if being strong is an advantage, then over successive generations, the strongest members of the group will tend to survive and breed more than weaker members, with the result that the whole species gradually becomes stronger.

To take another example, it is argued that the ancestor of the giraffe had a much shorter neck. Presumably at some point food became scarcer, so members of the species with longer necks (who could reach more leaves from trees) gained an advantage. Those favoured individuals who had longer necks were not consciously chosen – it just happened that they were born this way. However, if the longer necked animals were the ones who survived, then they were the ones who also got to breed, and *their* offspring in turn were also long necked (the shorter necked animals died before they could breed). If food got even scarcer, then a still longer neck would be an advantage, and so over generations, longer and longer necked animals would be favoured. Thus, over progressive generations, the necks got longer and longer, until the modern giraffe was created. This process was due to an entirely *random* process – the length of neck was the product of breeding and could not be, for example, consciously chosen during gestation. Although the end result may *appear* planned, the giraffe's neck is basically the result of chance differences between offspring.

Darwin's theory is controversial because it contradicts a *literal* interpretation of the Bible and some other religious texts, which state that the world and all living things were created by a deity in the form in which we see them today and have not been created by chance fluctuations.

## The selfish gene

Darwin's theory in its basic form has since been criticised and amended. For example, it is now felt unlikely by many commentators that changes are as gradual as Darwin thought. Instead, it is more likely that species change in 'bursts' (e.g. by genetic mutation a major change occurs in a small group of individuals, which, if advantageous, spreads quickly through the rest of the population by breeding[1]). Again, Darwin knew nothing of modern genetic theory, which weakened some of his arguments. For example, he had great difficulty in explaining *altruism* – behaviour which is apparently for others' benefit and which may be costly to the individual performing the behaviour. Why, for example, should a bird in a flock let out a warning cry when it sees a predator approach? This should make the bird conspicuous – why not just fly away and let one of the other birds be caught? By traditional Darwinian theory, this is behaviour which evolution should have wiped out. Surely a behavioural trait in which an animal puts itself at risk should not have survived?

To a certain extent, Darwin was being pessimistic; alarm calls in many cases can have an inherent value for the caller. For example, although an alarm call alerts others to danger, only the caller knows the source of the danger. Thus, when the group flees, only the caller knows the best direction in which to escape. By a similar token, the alarm calls of many species are hard to locate spatially, so a predator may not be able to easily get a 'fix' on the caller before the group begins to respond. However, other instances of alarm calls are harder to explain by traditional Darwinian theory. For example, Sherman's (1981) study of Belding's ground squirrels found that squirrels would give alarm calls which *did* place them at considerable danger, but were far more likely to do this if the nearby squirrels were close genetic relatives. Why?

The solution to this, and similar problems, lay in what has become known as *selfish gene theory* (Hamilton, 1964; Dawkins, 1982). This argues that what matters is not the survival of the individual member of a species, but the genes it carries. Take the example of warning cries. The Belding's ground squirrel mentioned above increases its chances of being caught by letting out a cry. However, the rest of the squirrels increase their chances of escaping. If those squirrels are close relatives, then they will contain all or most of the genes in the caller's body. Therefore, although the genes in one body might die, plenty of copies of the gene in other bodies will survive. The fact that an

---

1    Though this will obviously take many generations, in the time scale of the world, this will take a comparatively short time.

individual is more likely to let out a cry if the squirrels it warns are close relatives lends support to the argument that the behaviour is primarily one of preserving genes.

Thus, genes may in this sense be 'selfish' – they may drive an individual into acts dangerous to the individual in order that they (in the form of identical copies in other bodies) will survive. It should not be assumed that the genes consciously plan this – the term 'selfish' is of course a metaphor. However, it can be appreciated how through inheritance, successful genes will be transmitted and passed through the population. Often of course the needs of the genes and the individual host coincide (in most cases the gene has an obvious vested interest in the individual surviving at least until it has bred and, where appropriate, reared its young). However, if placed in a position where the choice is between the preservation of either the individual or a larger number of hosts carrying the same gene, then the individual will inevitably suffer.

The selfish gene theory helped to explain other aspects of animal behaviour which had defied traditional Darwinian theory. For example, another aspect of altruism is the case of Tasmanian native hens (Maynard Smith and Ridpath, 1972). Often a single female will be 'shared' between two males (almost always brothers). One male is usually dominant over the other. However, the dominant one allows the subservient one to mate with the female as well, though less often (it is important to note that a feature of hen breeding is that the offspring in a single clutch can have more than one father). It is at first difficult to see how this altruism by either male is advantageous. The subservient male is losing out by not having all the eggs fertilised by himself, whilst the dominant male, by allowing the subservient male to mate, is likewise not fertilising all the eggs himself. However, the arrangement makes far greater sense when a more pragmatic view is taken.[2]

If the dominant male kept the female to himself, then all of the offspring would be his. But he would have to expend more energy helping the chicks

---

2    It should be noted that discussions of animal behaviour can become very mechanistic and
     apparently very sexist. It must be stressed that findings are descriptive and not prescriptive of
     how humans 'should' behave.

and the female (the environment in which the hens live is sparse and collecting food is difficult). Indeed, Maynard Smith and Ridpath demonstrated that far more offspring survive in a breeding trio than in a breeding pair. A further point is that if the subservient male is a brother, then half of the subservient male's genes will belong to the dominant male in any case. Therefore, sharing of breeding rights will ensure that more copies of genes will survive.

Another anomaly which had baffled traditional Darwinism was that it had been difficult to explain why male bird plumage is often very bright and hence conspicuous. In many species of birds, the male attracts a mate through the brightness of its plumage; a well-known example of this is the peacock's tail feathers. These may be very good at attracting a mate, but they are also very good at attracting predators, who of course can also see the colourful plumage. Traditional theories could not adequately explain this apparently suicidal behaviour, but the selfish gene theory encounters no such difficulties. The fate of the individual male is less important than that he breeds and passes on his *genes*. Thus, a very brightly coloured male may die young, but before he is killed, he may successfully breed with a great many females. His genes have thus been passed on in greater number than those of a more drably coloured male, who may live longer, but equally, attracts fewer mates and hence produces far fewer offspring. In selfish gene theory, it is better to be fertile than long-lived.

Such a view creates a grim picture of evolutionary processes; species appear to progress through a forced march, trapped by the whims of their genes. Certainly evolutionary theory has led to some intellectually clumsy forms of social engineering. A sinister extrapolation of the early theory was a form of 'social Darwinism', which justified racism and severe social divisions because these were 'natural' and demonstrated the 'survival of the fittest'. Again, the selfish gene theory was perhaps taken too far by some commentators, who began to see *all* behaviour as determined by some basic 'natural' laws of survival and breeding success. Thus, the human male serial philanderer might be portrayed as only trying to maximise the spread of his genes. This gives a spurious justification to morally reprehensible behaviour as well as creating a more complex justification than may be necessary (that man likes sex and has an immature view of women and relationships is somewhat simpler but arguably equally valid). However, such views are often based upon an inaccurate view of evolutionary theory. There is *nothing* in Darwinian theory or its derivatives which justifies the argument that humans are the culmination of the evolutionary process. Every living thing has evolved in response to the conditions in which it finds itself. Each is adapted to its particular niche. Thus, the dung beetle is just as 'perfect' in its way as humans are in theirs. The concept that humans are the ultimate product in a fight for supremacy is wrong.

Again, it must be stressed that evolutionary change is blind. There is no deliberate planning. This argument has been taken even further in recent years to argue that many features may be even more accidental than even the blind chance of traditional theory would predict. For example, Gould (1991, 1997) has argued that some features of animals may have been accidental by-products of other changes which were being shaped by natural selection for quite different purposes. For example, it has been plausibly argued that bird's feathers probably began in structures in a distant ancestor designed to help temperature regulation. However, once this development had reached a certain stage, their use as a mechanism for flight (which was not being 'planned' by natural selection) took precedence (it must be stressed that this is not a *conscious* process). Gould goes further than this, and argues that these changes are of two types. The first, called *exaptations*, are akin to the feather example, where the feature is an existing alteration to structure which 'changes course' when a better use is created. The other form, the *spandrel*, occurs when a new feature occurs which is simply a by-product of other changes. It has not been planned, but simply happens. In an excellent review of the theory, Buss *et al.* (1998) use the analogy of the belly button. Everybody has one, but it is a by-product of the need for the umbilical cord to be attached to the stomach area. Gould argues that much of what we intuitively consider to be quintessentially human, such as language, artistic sense, even the ability to wage war, are spandrels; mere accidental by-products of other evolutionary processes, designed, for instance, to create bigger brains. Although there are criticisms of some aspects of this theory (see Buss *et al.*, 1998), it is an intriguing argument.

## Communication

Although evolutionary theory is an important aspect of comparative psychology and underpins almost all studies in the field, many studies simply take it as read, and instead concentrate on specific aspects of behaviour without especial regard for the forces which created them. For example, there is a sizeable literature on forms of communication. Of this, perhaps the best known example is the research on honey bees. This was initiated by Karl Ritter Von Frisch (1886–1983), Nobel laureate.[3] He found that when a worker bee finds a new source of food, she flies back to the nest and informs other workers. This is done by means of a pattern of movement which might anthropomorphically[4] be described as a 'dance'. Food near the hive is indicated by the bee walking round in a circle. Other bees then fly off and scout the immediate surroundings until the food is found. For food further away, such a strategy would be too time-consuming, so more specific directions are given. Two key pieces of information need to be given – how far away the food is and its direction. This is indicated in a set of movements which in effect describe a figure of eight; the so-called *waggle dance* (because whilst going along the central 'bar' of the figure of eight, the bee waggles her abdomen). The distance to the food is indicated by the speed at which the 'dance' is performed; the faster the dance, the *closer* the food is. The direction is indicated by the angle of the central 'bar' in the figure of eight pattern. In most species, bees perform the dance on the vertical plane of a honey comb inside the hive; the angle of movement along the bar relative to vertical indicates the direction relative to the position of the sun (e.g. if the movement of the bar is straight up, then this indicates that the food is in the direction of the sun; if straight down, then the food is directly away from the sun; at ninety degrees to the right, then the food is at ninety degrees to the right of the sun, etc).

---

3    Von Frisch shared the 1983 prize with Konrad Lorenz (1903–1982) and Nikolaas Tinbergen (1907–88).

4    Attributing human motivation and thoughts to non-human animals is (rightly) frowned upon in animal behaviour research; arguing that bees use dance movements describes what they *look* like; that is *all*.

There were some criticisms of Von Frisch's theory (e.g. that the waggle dance was an incidental by-product and the other bees simply followed a scent trail), but these were later refuted, leaving a firm conclusion that bees are capable of a fairly sophisticated form of communication. It should be stressed that the bees are not necessarily 'aware' of what they are doing; such behaviour could be genetically 'hard wired' as a set routine which is followed like an automaton whenever the need arises. This consideration leads to some problems in examining what is meant by 'communication'. It cannot be inferred that an animal making a signal to another necessarily has conscious intent. This may sound a trivial point, but if one pauses to consider that subjectively, the conscious intent to transfer information is precisely the point of much human communication, then the difficulty becomes apparent.

Instead, discussion of animal communication must lie in terms of the effect a communication has on a recipient. Since we cannot ask animals how they interpret signals, we are left to judge the effects of a communication purely in terms of changes in behaviour. For example, if a member of a particular species of bird spreads out its tail feathers, this might intuitively be seen by humans as an attempt at communication. However, if other birds do nothing when they see this action, then we would be led to conclude that spreading out tail feathers is not a communicative act – it may be no more than the human equivalent of stretching one's arms. However, if the spreading of tail feathers was reliably met with the same sort of response (e.g. it always or nearly always led to fighting, or it always or nearly always led to mating, etc), then it might be concluded that the act was a form of communication.

There is a danger with such a definition that it does not necessarily distinguish between accidental and designed communication. For example, suppose that an animal is hiding from a predator, moves, is detected by the predator, and killed. This is observed to occur with reliable frequency. Therefore, can we conclude that the animal is communicating with the predator? It is clear that such a problem places an undue strain on the definition of 'communication' we have adopted. However, to counteract this, we would have to amend the definition to include a statement that communication only occurs when the animal intends it, which creates more problems than it solves. The solution often adopted is to argue that communication occurs when there is evidence that the communicative act has specially evolved for that purpose (see Dawkins, 1986 for an excellent discussion of this issue). This allows for behaviour such as ritualistic courtship displays to be included, but accidentally attracting a predator to be excluded, without invoking concepts of conscious intent. However, there are still problems with this. Dawkins (1986) raises the point that only very 'obvious' displays can therefore be classified as communication, whilst a range of subtler signals may be excluded. This is a moot point (what does one classify as 'subtle'?) but Dawkins is correct in noting that many discussions of animal communication tend to be biased in this fashion. Another point is that there is a danger that the argument can become a tautology (a communicative act is apparent, therefore it has specially evolved for this purpose, because it is specially evolved ... etc).

The reason for this diversionary discussion is simply to stress that behind even apparently very simple ideas in animal behaviour there is usually a great deal of discussion. It is easy to argue that animal communication 'must' be taking place, but it is quite another thing to prove this on logical grounds. Notwithstanding these comments, it is clear that animals do use communication in a range of ways and to great effect. Courtship is an obvious example, alarm calls and bee waggle dances are others. Bird song, in spite of its romantic connotations, is basically about feeding, fighting and fornication. Many birds have a range of calls, which generally signal either: a warning to a rival to get away; a mating call to a prospective partner; a demand to be fed (in young birds); or an alarm call. Whether Keats would have thought the nightingale a 'light-winged Dryad of the trees' had he known its song is the avian equivalent of 'come on over here if you think you're hard enough'[5] is open to debate.

Communication is not solely limited to sound and vision. For example, scent plays an important role in many animals. Females of some species release a scent indicating when they are fertile and receptive to intercourse. Anyone with a dog will know the trouble which can be caused by a bitch on heat in the neighbourhood. Humans are less receptive to scent. Some years

5    A note for non-British readers: a polite chant often offered by some of our more Neanderthal football supporters to fans of a rival team.

ago, claims were made that a particular 'sex scent' spray would make men irresistible to women. This is unlikely, since human attraction is rather more complex and cerebral (see Chapter 4) but users should be wary of going near a pig farm – the main commercial use of at least one variety of spray is in attracting boars to sows.

Why communication should have evolved is a lengthy issue. Perhaps the main reason is to save energy and time. For example, Dawkins (1986) cites the case of stags bellowing at each other during mating season (basically, the stag which bellows longest and loudest wins; the bellowing is a good indicator of the stag's strength). Stags can and will fight over mates, in the process weakening themselves and sometimes causing serious injury or even death. A bellowing match is exhausting, but it is less exhausting and dangerous than fighting. Most confrontations are settled by bellowing, without escalating into a fight. In other cases, communication simply saves a lot of physical effort rather than avoiding injury. If a female animal wishes to indicate she is on heat, she could move around the neighbourhood actively finding mates. However, this would require more physical effort as well as increase the risk of predation as she moves around. A further consideration is that communication can be faster. For example, a ground squirrel seeing a predator could run up to each squirrel and push it away, but this would take a lot of time; an alarm call does the same job for all the squirrels in the vicinity in a fraction of the time.

## Mate selection and parenting

In any species reliant upon sexual reproduction for continuation of the species, there is a very obvious issue to be resolved – how and why do individuals select their sexual partners? The survival of the species depends upon breeding taking place. Mating and subsequently raising the young is not just simply a matter of male and female getting together. The issue creates a whole series of problems, some of which are considered below.

When mating should take place may seem an odd question to humans, since we are amongst a relatively small proportion of species who are potentially ready to breed throughout the year. Many species, however, are only fertile during a particular 'mating season'. This can be for several reasons.

One is concerned with availability of food. There is little point in giving birth to offspring when food is scarce. Therefore, a common time for births is in the warmer months of the year, when there is more plentiful vegetation. Animals which do not have a closed breeding season tend to be those for whom the availability of food and shelter do not pose problems. Other reasons also play a role, such as similar species having different breeding seasons to stop cross-species mating; and quite simply, investing time and energy into breeding for just one part of the year leaves the rest free for other things.

Another issue concerns the degree of fidelity mates show to each other and to the offspring. Some species show no involvement after initial fertilisation. For example, most fish and amphibians breed by the female depositing eggs, which are then fertilised by the male, and then the parents leave. Given such lack of protection for the developing eggs, it is small wonder that very few offspring survive. Hence, the number of fertilised eggs produced in mating will be large. In other species, the female will be responsible for tending the developing embryos, and also for caring for the offspring for some time after birth. However, what about the male? There are many different levels of male involvement, but two of the commonest consist of *polygamy* (the male shows little or no fidelity or help in raising young, but tries to mate with as many different females as possible) and by way of contrast, *monogamy* (the male remains faithful to one partner for the time of raising the offspring, or even for life).

The two systems have advantages and disadvantages for the male. The polygamous male will obviously be able to spread their genes further. A male who can breed with twenty females will produce far more offspring than a male who remains faithful to one mate. However, there are also disadvantages. For example, if a species is polygamous, then several males may mate with the same female, so a male cannot be sure that it is his sperm which have fertilised her eggs. Males in some species, such as dragonflies, try to combat this problem with specially-shaped penises, which contain barbs designed to scrape out sperm from any previous copulations.[6] Again, if males are compet-

6    The female dragonfly's view of this has not been sought.

ing for the females, the male has to invest a lot of energy in not only courting as many females as possible, but also perhaps in fighting other males. A monogamous bonding avoids these problems of paternity and effort, but carries the disadvantage that a male has fewer offspring than might *potentially* be the case in polygamy.

Whether a species is monogamous or polygamous tends to depend upon their environment. Where resources are poor, bondings tend to be monogamous, since it may require both parents successfully to raise the offspring to a state where they can fend for themselves. A polygamous male might make lots of females pregnant but, in a poor environment, a female by herself may not be able to raise the offspring successfully. Thus, few if any might reach maturity. On the other hand, in an environment rich in resources, and/or where the offspring need little care, a polygamous strategy might be the most effective. Here, the males can 'afford' to mate with as many females as possible, because there is a high chance that at least some of their offspring will survive to an age where they themselves can breed, without further male help being required.

What of the females in these two systems? In both cases, the energy required of the female in tending for the offspring is hypothesised to be roughly the same. However, criteria for accepting a male will be different. In monogamous species, competition for mates is usually fairly 'relaxed'. The argument is basically that there is no point in competing – once a female is bonded, that is that. However, in cases of polygamy, competition is far more intense. Since the male's involvement ceases with fertilisation, the female needs to ensure that the best mate is attained (since this is in effect the limit of the use she will get of the male). Thus, males may be required to engage in physically demanding courtship rituals, or provide gifts of food (in some species, such as some breeds of fly, copulation lasts for as long as it takes the female to eat the food gift). This regime will also help the female ensure that her male offspring are also likely to be good at courtship rituals (i.e. their chances of reproductive success will also be high and so the genes will survive). Males with poor courtship rituals will be less likely to breed because the female will reject their efforts as inadequate.

The physical state of the male is also important in female choice of a mate. An animal which looks healthy is more likely to be carrying 'healthy genes' than more bedraggled specimens. This extends to other aspects of physical display, such as plumage in birds (one of the reasons why male birds are often more brightly coloured than females of the same species). The case of the peacock's tail has already been mentioned. Another instance is the long-tailed widow bird of Africa. The male has a long tail which is involved in courtship display. Andersson (1982) removed the tails from a group of males and replaced them with tails of different lengths. It was found that the longer the tail (even when freakishly longer than normal), the higher the breeding success of the male. In some instances, size *does* matter.

## Competition

It can be surmised from what has been written so far that a lot of discussion about animal behaviour is couched in terms of the costs and benefits to animals of performing particular actions. Indeed, some topics are very explicitly analysed in terms of mathematical or economic models (see Krebs and Davies, 1987). One such example is the concept of the *evolutionary stable strategy (ESS)*. This is the set of behaviours exhibited by a species which is best for it given the situation in which they find themselves. This might be judged in terms of criteria such as survival (i.e. if this behaviour is adopted, then the largest number of individuals will live) or, more usually, reproductive success (i.e. this is the strategy which ultimately will produce the largest number of offspring). The ESS is best seen in terms of an example, such as the *Hawks and Doves* model of Maynard Smith (1972). Hawks and Doves is a deceptively simple problem used in a branch of mathematics called *game theory*. Two varieties of the same species are presumed to exist, or, a species can adopt one of two behaviours. The Hawks are aggressive and use physical force to show their aggression; Doves are more peaceful, and do not use force. Not surprisingly, a Hawk fighting a Dove will always win (in the face of physical aggression, the Dove withdraws without getting hurt). A Hawk fighting a Hawk *may* win, but victory may be Pyrrhic, since the victor may also get hurt. A Hawk defeated by a Hawk will not only lose, but may also be injured. A Dove fighting a Dove may win, and if so, then there will be gains, but losing will also be relatively painless. Given these fighting styles, what proportion of a population will be Hawks and what proportion Doves?

The answer is less obvious than it may first appear. It would clearly be very useful to be the only Hawk in a population of Doves, since this would guarantee victory every time. Equally, being the only Dove in a population of Hawks would be useful as the Dove would be the only animal to remain unscathed in combat (remember that the Dove always withdraws before being hurt). However, such a situation would not last for very long. If being a Hawk is advantageous, then more animals will become Hawks; if being a Dove is advantageous, then more animals will become Doves. This process will continue until there are too many Hawks or too many Doves, whereupon the advantage switches to being the other sort of animal. This process will continue until a balance is achieved, and the proportion of Hawks to Doves in the population is such that there is no incentive for the balance to alter.

Quite what this balance is depends upon how one defines the costs and benefits in the first place. For example, if the costs of injury are very high relative to the benefits of physically fighting, then the balance will tilt in favour of the Doves; costs in the other direction will favour an increase in Hawks. Again, one can conceive of situations in which an individual might begin like a Dove and then switch to being a Hawk if physical threat is made, etc. However, all these models essentially obey the same premise; namely, that the balance of reward to injury may dictate the type of aggressive behaviour shown.

This seems to be supported by various empirical studies which have used game theory to predict the outcomes of 'real life' animal conflicts. For example, stags will for most of the year be relatively unaggressive. However, during mating season, when stags fight each other for access to fertile does, the level of physical aggression displayed increases dramatically. In terms of game theory, the balance of costs and benefits have shifted so that it is now worth the risk of sustaining injury from fighting because the rewards of fighting have just got much much better.

ESS is not solely about aggression, however. Practically any behaviour can be analysed this way, where the individual is torn between conflicting options. A notable example of this research is work by Parker (1970) who examined male dung flies on cow pats. The female dung fly lays her eggs on newly 'laid' cow pats, which the male then fertilises; the older (and colder) the cow pat, the less likely the female is to lay her eggs. What does the male do? Obviously, the longer he waits, the greater the chance a female will turn up, but equally, the longer he waits, the colder the cow pat and the less likely it is that the female will lay her eggs. Parker found that the male dung flies in effect managed to balance out the two conflicting factors, and that reproductive success followed almost exactly the mathematical model of an ESS for this behaviour. This fitting of real data to mathematical models is found with remarkable frequency in ethological research. Although in some instances there is more than a whiff of post-hoc reasoning about it,[7] and many of the model's parameters have been intentionally simplified (see Dawkins, 1986) nonetheless, behaviour patterns which have evolved over time often do obey a simple equation.

## Genetics and behaviour

Throughout this chapter the important role of genetic inheritance has been stressed. Animals are viewed as using particular behaviours because genetic and evolutionary forces 'make' them do so. Certainly it is true that many species appear to be born with complex behaviours which are not learnt, but which 'spontaneously' appear at the appropriate point. For example, the elaborate courtship rituals of many animals appear to be instinctive – there is no sign that they have been taught to do them. This has important implications not only within comparative psychology but also by extension to other disciplines of psychology, and in particular the *nature–nurture debate* (see Chapter 2). If, the argument runs, we can demonstrate genetic inheritance of complex behaviours in other species, why should the same not be ascribed to humans? As we shall see, this proves to be a rather simplistic notion of the complexities of innate behaviour.

It is intuitively obvious that some very basic acts must be 'hard wired' from birth. For example, some *survival reflexes*, such as the ability to swallow in humans, are necessary for feeding to take place. Again, the eye blink reflex

---

7    I.e. the model has been made to fit the data; rather like arguing that people's heads are the shape they are to make sure that hats fit on them.

is necessary to prevent damage to sight. However, these cannot be said to shape behaviour except in the sense that the ability to digest food or use the voluntary muscles can be said to shape behaviour. More striking are identical behaviours which different members of a species exhibit no matter what environment they are raised in. For example, there are some species of crickets and birds which will produce the same song whether raised with their own kind, raised in isolation, or raised hearing only the songs of other species. Again, male sticklebacks will attempt to attack another male with a red belly whether they have been raised 'naturally' or in isolation. In other words, the behaviour will display itself in spite of the environment. Again, the behaviour will be identical in form in all individuals across all environments. This leads to the conclusion that the behaviour 'must' be genetically determined. To all intents and purposes, this is true. It is possible to argue that the environment must still play a role: for example, without the sensory input of the environment, the animal could not have developed the perceptual mechanisms necessary to produce the behaviour. However, even by the standards of ethology, this is splitting hairs.

Finding that some behaviours are genetically fixed to appear come what may (*fixed action patterns*) does not mean that *all* behaviour is so rigidly hard-wired. For example, some bird species will produce a song even if surgically deafened, but it will not be as 'refined' as in a hearing bird (i.e. they need the auditory feedback from the environment fully to develop their song). Other bird species will not produce a song at all unless they are reared with other birds of their species. The number of occasions where a behaviour is 'purely' genetically-determined are in fact relatively rare. For this reason, use of the term 'innate' has to be treated with caution (Dawkins, 1986).

This argument does not remove the case for genetic factors in behaviour, however. Although an animal's behaviour may not be *purely* genetic, it is certainly strongly *shaped* by inherited factors. At the very least, behaviour is restricted by genetically imposed limitations. This can be taken *reductio ad absurdum* (e.g. humans are shaped in their courtship rituals because they are not genetically endowed with tail feathers, etc). However, taken at a more pragmatic level, it makes sense. For example, some birds, such as chaffinches can only produce a certain set of sounds; anything not in the set of 'chaffinch sounds' cannot be learnt (Thorpe, 1961).

Again, it must not be assumed that a genetically-influenced behaviour is necessarily complex in origin. For example, male sticklebacks will attack other male sticklebacks during mating season because of their possession of a red belly. This sounds as if their genes have hard wired a very specific piece of behaviour ('attack red bellies'). However, the truth is rather simpler: male sticklebacks will attack practically anything red, including the red of a van passing the window and reflected in an aquarium tank (Tinbergen, 1951). Again, a young herring gull chick will peck at the red dot on its mother's beak to get the mother to regurgitate food. This again seems a very precise behaviour until one learns that chicks will also peck at many red stimuli, such as red knitting needles (though the chick become more selective in what it will peck at as it gets older – see Hailman, 1967).

The stimuli (usually simple) initiating behaviours were called *innate releasing mechanisms (IRMs)* by Tinbergen (e.g. Tinbergen, 1951). It is important to note that the stimulus does not even have to be very realistic, provided it contains the requisite colour, shape, etc. The stimulus may even be a grossly exaggerated version of 'the real thing', which will often produce a commensurately better bigger response (what Tinbergen called a *super-releaser*). This general concept is accepted by most ethologists (though the term *sign stimulus*, rather than IRM, is now more often used). However, the reason why animals respond to IRMs which Tinbergen and also Lorenz (e.g. Lorenz, 1950, 1958) advanced is rather more disputed.

Lorenz proposed that the energy to perform a particular action (*action-specific energy*) 'builds up', rather like water accumulating in a cistern. The more water which accumulates in the cistern the greater the potential force of the water which can be released. In a similar way, the longer since an action had been performed, the greater the force impelling the animal to do it again. For example, an animal which has just fed will have less drive to eat again than an animal which has not eaten for some time (and whose 'eating force' has therefore built up). Again, an animal which has not copulated for some time will have a higher potential 'copulation energy' than an animal which has just mated. Release of this energy will come when the situation signals itself in the form of an IRM. When an IRM appears, it is equivalent to a tap being turned – the more powerful the strength of the IRM, the more the tap is opened, and the greater the force of water which comes out. It should now be clear why the term 'innate *releasing* mechanism' was chosen – the stimulus is felt to release pent-up energy. Tinbergen refined the model to argue that different actions would be initiated according to the amount of energy released (a small release would result in relatively minor actions, etc).

The model is at first sight plausible. For example, animals which have just responded to IRMs are less likely to repeat them straight away; it is as if the energy or drive to perform them has temporarily drained away and must build back up. Again, there is the curious phenomenon of *displacement activity* – animals in the midst of an appropriate response to an IRM may suddenly break off from doing this and do something different (e.g. scratching themselves, wandering off, etc). The Lorenz-Tinbergen model explains this in terms of a build-up of energy which cannot be used up by the action in progress, so another act has to be initiated, in effect, to soak up the excess. By extension, animals may engage in displacement activity when they have a drive to do something completely different which they are denied doing. An example often given is of humans drumming their fingers on a table when they are angry with someone.

Although the *hydraulic model* is an attractive one, there are often much simpler explanations available. For example, there is little evidence that the drive to perform an act is governed by a build-up of energy. First, it is physiologically naive to argue that animal bodies contain reserves of energy building up and itching to be released. Second, following a response to an IRM, there is certainly a period during which the response to further IRMs is weaker. This may simply be due to the animal being too tired to respond strongly. Alternatively, it may be a matter of *habituation* rather than depletion of a hypothesised energy store. In other words, the animal is so used to seeing the IRM that it has ceased to be the novelty it once was. This was elegantly demonstrated by Prechtl (1953; cited Hayes, 1994) who showed that chaffinch nestlings would after a while offer fewer response cries to the sound of an adult chaffinch, but would cry with renewed vigour if their nest was vibrated instead. In other words, there was no sign of a decreased 'energy store'. Again, displacement activity need not be explained by an accumulation of energy. There is some evidence, for example, that the supposed displacement activity may be part of a display process (see McFarland, 1987). Again, Dawkins (1986; p.80) makes the sensible point that 'we should not jump to the conclusion that the behaviour we are watching is "irrelevant" just because we cannot immediately see what it is'.

It is easy to summarise work on comparative psychology as an attempt to prove that Darwin was right, and that to a greater or lesser extent it revolves around proof of the evolution of genetically-controlled behaviours. However, whilst evolutionary theory is undoubtedly central to the discipline, there is more to it than this. Furthermore, as has been seen, evidence indicates that although genetic factors can be shown to be important, the role of the environment is, in most instances, crucial.

FURTHER READING

Readers interested in pursuing the topics raised in this chapter have a wide field of books to choose from. Hayes (1994) provides a succinct overview of the key topics. Dawkins (1986) is a brief book concerned with the rationale of animal behaviour research rather more than examples of behaviour. However, it should be a key component of the reading list of anyone wishing to gain a deeper understanding of the subject. McFarland's *Oxford Companion to Animal Behaviour* is an excellent compendium of brief authoritative essays on key topics as well as being marvellous to 'dip into'. Krebs and Davies's *An Introduction to Behavioural Ecology* is a sound work perhaps best approached after some preliminary reading in other 'lighter' works, though newcomers should still find it readable.

# CHAPTER 12

# Mental Illness

## Introduction

Mental illness has been given a very poor image by the media. In fictional works, severe disturbances of thought and behaviour are almost solely seen in terms of the murderous psychopath. Such distinguished works as *Friday 13th, Halloween, Nightmare on Elm Street et al.* portray figures of evil whose prime motivation is a severely disturbed mind. The fact that the other common reason for killing presented in horror films is demonic possession does nothing to diminish the association of mental illness with evil. Non-fictional images of mental illness are little better. Although practically all mentally ill people are a danger to no-one but themselves, the images which appear in the media are of the *extremely rare* times when a severely disturbed individual commits a serious crime. In the case of UK residents, the words 'Hungerford' and 'Dunblane' are etched in the mind, and rightly so. However, it must be stressed that these are the *very rare* exception and not the rule.

To begin to understand the issues involved, it must first be established what is meant by 'mentally ill'. Some people believe that all forms of 'madness' are the same, and that the difference between mentally ill people is simply the degree to which they are ill. As will be seen, this is far from the case.

## Defining 'illness'

When it is said that a person is 'ill', what do we mean by this statement? At the heart of the matter is the recognition that illness is a state which is not normal, and should be treated so that the patient returns to normal. However, all this does is shift the issue onto defining another word, and immediately begs the question of what one means by the term 'normal'. It is clear that physical illnesses are not normal, since they impede normal physical functioning, and in some cases (e.g. cancer) will terminate life if not treated. However, with some mental illnesses, whether 'normal' functioning is impaired may be determined more by societal standards than objective criteria. For example, within most modern industrialised nations, legal and medical authorities consider homosexuality to be a normal sexual orientation, albeit one preferred by a minority of the population. However, in the past, and currently in many other countries, homosexuality was and is considered to be abnormal, requiring treatment or even punishment. The behaviour is the same in the two situations – whether it is an illness or not depends upon the view of the culture concerned.

Taking this argument further, it is possible to argue that a lot of what is perceived as mental *illness* is the product of societal labelling. This was a particularly popular argument in the 1960s amongst the *anti-psychiatry movement*, in part fuelled by the work of Thomas Szasz (e.g. Szasz, 1963) and RD Laing (e.g. Laing, 1959). The central argument is that much of what is considered a 'disease' of behaviour might be regarded as an alternative and interesting view of the world. If a person's behaviour is radically altered because of this, it may be inconvenient for family, friends and the community, but it does not mean that the person should be locked up against their will or forced into receiving treatment, since that person's view should be considered as a valid alternative to convention. Such a view provoked a considerable and at times intemperate debate. The majority of psychiatrists and psychologists opposed the anti-psychiatry movement, not, as was popularly suggested, because it attacked their status as (well paid) arbiters of who is sane and who is not, but because much mental illness manifestly causes distress to both the patient and his or her family and friends, and needs to be treated. This does not mean that the views of Laing, Szasz and others can be dismissed out of hand. By arguing strongly and cogently that mentally ill people are individuals with valid needs and wishes, their arguments helped create in many institutions a gentler, more humanistic face to patient care.

Notwithstanding these comments, the fact remains that illness in general and mental illness in particular still awaits a cogent definition. It might be thought that defining illness in terms of suffering would be adequate, but this is fallacious in the case of mental illness, since in several conditions, the patient does not appear to be in any distress.[1] Nor can mental illness be defined in terms of physical damage, since many conditions show no sign of injury or, for example, disordered brain activity or structure.[2] Again, mental illness cannot be defined in terms of failure to fulfil certain average standards, because this proposes a subjective judgement that what is average is the correct arbiter. The simple fact is that any definition based upon a single consideration is likely to raise criticisms (cf. Davison and Neale, 1996; Kendall, 1975). One workable definition is perhaps that mental illness is a behaviour which requires treatment for the immediate or longer-term benefit of the patient or for others. However, it should be noted that commentators who have produced similar concepts in the past have argued that this is less a definition of illness than a description of who should be treated (e.g. Kendall, 1975; Linder, 1965). In addition, it implies that a person with behaviours which offend a particular culture's standards may be mentally ill. However, any single sentence definition of mental illness is likely to fall apart if pushed to unrealistic extremes. Readers should be nonetheless aware that behind any definition of 'abnormal' *may* lie a cultural judgement.

This issue is brought into focus by the issue of criminal culpability. In other words, if someone commits a crime and they are also considered to be mentally ill, to what extent can they be considered responsible for their actions? Within the English and American legal systems at least, a general principle has long been established that a person judged insane is not responsible for their actions and that they therefore cannot be guilty of a crime (though this would not prevent them being incarcerated in a secure hospital for their or other people's safety). However, the precise definition of 'insane' for legal purposes has gone through several permutations, and what is 'obviously' a mental illness in one age is not necessarily recognised as such in another (e.g. until recent historical times, some forms of mental illness may have been interpreted as signs of diabolic possession and persecuted accordingly). Modern views stem from the *M'Naghten Rule* of 1843. David M'Naghten was a

---

1   Though they may pose a danger to themselves or others if untreated (e.g. a patient who thinks they can fly).

2   At least given the current state of medical tests – future technologies may change this.

severely disturbed man who formed the delusion that Sir Robert Peel (at the time Prime Minister of Great Britain) was persecuting him and accordingly tried to shoot him. Unfortunately, his aim was as accurate as his beliefs, and he shot Peel's secretary by mistake. At his subsequent trial, M'Naghten was judged insane and committed to an asylum. There is no doubt that M'Naghten was severely mentally disturbed, but given the status of the intended victim and attendant publicity, the case generated a governmental enquiry into how precisely a plea of insanity should be judged. This created a twofold definition – either a person must be so severely disturbed that they did not know what they were doing, or, they knew what they are doing, but do not know that it was wrong. This ruling stood for Anglo-American courts for the next hundred years, in some cases augmented by an irresistible impulse clause, which stated that the person was unable to control their behaviour (there are some instances where a mentally ill person may know that what they did was wrong when interviewed, but nonetheless could not stop doing it). More recently, and particularly in the United States, criteria have become more draconian. The irresistible impulse clause has largely been abandoned (on the grounds that anyone who has committed a crime, whether sane or otherwise might palpably claim it) and the criteria for demonstrating mental illness have been made more demanding (e.g. the illness must be severe enough to cause an almost total severance from reality, rather than e.g. a general predisposition to be anti-social).

The legal emphasis is thus not so much on the fact that an accused person has an illness as defined by clinicians (that may not be in doubt) but whether he or she is sufficiently in control of their actions that they could have been expected to use their free will to prevent an illegal act occurring. This explains why the apparently anomalous situation may arise where a person found guilty of a crime in spite of pleading insanity can be sentenced and simultaneously placed in a mental hospital for treatment. The court believes that the person could have controlled their actions but also recognises that they nonetheless need treatment. It is important to note that when a person is found not guilty due to insanity, this is not a case of being 'let off lightly' (much of the current tightening of definitions stems from American popular concerns that John Hinckley, the would-be assassin of President Reagan, was not sufficiently punished by being sent to a mental hospital rather than prison). The person is palpably ill and will be placed in an institution, perhaps against their will (there have been several instances where a person has spent longer in hospital than they would have spent in prison). It should also be noted that it is far commoner for a disturbed person to be judged mentally unfit to stand trial at all than it is for them to be subjected to a court case.

## Cataloguing mental illness

### Early attitudes and treatment

Most early historical cultures regarded mental illness as a God-given curse. Since humans were created in the image of God, it was blasphemy to consider that a mad person was a reflection of God's mind. Therefore, if someone became insane, this demonstrated demonic possession and/or loss of God's protection as a result of misdeeds. The writings of Hippocrates and other Ancient Greeks and Romans on the theory of humours (see Chapter 3) shifted the emphasis towards the concept that personality, and by extension, personality disorders, could be the result of physical imbalance. This concept gained ground in modern European thought from the Middle Ages onwards, notwithstanding two centuries[3] of vigorous persecution of suspected witches (in which odd behaviour was taken as a cardinal sign of diabolic possession, rather than of physical problems). Treatment was, however, crude. For example, an attempt to redress the balance of the humours might involve repeated bleeding or purging of the patient. This might make the patient docile through physical weakening, but it is unlikely that it had any effect on the underlying illness. In other cases, patients were not treated, but merely constrained (often in squalid surroundings), even to the point of being shackled to the wall, so that they were not a danger to the rest of the community. The community as a whole was content with this state of affairs. Its more fashionable members even found such lunatic asylums entertaining,

---

3    The onset is generally taken to be the publication of the *Malleus Maleficarum* (a DIY guide to spotting signs of diabolic possession) in 1486. By the mid-17th century, even the most inbred of European monarchs had recognised the stupidity of witch hunting, and the practice was officially discouraged.

and would pay to visit some of the more florid inmates whose behaviour was considered to be especially entertaining. One such institution was the hospital of St Mary's of Bethlehem in London, whose name became shortened to Bedlam.

Reform of mental hospitals began with the pioneering work of Philippe Pinel in the Revolutionary France of the 1790s, who removed many of the physical constraints from inmates,[4] and began to treat them more as patients than as prisoners. During the same period, William Tuke, a Quaker business-man, established a liberal treatment regime in Britain, at the York Retreat, which formed the basis of similar new hospitals elsewhere, notably in the USA (see Davison and Neale, 1996). It should be noted that the treatments offered at such institutions were not necessarily effective – recovery was far from guaranteed, and instead of shackles, many patients were subdued with sedative drugs. However, a crucial move had been made away from the idea of mental illness being a punishment towards the concept of it being a dis-ease.

Systematic study of mental illness from the 19th century onwards began to identify different types of disease, which in turn led to a variety of classifi-catory systems. Some early systems, such as that devised by Emil Kraepelin (1856–1926) would now been seen as overly-simplistic: Kraepelin argued that all mental illness could be explained by two root causes – *dementia praecox* (now called *schizophrenia*) and *manic-depressive psychosis* (now termed *bipolar disorder*[5]). However, it was a start, and as more people began to work on the issue, larger, more sophisticated classificatory systems were estab-lished.

### The DSM

The modern classificatory methods which have gained the greatest acceptance are: the *International Classification of Diseases (ICD)* (World Health Organisation, 1993); and the *Diagnostic and Statistical Manual of Mental*

---

4   Or at least the patients from wealthy homes – in a distinctly un-Revolutionary gesture, the working class patients received rather shabbier treatment.

5   The terms are defined later in the chapter.

the edition of the system being referred to. At the time of writing, the current versions are ICD-10 and DSM-IV. The two systems are now (intentionally) very similar. In this chapter, discussion will be confined to the DSM-IV, because this is the one which most readers are likely to encounter.

The DSM-IV is divided into 5 axes. The grading of a patient's behaviour and recent life history on these describes not only the type of illness from which the patient is suffering, but also his or her general state, and from this, the type, the intensity and the urgency of treatment which is required. *Axes I* and *II* describe the disease the patient is suffering from. Axis II consists of two types of mental disorder: mental retardation; and all *personalty disorders.* Axis I consists of all other mental disorders. *Axes III* and *IV* provide information on factors which may exacerbate or ameliorate the condition. Axis III describes all other physical conditions the patient may suffer from, and by extension, may provide information on possible causes of the mental illness (e.g. side-effects of tablets being given to treat a physical ailment). Axis IV describes problems in the patient's social surroundings and/or monetary problems. These again may have a bearing on the illness (e.g. a patient may be depressed because of marital problems or financial insolvency). *Axis V* describes the highest level at which the patient coped in the past year, on a scale of 1 (serious danger of death/hurting self or others) to 100 (no symptoms of inadequate coping). Axes III–V are obviously of great importance to clinicians gauging the severity of a patient's case and its likely causes. However, to the general reader, they are of less importance than Axes I and II which between them categorise the principal mental illnesses.

In addition to formal classificatory systems, other terms have entered into usage as fairly broad descriptions. For example, illnesses are sometimes divided into *psychoses* and *neuroses.* The former refers to all conditions where in essence the patient has lost significant contact with reality, whilst the latter is reserved for patients who have a single appreciable problem but whose behaviour and attitudes are otherwise relatively normal.[6] For example, a psychotic patient who believes that everything around them is evidence that the

---

6    One should be careful about using the term 'normal' in this context because it carries a value
      judgement. Equally, not using it is patronising and naive. Accordingly, the word will be used as
      a gauge, but reader caution is advised.

Antichrist is plotting to kill them and is not aware that their condition is unusual might be said to have lost contact with reality. On the other hand, a neurotic patient might have a morbid fear of spiders but otherwise is fully aware of their surroundings (and is probably aware that their fear is illogical). Clinicians and researchers are not always happy with this division, because it is too neat and glosses over subtle but important distinctions between illnesses. Accordingly, whilst it is convenient shorthand, it should generally be avoided.

It is not possible or desirable to present a catalogue of every single type of mental illness in a general introductory text. Those interested in seeing the full range are recommended to an introduction to abnormal psychology, such as Davison and Neale (1996). Nonetheless, because mental illness is often a prime reason for people being interested in psychology,[7] some consideration is needed of at least the 'best known' and most illustrative illnesses. A selection has therefore been made of some conditions which demonstrate different degrees to which a person's thoughts, mood and behaviour can be damaged by illness.

However, one must avoid treating some of the more unusual conditions as curious specimens. Although some symptoms can be bizarre, it must be recalled that there are real people *suffering* because of them. If mental illness is treated as entertainment, then we become no better than the society folk who visited the inmates of Bedlam. It is also important to be aware of 'medical student syndrome'. People reading about illness for the first time can become convinced that they have every disease in the book. This is, to say the least, unlikely, but anyone who has doubts about their mental health should seek professional advice, in spite of Samuel Goldwyn's famous dictum that 'any man who goes to a psychiatrist needs his head examined'.

---

7    The statement is meant in the kindest possible way.

# Some examples of mental illness

## Schizophrenia

It is hard to imagine any adult who has not heard of schizophrenia, and yet it is an illness which is often woefully misunderstood. First, it is important to state that the term does *not* mean 'split personality'. This arises from a twofold misunderstanding. First, 'schizophrenia' means 'cloven mind'; it is easy to see how this might be misinterpreted as 'split mind', but the term is intended to mean a broken or fragmented mind. Second, there are instances of patients with 'split personalities' (or more accurately, *multiple personality disorder*) who at different times can assume radically different personas, each often unaware of the others.[8] Such cases are an obvious gift to Hollywood scriptwriters and actors wishing to show their range of skills,[9] but real cases of multiple personality disorder are extremely rare and usually less florid than fiction would have one believe.[10] In addition, they are *not* related to schizophrenia.

A further point is that schizophrenia is usually seen as synonymous with violence. Whilst it is true that some of the more distressing crimes by mentally ill people have been by patients suffering from schizophrenia, the illness takes many different forms, and the majority of patients offer no threat to other people.

There is no single snappy definition of schizophrenia. Broadly speaking, it is 'a *psychosis* characterised by profound disorders of thought and language (though without signs of mental retardation), loss of perception of reality, and concomitant changes in emotions and behaviour' (Stuart-Hamilton, 1996). The DSM requires that the symptoms must be present for a minimum of 6 months to be classified as schizophrenia (briefer episodes with similar

---

8 The term should also be distinguished from 'split brain', in which a patient's right and left brain hemispheres have become disconnected (typically deliberately severed in surgery on some very rare forms of epilepsy). Such patients often possess two simultaneous and different conscious perceptions of the same event.

9 Usually limited.

10 In recent years there has been a huge increase in the number of reported cases of MPD (now termed *dissociative identity disorder*) in the USA. This increase in diagnosis is controversial – most of these new cases of 'extra' personalities are only found under hypnosis, leading to arguments that they are a product of hypnotic suggestion, picking up on cultural expectations, etc.

symptoms are classified under such headings as *schizophreniform disorder* and *brief reactive psychosis*). We are thus considering a serious long-term break-down of reality and the attendant misery which this brings. Most patients are unaware that their belief systems are illogical, although they may be aware that they are considered ill. The said beliefs are varied, but nearly always unpleasant. A frequent, but not universal element, for example, is a feeling of persecution. Others include the belief that other beings (either human, spiritual, or extraterrestrial) are controlling the patient's thoughts and deeds. This is a familiar phenomenon from newspaper reports, since it is often cited as the motive in crimes committed by schizophrenic patients; namely, that they were not in rational control and were ordered to do their acts by 'voices' in the head. It is small wonder that it is now often argued that cases of supposed demonic possession throughout history may have been cases of schizophrenia rather than the actions of Satan. By the same token, the religious visions and actions of some holy men and women may also have been the by-products of a schizophrenic disturbance.[11] However, once again it must be stressed that such behaviour is rarely very florid. Relatively few schizophrenics are prompted to act violently to others, or for that matter, see visions of the Heavenly Host. For many, the experience is of having a nasty peevish voice in the head which will never leave one alone or let one enjoy life.

Another relatively common problem is that the patient becomes convinced that their thoughts are being read by other people, and that (entirely innocent) remarks by others are directed at the patient (*ideas of reference*). This illustrates the point made earlier in this chapter that mental illness can be seen as a continuum. Most people have at some time misinterpreted other people's behaviour as being directed at oneself. This commonly occurs when someone has done something embarrassing and is convinced that everybody else knows. In everyday life, this is little more than a guilty conscience, and in time will pass. The difference in schizophrenia is one of degree – the belief is more strongly held and does not go away. Added to these problems, there are

---

11    This is not intended to offend anyone's faith; there have also been a great many palpably sane religious figures who outnumber their more florid companions in faith.

often *delusions* (false beliefs about the world and people around the patient) and *hallucinations* (a misperception of sensory information, such as seeing people with grossly distorted faces).

Given such a mental world, it is not surprising that the schizophrenic patient often behaves and talks in an unusual manner. For example, responses to questions may often be classed as 'surreal', either because they appear at best to be only tangentially connected with the question, or because the answers, whilst obeying the rules of conversation, are magnificently false (e.g. "where are we?" – "Egypt in 54BC"). This can make communication difficult, but it may be worsened by a tendency to produce made-up words (*neologisms*) and *clang association* (producing strings of real words and neologisms whose only link is that they sound similar). Since a clinician cannot readily understand the language, it makes understanding the patients' problems and 'getting through' to them all the more difficult. Alternatively, language may be severely impoverished, with a limited vocabulary, or statements which 'tail off' before they are completed. This is not helped by the fact that in most cases, emotional expression is usually either limited, or otherwise may be inappropriate for the situation. Given this catalogue of problems, it is small wonder that many schizophrenic patients are also depressed.

There are many types of schizophrenia, which are classified according to the most prevalent symptom (though symptoms found in other forms of the illness may also be present in a less pronounced fashion). The following are amongst the most often encountered.

*Catatonic schizophrenia* is characterised by extremes of motor activity – the patient alternates between high activity and periods of extraordinary immobility, 'freezing' into postures which are maintained for several hours. *Disorganised schizophrenia* is characterised by a disorganisation of thought, inconsistent and extreme moods, and a general lack of control (e.g. of personal hygiene). In cases of *paranoid schizophrenia*, the patient has delusions of persecution and/or of self-importance, and/or has *delusional jealousy* (an extreme and illogical delusion of one's partner's infidelity). Ideas of reference are also often present. *Residual schizophrenia* describes a state in which the patient has suffered from schizophrenia in the past, who now could not be described as suffering from the illness in its full-blown form, but who nonetheless continues to exhibit some symptoms. *Undifferentiated schizophrenia* is a rather nebulously defined condition, in which the patient possesses symptoms characteristic of more than one of the other types of schizophrenia. The illness can also be sub-categorised according to rate of onset. *Process schizophrenia* has a very slow and gradual onset, whilst *reactive schizophrenia* has a sudden and dramatic onset (and may be triggered by a stressful or otherwise distressing event). Recovery is less good from the former condition [source: Stuart-Hamilton, 1996].

The debate about the causes of schizophrenia is a lengthy one. It is worth noting that the illness is commoner than many people believe, and studies usually find an incidence between 1 and 2 per cent. Generally, proportions increase the lower the socio-economic group being considered, and also tend to be higher amongst ethnic minorities (though this can be confounded with socio-economic status). The explanations for these figures vary, but all are essentially permutations of the nature–nurture debate (see Chapter 2). It is possible, for example, that people are born predestined to become schizophrenic, and that peculiarities in their behaviour before the illness becomes apparent ensure that they remain unemployed or can only find low status jobs. Hence, their schizophrenic minds have in effect lowered their social status. The converse of this argument is that people in poor living conditions are made schizophrenic by the stress they receive from the environment. This is exacerbated by a tendency of a predominantly white middle-class medical profession to regard working class and racial minority behaviour with less tolerance, and thus be more prepared to slap a label of 'mentally ill' upon it.

There is some justification for both these viewpoints. Let us first consider the case for environmental factors. It must be stressed that there are no truly objective measures of schizophrenia – there is no blood test or body scan, for example, which will unambiguously prove a diagnosis. This means that, ultimately, the judgement on who is sane and who is insane is down to the clinician, and this judgement can be very fallible indeed. In a classic study by Rosenhan (1973) a group of eight sane individuals (many of them psychiatric professionals) applied for admission as patients to mental hospitals complaining of hearing 'voices in the head'. Once admitted, they claimed the symptoms had stopped, and behaved in all ways as 'normal' individuals. In all cases, the pretence of the pseudopatients was undetected by the staff (though interestingly, an appreciable proportion of fellow patients detected the deception). All but one was diagnosed as 'schizophrenic' and took an average of 19 days to be released from hospital 'care' with a typical diagnosis of 'schizophrenia in remission' (i.e. it might return). What this study demonstrates is that it is very easy to label a person as schizophrenic on inadequate evidence. If we follow this argument to its logical conclusion, it only requires a relatively mild bias against people from working class or ethnic minority backgrounds for a disproportionate number to be diagnosed as schizophrenic. It should be stressed that this bias need not be derived from snobbery or racism. A simple incomprehension of different attitudes and behaviours, which may be appropriate in one social setting but not another, could be a large contributory factor. For example, studies have found a higher probability of being diagnosed by UK clinicians as being mentally ill if one is of Afro-Caribbean descent (e.g. Harrison *et al.*, 1988), which may imply a racist element. However, one of the first studies of this subject found a similarly higher rate of mental illness amongst Norwegian emigrants to the United States (Odegaard, 1932).

Another aspect of the environmental argument is to consider the potential causes of schizophrenia. It has long been argued, for example, that schizophrenic patients tend to come from rather emotionally 'cold' and domineering families (the term *refrigerator parent* was for a time in vogue). A manifestation of this is the *double bind*, in which family members express emotions ambiguously. Thus, expressions of love might be coupled with warnings of not to misbehave or the love will be withdrawn. Falloon *et al.* (1985) found that if the whole household in which a schizophrenic patient lived was treated in therapeutic sessions, then the level of remission amongst the schizophrenic patients was significantly lower. Therefore, the familial background is an important contributory factor. However, taken by itself such a statement might be interpreted as a stigma on families of schizophrenic patients. It must be stressed that not all families with a schizophrenic member are dysfunctional, nor is there evidence that families of schizophrenic patients are any different from non-schizophrenic families in their belief that they are doing their best. Any dysfunction is thus *not* deliberate.

However, none of the above arguments presents an overwhelming case for the environmental viewpoint. First, consider the evidence on misdiagnosis. Although clinicians are capable of bad judgement, it must be stressed that the pseudopatients in Rosenhan's study were deliberately trying to get admitted to hospital. In normal circumstances, a person is only considered for hospitalisation if their everyday behaviour has given cause for concern. In other words, if there are genuine grounds for concern. It is also worth noting that whilst it is right and proper that there should be concern that over racial and social bias may be marring diagnosis, it is also highly divisive to assume that it is 'natural' that particular social and racial groups contain higher proportions of people behaving in an aberrant manner. If poor living conditions are causing some groups to have a higher level of mental illness, then this is cause for concern, but that is a rather different argument. Again, evidence that familial factors often play an important role in schizophrenia cannot be denied but, equally, there may be a strong genetic role. For example, parents of schizophrenic patients may have provided a dysfunctional environment, but they also share genes in common with the patient. Is the dysfunctional household simply a product of dysfunctional genes? The total evidence points to there being strong environmental contributory factors, but in themselves they are not *necessarily* the sole causes.

However, the evidence for genetic factors is equally ambiguous. It can be easily demonstrated that one's chances of developing schizophrenia rise if one has a close genetic relative who is schizophrenic (e.g. Gottesman, 1991). Furthermore, the chances are still higher than average if one has a schizophrenic parent but one is raised by foster parents. In short, there is a genetic influence beyond the effects of being raised in a household with dysfunctional parents. However, although the chances of developing schizophrenia are higher if one has a genetic relative with the illness, they are not overwhelming. For example, if one identical twin succumbs to the illness, the chances are under half that the other twin will also become schizophrenic (see Gottesman, 1991). Since identical twins are genetically the same, there must be more to developing schizophrenia than one's genes. In other words, the cause must be an interaction between genes and environment, a conclusion which permeates the nature–nurture debate. Indeed, all the evidence points to this. Poor living conditions and dysfunctional families raise the probability of becoming schizophrenic, but do not make it a certainty (and faulty diagnosis may also artificially raise figures for some groups). The same can be said for having a 'schizophrenic gene'. Therefore, the most pragmatic solution is that a mixture of opportunity and circumstance are needed before the illness manifests itself. That about one in fifty of the population will develop the illness displays how surprisingly often this conjunction can occur.

### Delirium and dementia

A large collection of conditions fall under this heading, but a defining factor is one of intellectual or perceptual handicap rather than abnormal behaviour *per se*. Delirium (sometimes called *acute confusional state* though, to be pedantic, this describes just one form of the illness) refers to a severe loss of intellectual and mnemonic functioning, and an apparent 'clouding' of consciousness. Symptoms vary widely – for example, patients may appear drowsy and with slurred speech, they may be very absent-minded and incapable of attending to anything, or they may be restless and very agitated. Hallucinations and paranoid delusions of persecution are also common. What is common to all conditions is that the person has veered away from their normal behavioural *and* intellectual state. The condition is often the result of a mishap – typical causes include illness (such as high fever), malnutrition, and drug-related problems (either from taking drugs or from withdrawal of a drug to which the patient has become addicted). This does not necessarily mean 'illegal' drugs. Prescription drugs can also affect susceptible individuals. An extremely fine description of paranoid delusions created by legal drug taking is Evelyn Waugh's *The Ordeal of Gilbert Pinfold* (Waugh, 1957). Delusions are commoner amongst older adults, who, because of frailer physical systems, may be more prone to extreme mental reactions to physical ailments.

Delusions can be removed by treatment of the underlying cause – thus, the delusional state will usually disappear once the offending drug has been flushed out of the system, the fever has abated, etc. Another cause of intellectual decline – *dementia* – cannot be so easily treated. Dementia describes a wide range of conditions all of which have one thing in common – there is a deterioration in intellectual or mnemonic skills (often accompanied by changes in behaviour) which are the result of atrophy of brain tissue. There are many different forms of dementia, most of which are quite rare. The most frequently encountered is *dementia of the Alzheimer type*, also known as *Alzheimer's disease*. The disease is named after Alois Alzheimer, who was the first to describe the condition. Typically, the first symptom is *amnesia* (memory loss) followed by *aphasia* (loss of language) and a general loss of intellectual functioning. Disturbance of language and visuo-spatial skills also typically occur early in the course of the disease. As the disease progresses, the patient gradually loses all discernable intellectual and linguistic functions, until in the final stages, he or she is very impaired. There is no known cure for the disease.

The illness is insidious and highly unpleasant. Patients are gradually and inexorably stripped of their dignity as not only do they become incapable of looking after themselves, but they also become incapable of remembering not only recent information but also of recalling items and events from the past. Amongst these are the faces and voices of relatives and partners. A patient suffering from Alzheimer's disease may become (literally) terrified at the sight of their partner, because they no longer recognise them. Since most 'civilised' nations leave much of the burden of caring for a demented patient on the shoulders of relatives and partners, it is not only the patient who suffers. The partner must, day in day out, tend to the needs of a body which looks like the person they have loved for years, but which is occupied by a mind which is increasingly incapable of recognition or affection. Add to this the fact that Alzheimer patients become doubly incontinent and are prone to wandering, leaving on gas taps, etc, and the burden placed by most health care systems on individuals is all too apparent.

Alzheimer's disease can strike at any time in adulthood, but increases in its frequency markedly past the age of seventy. The physical causes of the illness are not fully understood, though it involves a progressive deterioration of brain tissue, particularly in the cortex and the hippocampus (see Stuart-Hamilton, 1994), areas known to be heavily involved in intellectual processes, language and memory. Other dementias have different physical causes. For example, *vascular dementia* is caused by damage to the blood supply to the brain (a *stroke*). Since the blood supply in effect 'feeds' brain tissue with nutrients and oxygen, termination of this causes the death of the affected brain tissue. In *multi-infarct dementia*, the patient suffers repeated very tiny strokes, each of which only affects a tiny portion of brain tissue. Each stroke in itself is usually unnoticed and relatively harmless, but the cumulative effect seriously damages the brain and with it mental functioning. Where damage occurs in the brains of vascular demented patients varies and is to a certain extent unpredictable. However, in general, the areas of the brain damaged in Alzheimer's disease are also affected in vascular dementia, which accordingly has the same general symptoms of loss of intellect and mnemonic ability.

A dementia which has at the time of writing caught the public's attention is *Creutzfeldt Jacob disease (CJD)*. This is unusual amongst the dementias in that the illness first manifests itself as a movement disorder – intellectual and mnemonic deterioration come later. This is a very rare illness (circa 1 person per million per year will die from it), but there is a current concern in Britain that it can be caught from eating beef from cattle infected with *Bovine Spongiform Encephalopathy (BSE)*, popularly known as 'mad cow disease'. At the time of writing, relatively little is known about the illness or its methods of transmission, and much of what passes for hard fact is speculation. However, because of the current media interest, the next couple of pages will be devoted to a general overview of the topic.

BSE appears to be largely confined to Britain, and was officially diagnosed in the mid 1980s – afflicted cattle stagger and cannot control their limbs, and progressively lose awareness of their surroundings. The illness is similar to a disease in sheep called *scrapie* (which has been known about for hundreds of years, and which is believed not to infect humans), and a link was suggested. Normally, it is difficult for a disease which affects one species to infect another, but a new cattle foodstuff, which contained a protein supplement derived from animal carcasses, had been introduced a few years earlier, and might have been the infectious agent. Whatever the cause, BSE spread through British cattle herds. The obvious question which was asked was if the disease could be spread into humans. Beef is a popular meat in its own right, but beef derivatives (e.g. gelatin) are used in many foodstuffs, including apparently meat-free products. Only the most assiduous British vegetarian or vegan is likely to have avoided eating beef in *any* form since BSE was first identified. The British Government has gradually (some would say too slowly) removed certain parts of beef carcasses felt to be particularly BSE-laden from sale, and the danger of beef products reaching the shops today containing BSE is felt to be minimal. However, could people have contracted BSE before these bans were enforced?

At first, this seemed to be mere scare-mongering. However, in the 1990s, about twenty or so[12] people in Britain and a few people in other countries have contracted a new form of CJD (*new variant CJD* or *nvCJD*) unlike any previously seen. The course of the illness is different from 'normal' CJD and autopsy samples of brain tissue show that much of it has died, giving the surviving brain tissue a spongy appearance, similar to that found in the brains of cattle affected with BSE (hence the term 'spongiform'). The majority of victims have been in their teens or twenties – precisely the age groups most likely to eat cheap meat products such as hamburgers and other convenience foods which contain reconstituted offal (felt to be a particularly infectious source of BSE). With only a handful of cases so far identified, scientists are faced with a dilemma – are these *all* the cases which will be found, or are these the first of a flood (NB when AIDS was first identified, it only affected a few people in one particular section of the population)?

The most pessimistic view is that these first victims are harbingers of a pandemic. Something in their physical constitution prevented them fighting off the BSE infection and they succumbed rapidly. Other infected people will be able to stave off the infection for many years (perhaps, like syphilis, BSE will remain dormant for decades before entering its final deadly phase) before they too will die. According to some of the more alarmist UK newspapers, because beef products have been eaten so widely in the UK, almost everyone will eventually contract the illness, officially-sanctioned euthanasia clinics will be established for those who cannot face the lingering death, the Channel Tunnel will be blocked up to prevent BSE-crazed zombies invading France, etc. A more optimistic view is that whilst BSE should not be taken lightly, it is unlikely to be a mass killer. First, at the time of writing, there is lit-

---

12    The exact number is unclear – some patients are still alive, and may have rare brain disorders which have the *appearance* of CJD – the only accurate diagnosis is an autopsy.

tle evidence from primate studies that *eating* BSE infected food will cause brain damage (injecting BSE into the brain causes brain damage, but this is hardly a behaviour which humans are likely to indulge in). Second, if the disease was likely to be a mass killer, it is very unlikely that, even allowing for an exponential growth pattern and the slow growth of the disease itself, the number of deaths would be so low at this stage. A more feasible explanation is that BSE can cause CJD in humans, but an individual would have to be very unlucky to get it. However, given the uncertainty surrounding the issue, it would be foolish to make any firm diagnosis in any direction until more evidence is available. This should in no manner compromise sympathy for the victims of the illness.

## Autism

A set of abnormal behaviours which are manifest across all aspects of the patient's life are the *pervasive developmental disorders*. The best known of these is *autism*. The term originally meant an obsessional interest in the self to the exclusion of others, and is still sometimes used in this sense. However, more commonly it refers to the rare (approximately 4 per 10, 000 live births; four times commoner in boys) but serious condition arising in infancy. It was first identified by Kanner (1943), though an independent and contemporaneous paper by Asperger (1944; cited Frith, 1991) also identifies the condition. Amongst the earliest signs of autism are that the patient as a baby may have lacked 'cuddliness', and as a young child, he or she avoided social contact. As the child grows and the condition becomes more apparent, he or she often seeks a monotony of environment and action (resulting in repetitive stereotyped movements) which appear to provide some comfort. There is usually a strong linguistic handicap (speech may be non-existent or apparently garbled), and social skills are poor. The film *Rainman* and media coverage of 'real' autistic children with remarkably good (by any standards) artistic or arithmetical talents can create the impression that the disease always has compensations. This recollects the oxymoronic term *idiot savant* (a term now largely avoided) – a mentally disadvantaged individual with a single exceptional talent. However, most autistic children have poor abilities, and are severely mentally disadvantaged. Autism is usually genetically inherited, but cases resulting from brain damage have been reported.

A condition closely related to autism is *Asperger's Syndrome*. The symptoms of the complaint are very similar to those of autism. Indeed, sometimes the two conditions are found in the same family, indicating a genetic component. The principal differences between them are that the person with Asperger's Syndrome possesses near-normal language, and usually has a higher degree of social skills. Sufferers are often perceived as normal, if eccentric. It has been suggested that one outlet for such a person's interests is a hobby requiring what to most people would appear to be tedious cataloguing. For example, in Britain, a pastime known as trainspotting[13] has become popular with a small but enthusiastic section of the population (predominantly male). This involves standing on railway platforms making a note of the serial numbers of engines and carriages as they enter the station. Enthusiasts travel the length and breadth of the country to see as many different trains as possible and vie with each other to collect a commensurately-sized set of serial numbers. They then meet in groups and compare notes with fellow trainspotters of serial numbers they have seen – an activity of brain-frying tedium to anyone not caught up in this hobby.[14] Some enthusiasts have taken matters even further, and at least one enterprising person is making a collection of the serial numbers of light fitments in carriages. Authorities on Asperger's Syndrome have plausibly argued that a higher than average proportion of trainspotters probably suffer from the complaint (e.g. Frith, 1991).

*Bipolar disorder*

This is better known under its older name of *manic depression*, and refers to a condition in which the patient alternates between extremes of intense elation and activity, and depression, (usually) with periods of relative 'normality' in between. Depression is a state which practically everybody has experienced to some extent and can thus empathise with. Fortunately, many people's

13　The term is now also being used as slang for drug abuse, but this is a secondary meaning.
14　On a crowded train with the batteries of his personal stereo exhausted, the author once had to spend a rail journey surrounded by a group of trainspotters who spent *five hours* reciting to each other serial numbers they had seen.

experience consists of feeling 'a bit miserable' for a few days, followed by recovery. However, in its more pronounced form, symptoms are considerably more unpleasant, and include disorders of sleep, loss of energy and perseverance, loss of enthusiasm, poor self-image, and changes in appetite and weight. To be classified as meriting concerted professional treatment (often loosely termed *clinical depression*), these symptoms must be more than transitory. The DSM classifies depression occurring by itself as *unipolar disorder*, and states that the patient solely exhibits this condition (i.e. there are no other forms of mental illness present as well), which is long-lasting (e.g. a minimum of two months), and severe enough to interfere with normal functioning. The condition is a serious one, and it is often difficult to persuade others that a depressed patient cannot just 'pull themselves together'. Because most people who feel depressed recover quickly, they cannot see why a severely depressed patient will not do the same. However, whilst the two situations are qualitatively similar, the depth of the depression is radically different. To illustrate this point – anyone who has ever felt 'down' for a few days and then recovered has not felt so worthless and drained of energy that they have urinated in their pants rather than go to the lavatory.

Related to unipolar disorder is *dysthymic disorder*, in which the episodes of depression last a relatively short time period (a couple of months at maximum), or last for a few days, but recur at regular intervals. This should not be confused with *bipolar disorder*, where, as said, the patient swings between episodes of depression and *mania* (an extremely elated mood, usually coupled with extreme levels of activity and energy and unrealistic plans), often with periods of relative normality in between (the episodes can vary in length from days to months). A further variation is *bipolar II disorder*, in which the patient swings between depression and a relatively mild form of mania known as *hypomania*. This may be contrasted with *cyclothymic disorder*, in which both the depression and mania are relatively mild in their impact.

Some commentators distinguish between *reactive depression* (depression arising after a distressing event) and *endogenous depression* (depression which arises for no apparent reason). This is an important distinction in that the treatments of the two conditions may be radically different. For example, if a person is depressed because of a miserable home life, then tackling the miserable home life may alleviate the depression. On the other hand, a person who has become depressed in a happy, supportive and trouble-free background (i.e. has become depressed in spite of their surroundings) may be more responsive to drug treatments to cope with an imbalance in their brain chemistry. However, it would be overly-simplistic to think of depression as being purely endogenous or purely reactive. Whilst depressing surroundings may undoubtedly cause some people to become depressed, others in the same or even worse circumstances will not show a lowered mood. Likewise, imbalanced brain chemistry or not, there is often some environmental triger for a depressive episode. Thus, these terms, whilst providing useful rules of thumb, should not be taken as watertight statements about causation. Furthermore, the endogenous/reactive distinction can be sub-divided. The depression may be the only symptom of mental illness (*primary depression*) or it may be a 'side effect' of another mental illness (*secondary depression*). Again, treatments will vary according to the category.

It is also worth noting that several specific types of depression have also been identified. These include *seasonal affective disorder (SAD)*, in which the patient's mood worsens during the winter months and is alleviated during the summer months. The condition is probably linked to exposure to sunlight – when there is relatively little light (as during the winter months), a brain chemical called *melatonin* is not released in sufficient quantities, and this causes the feeling of depression. The symptoms can often be alleviated by exposing the patients to bright artificial lights which mimic the sun's rays. Another well-documented condition is *postnatal depression* (also known as *postpartum depression*), commonly known as the 'baby blues'. Many mothers after giving birth experience a feeling of inadequacy and depression, due to a combination of hormonal factors and the general stress of the event. This is usually relatively short-lived. However, in some instances this depressed feeling persists, giving cause for concern for both the mother's and the baby's welfare.

Discussions of depression often lead to a consideration of the issue of suicide, and with good reason, since most people who attempt suicide are depressed. Media images tend to portray suicide as a young person's death. To some extent this is true – suicide is one of the commonest causes of mortality in teenagers and young adults. However, the overall death rate amongst teenagers and young adults is low so, in absolute terms, the figures are less dramatic. In reality, suicide becomes increasingly common the *older* the age group considered, with white elderly men the most likely group to kill themselves (see MacLeod *et al.*, 1992; Stuart-Hamilton, 1994). Furthermore, the older the person attempting to kill themselves, the more likely they are to 'succeed' (i.e. dying rather than surviving). Reasons for suicide vary, and it is dangerous to generalise, since each case is unique. However, it is certainly true that many people attempting to kill themselves (particularly younger adults) have an ambivalent attitude towards whether they really want to die. Methods chosen by such people are often surprisingly inefficient, such as drug overdoses,[15] which leave time for them to call for assistance before they can take effect. Often they will also leave opportunities to be discovered before it is too late. It is easy to encapsulate this in the phrase 'a cry for help', but there is a danger that this dismisses it as a petulant piece of attention seeking. It is certainly more than this, even if one argues that the ultimate aim of the person attempting suicide is to improve their life rather than escape it. Conversely, people with fewer doubts about death include all or most of those who choose a very immediate method of death, such as shooting oneself, and who take measures to avoid discovery until after death. This group generally includes those people who want an end to their suffering, such as the pain of an incurable disease (this is one reason why suicide rates increase with age). Fremouw *et al.* (1990) categorise suicide attempters who have doubts about death as possessing 'depression with anger', whilst those with firmer intentions are said to have 'depression with hopelessness'. Rephrasing this: the first group attempt suicide to alter their situation; the latter attempt suicide to escape their situation.

Anyone who is announcing plans to kill themselves should be taken seriously. Perversely, suicide attempts are most likely when a person appears to

15 Though note that these can still succeed. Anyone under the illusion that death from a drug overdose is like falling into a deep sleep should note that the patient is often conscious and dies in agony.

be recovering from a bout of depression (i.e. at a time when people are less likely to be concerned). A reader who is themselves troubled by thoughts of suicide should seek help at once. It is a cliche, but the hardest step is the first one of admitting to someone that you have a problem.

*Personality disorders*

The final group of mental illnesses to be considered are the *personality disorders*, a general term for a group of illnesses whose principal symptom is a personality trait which is sufficiently extreme and at odds with societal norms to cause distress to the patient and/or to those whom he or she comes into contact with. It is important to note that these personalities go considerably beyond the bounds of what might be considered 'eccentric' but nonetheless tolerable behaviour. However, it is also possible to see that many personality disorders are in essence exaggerations of 'normal' personality types. For example, *avoidant personality disorder* describes a person who has an abnormally poor self-image and who avoids social contact with others. Many people may have some doubts about themselves and feel shy and awkward in company, but few are so cripplingly shy and avoidant that they cannot function in social situations. Again, most people can list amongst their acquaintances someone who is subject to changeable moods, but few reach the levels of a patient with *borderline personality disorder*, where the mood changes are sudden, unpredictable and dramatic.

The list of other personality disorders, where in essence a minor irritating trait has been magnified into a major problem is a long one. Further examples include: desire for perfection in everything done by the patient (*compulsive personality disorder*);[16] an extreme willingness to let others decide everything for the patient (*dependent personality disorder*); over-dramatic moods and reactions (*histrionic personality disorder*); extreme self-preoccupation (*narcissistic personality disorder*); irrational suspicion of others (*paranoid personality disorder*); avoiding following other people's requests (*passive–*

16    Not to be confused with *obsessive–compulsive disorder*, in which the patient feels compelled through feelings of extreme anxiety constantly to repeat meaningless and sometimes painful rituals, such as repeatedly washing their hands.

*aggressive personality disorder*); and an insensitivity to others accompanied by some 'eccentric' thoughts and behaviour (*schizotypal personality disorder*).

Not mentioned in the above list is *antisocial personality disorder*, characterised by a profound lack of moral sense and a low emotional range, often resulting in illegal and/or violent behaviour. The condition is better known as *psychopathy* (the latter term is derived from a slightly different classificatory system than the DSM, but at a broad level, the terms are largely interchangeable). Practically any violent crime is described in the media as the work of a psychopath, and often with good reason, since the proportion of criminals with psychopathic tendencies is very high. However, it would be misleading to suggest that all people with psychopathic personalities are inevitably waiting to star in their own version of *Silence of the Lambs* or *American Psycho*. Although psychopathy is obviously suited to a life of crime, it can also be channelled into legitimate pursuits, such as dangerous sports or dangerous careers (e.g. some of the more hazardous branches of the armed forces). There is reasonable evidence that psychopathy is genetically inherited, but once again, there is also evidence of a mediating influence of environment (see Davison and Neale, 1996).

## Summary

From the above survey, it is apparent that at its most basic, a mental illness has one of four causes: (1) the patient is born predestined to have problems (arguably the case with many instances of autism); (2) the patient suffers brain damage resulting in illness (e.g. personality change following brain damage); (3) the patient becomes ill following environmental pressures (e.g. depression at the loss of a partner); (4) the patient experiences an interaction of two or more of the above factors (see e.g. the studies of schizophrenia cited above). To a certain extent, this is yet another replaying of the nature–nurture debate of individual differences (see Chapter 2). In other words, how much of mental illness is due to the environment, and how much is due to genetics? Compounding this are problems over the accuracy of diagnosis and the influence of clinician's expectations.

Given such a variety of causes, it would not be surprising to find a variety of treatment methods, and that is indeed what is found. Treatments can be roughly categorised according to their level of direct physical contact and as to whether they are primarily directed at the cause or the symptoms of the illness.

## Treatment of mental illness

*Biological therapies*

A variety of methods of treating mental illness are available which operate physically upon biological mechanisms. These are largely the concern of medical practitioners rather than psychologists, since their use requires medical training. Nonetheless, for the sake of completeness, some knowledge of them is required. In addition, psychologists may be involved in evaluating the effectiveness of such treatments.

Amongst the biological therapies, none is more direct than *psychosurgery*. This refers to any surgical procedure in which the patient is operated upon in an attempt to cure their psychological problems. The best-known operation is the *frontal lobotomy*,[17] in which the neural connections to the frontal lobes of the brain (see Chapter 10) are severed. The reasoning behind this operation is lengthy, but in essence, it was felt that 'faulty' instructions from this part of the brain were responsible for several forms of serious illness, including schizophrenia; hence, by severing the links, the faulty instructions should cease, and the patient would be cured. The operation became popular (with neurosurgeons rather than patients) in the 1940s and 1950s and was hailed as a cure for several forms of mental illness. However, the reality was that the operation was probably no better than non-surgical treatments, and in addition, about 2 per cent of patients died (see Robin and MacDonald, 1975). Gradually, the operation fell in popularity. However, it would be wrong to write off this surgical technique altogether. In part the failure may have been due to its misapplication, with patients who were unresponsive to other treatments being operated upon as a method of last resort or because clinicians were anxious to try out a new technique, regardless of whether the patient's symptoms truly merited it. To make an analogy – no-one would deny the

17    More accurately, the surgical technique most frequently used was a *frontal leucotomy*, which is a *partial* severing of links.

value of antibiotics, even if some doctors over-prescribed them after they were introduced. Today, frontal leucotomies are still used, but usually far more selectively than before. It should also be noted that selective severance of areas of the frontal lobes is also used in the treatment of some forms of epilepsy, with a high degree of success. Nonetheless, the image of patients being irretrievably altered because of brain surgery makes people apprehensive of the subject. However, surgery is always the method of last resort and is not entered into lightly by any clinician. There is always a risk that the patient will be transformed into a mental vegetable by psychosurgery. However, one can turn this argument on its head – what is the patient's life like if this is considered to be an acceptable risk?

Another physical treatment which has captured the public imagination is *electro-convulsive therapy (ECT)*. This involves applying electric shocks to the brain. Again, the reasoning behind this is complex but, in essence, it is hoped that the gross disruption to the brain's own electrical activity will 'jolt' the patient out of their maladaptive state. Several other techniques have also been tried in the past with similar aims, including *insulin therapy* (giving patients an overdose of this substance made them extremely ill and, it was hoped, would provide the necessary shock to the system). Connoisseurs of a certain type of horror film have an image of the patient being strapped down screaming and a massive dose of electricity being applied whilst the patient is fully conscious. The reality is rather more prosaic – patients are given a muscle relaxant to prevent involuntary muscular contractions when the shocks are given, and he or she is anaesthetised before the treatment is given. Evidence for the effectiveness of ECT is equivocal. It can appreciably disrupt memory and lead to general feelings of disorientation (though this can be minimised by applying shocks to only one side of the brain). Again, it is not very effective in treating some forms of mental illness, and, like psychosurgery, it was over-used in the past. However, there is good evidence that in cases of very severe depression, it can be effective (see e.g. Klerman, 1988).

A third and final aspect of physical treatments to consider is *drug therapy* – the treatment of illness by drugs. The range of treatments available to the clinician is large, and there is little doubt that *psychotropic drug* [a drug which affects psychological functioning] treatments have revolutionised the care of many mentally ill people. Most notable, perhaps, was the effect of new drug therapies introduced in the 1950s which radically reduced the severity of symptoms in many schizophrenic and other psychotic patients. People who attended mental hospitals before and after the drugs were introduced often commented upon how much quieter they had become.

Psychotropic drugs work by altering the production and/or uptake of *neurotransmitters* (the chemical messengers neurons use to communicate with each other – see Chapter 10). It has been found that patients suffering from some mental illnesses show an unusual excess or depletion of certain neurotransmitters relative to 'normal' people. For example, many patients with schizophrenia have an unusually high level of a neurotransmitter called *dopamine*, and pharmacologically reducing this level can alleviate symptoms in many cases (see Davison and Neale, 1996, for an excellent summary). Again, *lithium* is commonly used to treat bipolar disorder because it is felt to restore a normal chemical balance in the brains of affected patients. Depressive disorders in general have a wide range of chemical treatments – amongst the best known is *fluoxetine*, sold under the trade name *Prozac*.

Drug therapies undoubtedly work in many cases, and have enabled millions of people to leave institutional care and lead relatively normal lives in the community. However, it must not be assumed that they are a panacea. Several arguments can be raised. First, the drugs do not alleviate every patient's symptoms, and some remain doggedly unaffected by drug treatments. Second, many of the drugs may have unpleasant side-effects. For example, reducing dopamine levels in schizophrenic patients can induce *Parkinson's syndrome*, characterised by an uncontrollable shaking of the limbs. Again, many of the antidepressant drugs can damage the cardiovascular system and blur vision. Third, symptoms of mental illness may not be removed as much as brought under control. For example, some anti-schizophrenic drugs do not remove hallucinations in patients, but they make them non-worrying. Fourth, the drug therapies rely upon the patient continuing to take the medicine. If the patient forgets or refuses, then the symptoms are likely to return.

These arguments do not deny the value of drug therapy – many of the same arguments can be made against drugs for the treatment of physical ailments, and no-one would deny the value of, for example, antibiotics or anti-arthritic drugs. However, they do make the point that drug therapy in particular and biological therapies in general cannot offer solutions to all problems. In other words, non-biological therapies are also necessary, if only for those instances where there is either no biological treatment available, or the biological treatment does not work. There are other reasons as well why non-biological treatments are desirable. Three will be cited here. First, it cannot be denied that all mental illness is associated with some form of structural change in the brain, no matter how slight (e.g. ranging from a general loss of neurotransmitter to the formation of 'faulty' ideas on a neural net). However, is the physical change the cause of the illness, or is the illness the cause of the change (this in part echoes the *mind–body problem* – see Chapter 10)? Suppose that a person becomes depressed following the death of their partner. Did that person's brain structure predispose them to become depressed, or did they become depressed, causing a change in brain structure? The debate can ultimately be as futile as the chicken and egg problem, but the point has, it is hoped, been made, that pinning mental illness purely on the patient's physical state may not be wise. Second, a more pragmatic consideration is that in treating mental illness, it is desirable to treat the patient rather than the disease. Thus, whilst drug therapies and more extreme biological treatment can affect the condition, they in themselves ignore the state of the patient as a *person*. Hence, treatments which acknowledge the patient's thoughts and wishes and their situation are also necessary. The third consideration is that by their very nature, biological treatments cannot cope with any environmental causes of illness. For example, it can be reasonably argued that schizophrenia may often have a genetic trigger, but environmental factors are necessary for it to develop. Therefore, a schizophrenic patient may need assistance in learning to cope with their environment and recognising the causes of their illness. This cannot be done by drugs, surgery, or ECT.

*Psychological therapies*
The above arguments lead into a consideration of the *psychological therapies*, a blanket term for any therapeutic methods which contain an appreciable

element of psychological theory or practice. As will be seen, these differ enormously in their theory and methodology.

The therapeutic method which most people associate with psychology is *psychoanalysis*, which in fact has little to do with psychology at all. The founder of psychoanalysis, Sigmund Freud, devised a rich theory of mental development which is outlined in Chapter 3. In essence, this argued that people form conceptions of correct behaviour and preferred sexual attitudes in early childhood. These early experiences are stored deep in the unconscious mind, and although they have a profound effect upon behaviour, the patient is unaware of this. Freud thus saw early childhood as a minefield of difficult choices and failure in any of these sowed the seeds for a 'faulty' personality in adulthood. A simplistic example of this is that a male patient as a boy formed a too deep attachment to his mother, and that this was not put into proper perspective by, for example, forming attachments to others (the famous *Oedipus complex*). In adult life, the patient may, for example, show an inability to form satisfactory relationships, or have an unhealthy interest in women who look like his mother.

A key premise of Freudian theory is that although the patient cannot recall the reasons why they behave as they do, it is nonetheless locked in the subconscious waiting to be extracted. To adapt a well-known quotation from a certain television series – the truth is in there. The subconscious by its very nature cannot be explicitly reached, but Freudian theory says that it may at times break through into a person's awareness, such as through slips of the tongue (the famous *Freudian slip*) or through imagery in dreams. A Freudian therapist will spend considerable time with patients analysing their dreams and exploring the meanings of the imagery. Because the subconscious may contain thoughts shocking to the patient, they are portrayed in dreams in a milder, symbolic form. Hence, dreams of large Zeppelin balloons going into tunnels may be a representation of a quite different activity. This can be overplayed, however, and not all symbolism is quite so crude; as Freud himself said, sometimes a cigar is just a cigar. It would also be wrong to trivialise Freudian therapy as consisting of therapists interpreting patients' mucky dreams – the process is rather more sophisticated than that, and the task of teasing apart the trivial from the meaningful is an arduous one. This is one reason why Freudian therapy can take years to complete. Another is that because the subconscious can only be accessed in a piecemeal fashion, the patient will only slowly gain insight into his or her problems.

There are, however, major problems with Freudian therapy. The first, and most damning criticism is that the theory upon which it is based, and hence the therapist's interpretation of the illness are untestable (see Chapter 3). One cannot prove they are either wrong or right, and the same applies to the therapies and treatments derived from Freud's basic model, such as those by Jung and Adler. A second problem is that it is a very limited therapy in that it is only really effective in cases where the patient is capable of considerable insight into their own problems. Mental illnesses in which there is considerable loss of contact from reality are not as amenable to treatment (though that has not stopped laudable attempts by some therapists). This has led to the popular (though unfair) criticism that it is a therapy for neurotic people who really have nothing wrong with them beyond the need to talk to someone about their problems. A third problem is that the therapy is long and typically requires one-to-one sessions. This is expensive and psychoanalysis is usually only available to the very rich. A fourth problem is that it may not be a very effective method of treatment. A famous study by Eysenck (1952) found that patients stood about the same chance of recovery if left alone or getting pills and sympathy from their GP than if given psychotherapy. Although the strength of this claim has subsequently been challenged (e.g. Bergin, 1971 reanalysed Eysenck's data and argued that a slightly more favourable interpretation could be made), the fact remains that the method is not hugely successful relative to other (and far cheaper) methods. Against this it must be said that this is only really valid if a rather narrow view of 'recovery' is taken, and one might argue that the process of self-discovery is enriching in ways other than treatment of the immediate problem.

Overall, psychologists tend to be dismissive of psychoanalysis, because it is unscientific, economically inefficient and is no more effective than other more 'scientific' and cost-effective therapeutic methods. However, for all this, there is still something appealing about psychoanalysis – it has a central theme of exploration and discovery which is often lacking in other therapies, which in comparison, can appear rather mechanistic and cold.

The antithesis of psychoanalysis is arguably *behaviour therapy*, which has its roots in *behaviourism* (see Chapter 7). In essence, behaviourism argues that the subjective mind should be ignored – what matters is the observation of stimuli and the responses given to those stimuli; contemplation of the mental processes which take place in giving the response is shunned. Behaviour therapy picks up this theme and treats mental illness by attempting to modify the behaviours which are manifestations of the illness, rather than trying to cure the causes of the behaviour. To take an example: suppose that a man has a fetish about women's shoes. Psychoanalysis might treat the patient by searching for the roots of the behaviour in the patient's past, getting him to recognise the cause, and then directing the patient's thoughts towards more wholesome attitudes. Behaviour therapy would simply try to stop the patient liking women's shoes. For example, one method used in the past (though not often used now) was to show the patient pictures of shoes and give him electric shocks at the same time. The patient thus became conditioned to associate his fetishistic object with pain, leading to a loss of arousal. Note that there is no interest shown in the causes of the fetish – all that matters is the treatment of the symptoms.

Some other forms of behaviour therapy can also be quite dramatic. For example, there is a technique called *flooding*, in which the patient is suddenly immersed in a situation which produces severe anxiety. An extreme example (though as far as the author is aware, this has never really been done) might be to take a patient suffering from *agoraphobia* (fear of open spaces), tie them up, and leave them in the middle of a field. The exposure to the aversive situation continues until the anxiety is reduced (loosely, until the patient realises that the event is not harmful). This is a traumatic experience, but it can be effective in some circumstances (a variant of the technique is *implosion*, in which the patient is made to imagine the event or object). Flooding works by making patients change their association between the feared object and their response to it from one of anxiety to something more acceptable. Put more loosely, the technique forces people to recognise that their fear is irrational.

Not all behaviour therapies are quite so extreme, however. An alternative to flooding is *systematic desensitisation*. This presents the patient with very mild examples of the threatening stimulus (e.g., in the case of an *arachnophobic* patient, a drawing of a spider in a case at the other end of a room), and gradually exposes the patient to more 'threatening' examples of it (an *anxiety hierarchy*). Thus, from viewing pictures of spiders, the patient may progress to tolerating a spider in a container at the other end of the room, and so on, until he or she can comfortably handle spiders (literally and metaphorically). At each stage in the process, the patient practises relaxing and shedding their feelings of fear, so that he or she comes to associate the situation with neutral or even positive feelings.

Behaviour therapy is used extensively in many clinical settings. There is no doubt that it can be highly effective in changing specific behaviours. However, in itself it can also be limited. For example, by concentrating on the behaviour rather than its cause, it might be argued that the therapist is simply papering over the cracks, and that the root cause of the patient's distress is still there and may manifest itself in other ways. In fact, there is only mixed evidence for this, and in most cases, behaviour therapy is used in conjunction with other techniques. For example, a sexual fetishist may not only need to be cured of their problem, but also need help in social skills training, so that they stand an improved chance of meeting a partner. Again, it is not necessary to accept the strictures of rigid behaviourism to use behaviour therapy. Indeed, many therapists use an *eclectic therapy*, in which they will deliberately select the 'best' aspects of several different methods of treatment to design a 'tailor made' package for each patient. Thus, behaviour therapy may be used to tackle the outward manifestations of a maladaptive behaviour whilst the therapist uses other techniques to discover the underlying cause.

Historically, behaviour therapy arose out of a dissatisfaction with the introspective methods of psychoanalysis. However, later therapists argued that in effect, a 'half way house' between these positions could be created, called *cognitive therapy*. Its essence is captured in an oft-quoted aphorism by the Stoic philosopher Epictetus (c60–c100 AD) – 'men are not frightened of things but their view of things'. Or put, another way, we have nothing to fear but fear itself. Any object in itself is not frightening, pleasing, arousing, or invested with any other emotion, until we decide how to interpret it. For example, a wide open space is pleasing to many people and frightening to a minority – it is the same item in both cases, and it is the interpretation by the individual which gives it its emotional value. It follows from this that the cause of many mental problems may be the cognitive processes which have produced a faulty interpretation of items or events which to others carry neutral or even pleasant overtones. For example, some people are shy of social gatherings to the point of feeling ill when confronted with them. One explanation of their behaviour is that they have too high a set of expectations in such settings. They overestimate the attention other people are paying to them and believe that they have 'failed' to impress. This is a type of shyness which the writer Hesketh Pearson rather unkindly described as 'egotism out of its depth'. Since such behaviour results in shying away from social contact, this further reinforces the person's view that nobody likes them and that they are hopeless in social gatherings. In such a situation, a psychoanalyst might wish to explore the childhood roots of such maladaptive behaviour, whilst a behavioral therapist would wish to condition the patient to reduce feelings of shyness. The cognitive therapist, however, would wish to make the patient analyse their thoughts which lead to the behaviour and modify these, often using conditioning techniques and practical examples. It thus neither probes into the routes of the problems as deeply as psychoanalysis nor does it ignore thought processes in the manner behaviour therapy does.

There are many forms of cognitive therapy, with new variants being created every year. At the core of all is the desire for the patient to think about their problems and to adjust their way of living through therapeutic exercises. For example, in *rational-emotive therapy*, (founder, Albert Ellis) the therapist explicitly directs the patient in restructuring their 'faulty' thoughts and concepts held to underlie problem behaviours and attitudes. This can take the form of fairly colourful and direct language (Ellis in the past was accused of using 'obscene' language), but therapists differ. A central tenet of *RET* is that a frequent cause of mental distress is a hopelessly unrealistic expectation of perfection. Thus, people feel they have 'failed' because they are not universally loved, have not gained the job promotion they wanted, etc, even though rationally no-one can expect to be popular with everyone nor can one possibly win every job. The task of RET is often to persuade patients to accept realistic goals, so that they cease to judge themselves too harshly. The danger with a brief description like this is that it makes RET sound like a justification for failure (e.g. 'if you don't want to try, it's okay – be a complete couch potato and nobody has the right to criticise you'). However, this would be wrong – RET does not seek to stifle healthy ambition, but rather, to stop it becoming an unrealistic force dominating a person's life.

Cognitive therapy, as already stated, can take other forms. For example, *social problems solving (SPS)* encourages patients to regard social situations they find aversive as intellectual challenges and to think through alternative solutions until they calculate the method which will reach the desired goal. In this way, the problem becomes a manageable task rather than a cause for 'blind' panic. Again, in *assertiveness training*, patients are trained to interpret situations which displease them but about which they are too afraid to complain, and then to make their objections or wishes heard. The technique is often misinterpreted because of the fictional stereotype of spoilt Californians being aggressive over ridiculously trivial matters. This is fair to neither Californians nor assertiveness training, which is intended for those whose voice should be heard but which is unfairly being ignored.

Tackling a different problem, *Beck's depression theory* (e.g. Beck, 1976) argues that depressed patients become that way because they develop a maladaptive interpretation of the world, called the *negative triad*. Essentially, this argues that the patient has an unrealistically negative view of themselves, the world, and the future. Thus, events are blown out of proportion or contracted to fit the depressed state. Slight mishaps become 'evidence' of gross incompetence, compliments are dismissed, saddening world events over which the patient has no control are a reflection of the patient's own state, and in the future, things can only get worse. This is often contrasted with the *hopelessness* model (Abramson, Metalsky and Alloy, 1989). In its original format, this was very much a behavioural theory, in which depression was felt to be caused by inappropriate conditioning that no matter what the patient did, bad things happened. This feeling of *learned helplessness* (Seligman, 1974) created depression. Subsequent models have placed an increasingly important role on maladaptive thought, so that depression arises as much from a self-perceived cognitive failure to find solutions as it does from simply being conditioned.

The cognitive therapies are enormously popular amongst psychologists, and the success rates of such treatments can be high (see Davison and Neale, 1996; Lindsay and Powell, 1994). However, there are caveats, of which three will be mentioned here. The first is that cognitive therapies require patients capable of insight into their own problems. This calls to mind the clinician's abbreviation for an ideal patient – YAVIS, which stands for 'young, attractive, verbal, intelligent, and successful' (the reasoning being that educated and literate people are better equipped to analyse themselves and not object to the process; if they are attractive and likely to pay their fees promptly, then so much the better). A patient who is incapable of much insight (whether through lack of intellectual skills or a seriously disturbed mind) is unlikely to be a very good prospect for treatment. A second problem is that cognitive therapy may not tackle the root cause of the illness. For example, a woman suffering from feelings of inadequacy because of a bullying husband may learn one set of coping strategies, only to have her confidence undermined in a fresh set of ways as the husband changes his tactics. A third and related problem is the familiar chicken and egg problem – is a change of behaviour the result of maladaptive thoughts, or are the maladaptive thoughts a product of the change in behaviour? Attacking cognitive problems in depression may be inappropriate if the cause of the depression is a biochemical disorder. However, as with behaviour therapy, this points to the need for eclectic therapies, which is the option many clincians will adopt.

A final group of therapies to be considered is the *humanistic therapies*, which are concerned with the growth of the individual and the right of each person to define and find their own particular niche in the world. Therapists from other disciplines might argue that this is their ultimate goal as well, but one cannot help but detect a feeling of patients being made to conform to particular desired 'correct' types of behaviour and attitudes. This does not mean that humanistic therapists advocate clearly maladaptive behaviours because they define the person as an individual, but rather, there is less emphasis on ideals (e.g. it might be argued that by persuading people to be less critical of themselves, this is in itself an ideal to be lived up to). At this point it should be noted that there is a related set of therapies called *existential therapies*. The boundaries of humanistic and existential therapy are blurred, since both have a central tenet of the growth of the individual. However, whilst humanistic thought emphasises the joy and vigour of life, existential philosophy is concerned with the angst of the individual faced with making decisions for him- or herself upon realising that, ultimately, each individual has the moral responsibility for deciding their own fate. This can make humanistic therapies seem rather jollier than existential ones, a mind set reinforced by visions of gloomy French intellectuals discussing the pointlessness of life.[18] However, in practice, the distinction is less pronounced than it might appear here.

Like cognitive therapy, there are many sub-divisions of humanistic psychology. One of the best-known is *client-centred therapy*, based upon *Roger's self theory of personality* (e.g. Rogers, 1961). Not surprisingly, the central tenet of the theory is that everyone has a goal of self-actualization, which is the full realisation of one's (positive) attributes and potential. This in turn is built upon an older theory by Abraham Maslow (1908–1970), who devised a *hierarchy of needs* (e.g. Maslow, 1954). As the title suggests, this proposed that humans have a hierarchy of needs and drives, which can be symbolically represented as a pyramid. At the 'base' are physiological needs for food, shelter, etc. Above these are safety needs, followed by social needs (e.g. to form friendships, to fit into the social world, etc). Above these are self-esteem, and at the top of the pyramid lies self actualisation, an individual's highest goal. However, this is difficult to achieve (Maslow himself found few people who had achieved it). How can a therapist help? Rogers argued that central to the process is that the person should receive *unconditional positive regard*. In other words, an uncritical acceptance and feeling of warmth towards the person, which enables the person to be true to his or her feelings. This at first sounds like a carte blanche for selfishness, but it is meant rather more in the spirit of accepting a person for who they are rather than letting them do what they like. Since other goals include *congruence* (the harmony of self with experience) and *empathic understanding* (the ability to perceive the needs and feelings of others) it is clear that a purely selfish individual could not attain these. Rogers argues that people are deflected from self-actualization by faulty de-

18    And typically being well paid for it.

velopment. In particular, authority figures (parents, teachers, etc) place value judgements on acts, which may not coincide with the child's true motivations and beliefs. This is known as *conditional positive regard* – in other words, the child only receives praise and affection when they do what the authority figure wants. Again, it is important to stress that pragmatism is needed here. For example, stopping a child putting their hand in a fire is not blunting their personal development. However, blocking legitimate exploration solely because it is 'against the rules' probably is. A child thus learns that personal wishes may have to be suppressed in order to gain affection. Such conflicts between what is desired and what has to be done mean that the person behaves in one manner because that is the one which will be rewarded (the *condition of worth*), even though he or she may really want to do something different. Such conflicts, Rogers argues, retard personality development. In time this leads to problems, because the person's self image, which has been built on inconsistencies, does not match up with reality, and in order to protect the self image, the person experiences anxiety, and has to create defences.

To cope with these problems, client-centered therapy was devised. This assumes that the best person to resolve a patient's internal conflict is the patient him- or herself. Accordingly, the therapy principally consists of the patient talking to the therapist, with the therapist making minimal interjections, such as to amplify discretely a key point by asking the patient to go into greater detail. The therapist holds the client in unconditional positive regard, since this is the ideal state in which to be viewed and the ultimate goal of the therapy. Because the technique relies on little vocal interjection by the therapist, and the interjections being fairly basic requests for elaboration, it is relatively easy to programme a computer to resemble a Rogerian therapist. Thus, the 'patient' types in statements about him- or herself which the computer responds to with statements such as 'tell me more about that' or 'can you amplify that point?'. The computer is also programmed to respond to key words, such as 'mother' with questions such as 'tell me more about your family'. Such programmes (the original version of which was called *Eliza*) are remarkably realistic and users often report a great attachment to them. They are not foolproof, however. Typing in lyrics to well-known pop songs of the 'confessional' type (Elton John's 'Your Song' being one such instance) can create rather surreal dialogue (readers with access to the Eliza computer programme are recommended to try it).

The plethora of therapies can appear daunting to anyone approaching the subject of mental illness for the first time, and for each listed here, there are at least tens of permutations. In addition, this excludes the related issue of *counselling*, which ranges from therapeutic methods with a rigid code of practice and sound grounding in theory to little more than having a comforting chat.[19] The reason for this wide variety of methods is that, put simply, none of them is totally effective in every situation. Thus, it would be foolhardy to assume that client-centered therapy would be the first choice for the treatment of schizophrenia. Likewise, nobody would seriously countenance giving a person with low feelings of self-esteem a course of electric shocks. To adopt a phrase, it is a case of horses for courses.

FURTHER READING

The range of books available on the topic of mental illness is vast. For those who want a sensible overview of all types of illness and treatments, then Davison and Neale (1996) can be warmly recommended. For those who want a briefer catalogue, then many of the larger introductory textbooks contain impressive lists of the main illnesses and their symptoms. A more advanced text is that by Lindsay and Powell (1994). This is rather more 'clinically based', but provides a good introduction to some more complex ideas. Fictional accounts of mental illness are legion, though often the illness is used as a dramatic device rather than for its own sake. However, there are exceptions. Waugh's *The Ordeal of Gilbert Pinfold* has already been mentioned. Also frequently recommended are *I Never Promised You a Rose Garden* (Green, 1964) and *The Bell Jar* (Plath, 1963). Films about mental illness are often less satisfactory than books. *One Flew Over the Cuckoo's Nest* and *Rainman* are often praised, but they are largely a matter of personal taste. A rather more modest TV movie, *Do You Remember Love?*, in spite of its rather

---

19    In fairness, counselling's professional bodies are making earnest efforts to regulate matters so
      that only adequately trained counsellors will be permitted to practise.

saccharin (and implausible) ending is a brilliant examination of a woman succumbing to dementia and is well worth seeking out.

# CHAPTER 13

# Statistics

## Introduction

At its simplest, statistics is a method of summarising the findings of research, and judging whether one would find the same thing again if this study was repeated on different people. The problem with statistics for most people is that they get put off by the thought of the mathematics involved. In fact, to understand statistics, at least at the introductory stages, relatively little mathematics is involved, and most of it falls under the description of 'common sense'.

## Summarising data

When we look at data, we need to be able to see what the data 'mean'. We cannot just look at a collection of figures – we have to manipulate them so that they assume a form we recognise. The method we use to do this very much depends upon the type of data we are dealing with. One type of data is *categorical data*. These consist of items each of which can be classified as belonging to one category and not to any of the others. For example, if we were to categorise people by country of birth, then people belong to one country and one country only – one cannot be a member of more than one category. Another type of data is *continuous data*, in which all the items are measured on the same scale. Common everyday examples include height and weight, which can be measured in metres and grams. No matter what size the item in question, it is measured on the same scale (e.g. an elephant and a mouse can both have their weights described in terms of the number of grams).

An important consideration in discussing continuous data is the shape of the graph which it produces. In many instances, the graph will take a shape known as the *normal distribution* (also known as the Gaussian curve and the bell-shaped curve). The typical shape of the normal distribution graph is shown in Figure 3.1. As can be seen, it is symmetrical – in other words, the left hand side of the graph is a mirror image of the right hand side. The bulk of the graph is immediately around the central peak, and gets progressively smaller the further from the peak one moves. The normal distribution is found in many instances of measurement in the 'real world' – data on such things as height and weight will typically produce the bell-shaped graph. So will other, less obvious events. For example, suppose one were to toss a coin a hundred times and note how many times it came down 'heads'. Suppose now that one repeated this exercise many many times, each time noting how many times the coin came down heads. If, after several thousand repetitions, one were to plot a graph of how many times heads came up in each particular set of trials (i.e. from 'zero' to '100'), then the graph would look very similar to a normal distribution. Because of the normal distribution is seen so regularly, many statistical tests are built around the supposition that the data being tested have a normal distribution. This creates problems when data do not have a normal distribution, but we shall return to this point later.

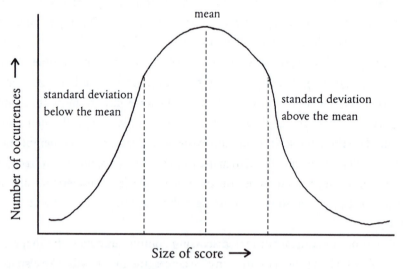

Figure 13.1 The Normal Distribution

One of the simplest uses of statistics, which everybody has encountered, is the use of the average. The average is an attempt to describe what the typical item in whatever one is considering is like. We thus talk about such things as 'average height', 'average rainfall', 'average age' in everyday language. In statistics, the term 'average' is used, but more often another word, called 'mean' is employed. 'Mean' and 'average' are interchangeable. It is a matter of habit that 'mean' tends to be used in statistics and 'average' in everyday speech. For the sake of convention, we will use 'mean' in the rest of this chapter.

The mean is measured by adding together all the measurements and then dividing by the number of those measurements. For example, the mean of 3, 2, 7, 4, 8, 4, 4, 6, 6, and 1 is 4.5. If you add the numbers together you get a total of 45. There are 10 numbers in total, so if you divide 45 by 10, you get an answer of 4.5. This is a measure of what a 'typical' member of the set we have measured is like. Note that the mean does not have to be exactly the same as any member of the set in question. For instance, in our example, there is no number '4.5' in the list of numbers.

The mean is the best known method of summarising data, but it is not the only one. The mean is one of a collection of measures known as *measures of central tendency*. They are called this because if one drew a graph of the figures being measured, a measure of central tendency usually lies roughly in the middle of the graph (i.e. half the numbers are smaller than it and half are bigger). Other measures of central tendency in common use are the *mode* (the most frequently occurring number – in our example above, the mode is 4) and the *median* (the value which falls exactly in the middle of the numbers – i.e. exactly 50 per cent of the numbers are bigger and 50 per cent are smaller). One of the features of the normal distribution described above is that in a perfect instance of it, the mean, the median and the mode are exactly equal.

Measures of central tendency provide a useful way of judging what is 'typical' of a particular sample, but they can be misleading. If we are told that the mean score on a test is 10, it is tempting to think that typically, people score 10, or a number close to it, such as 11, 12, 8 or 9. However, consider the following two lists of numbers: (a) 20, 20, 20, 20, 20, 0, 0, 0, 0, 0; (b) 10, 11, 9, 12, 8, 11, 9, 10, 8, 12. Both these lists have a mean value of 10, but they are obviously very different. In one case, people either score 20 or 0; in the other, they score a range of scores which all tend to be fairly close to the mean. This brings us to another important feature of statistics – the measure of *variability*. This is simply a measure of how widespread the scores are. If all scores tend to be close to the mean, then there is said to be low variability, whilst if an appreciable proportion of the scores can stray far away from the mean, then there is high variability. This is obviously a useful measure, since it tells us how far away from the mean we are likely to find scores. For example, if you are a ready-to-wear clothing manufacturer, there is no point in simply making clothing to fit the average figure – you also need to know a lot about the variability in sizes so that you can make clothes which everybody can buy.

There are a variety of ways of measuring variability, and thankfully none of them is complicated. The simplest and most direct measure is the *range*. This is simply the difference in size between the smallest item in your sample and the largest, and gives a rough-and-ready idea of the spread of scores. However, it is limited in its uses, since it only requires one very exceptional score to give an enormous range which does not reflect the typical nature of the sample. For example, if one was measuring height, then most people would fall between about 4 feet 10 inches and 6 feet 6 inches. However, there are some exceptionally tall people over 7 feet in height, and it would only require one such person, measuring, for example, 7 feet 3 inches, to increase the range by 9 inches. Whilst this is a fair reflection of what was found, it makes the variability of a 'typical' sample of people appear far larger than it actually is. Therefore, there must be a method of measuring variability which compensates for exceptional cases so that they do not distort the results.

This brings us to the next method of measuring variability – the *mean variance*. This is the mean difference between each number in the sample and the sample's mean, and is simpler than this definition at first sounds. Let us consider the figures we used in the example of calculating the mean. These have been set out in the far left hand column (titled 'Score') in Table 3.1. You will recall that the mean of these figures is 4.5. To find the mean variance, one finds the difference between each score and the mean, and the resulting figures are put in a new column (the middle one marked 'Score–Mean'). The

Plus or minus signs are ignored (i.e. if the mean is bigger than the score, the size of the difference is noted down, but a minus sign is not put in front of it). Take the first number in the 'Score' column – 3. The mean is 4.5, so the difference between the score and the mean is the difference between 4.5 and 3 – i.e. 1.5. This number is entered into the 'Score–Mean' column. The exercise is repeated for the other nine numbers in the column. When this is done, we have a new collection of numbers, which give the sizes of the differences between the mean and each number in the set. If the mean is a good representation of the numbers, then this new column should contain small numbers (because the differences between the mean and the numbers in the sample should be small). To work out the typical size of the difference between the mean and the numbers, we calculate the mean of these differences. In other words, we calculate the mean of the numbers in the 'Score–Mean' column. What we get is called the mean variance. In our example, the mean variance is 1.8. So therefore, any number in the sample is typically different from the mean by 1.8.

The mean variance seems to many people to be an intuitively obvious way of measuring variability, since it tells us what is the typical difference between the numbers and the mean which supposedly represents them (the smaller the number, the lower the variability). However, useful as the mean variance is, a refinement of it is usually used. The first step towards this is to find the *variance*. This is gained by first taking the values in the 'Score–Mean' column, and squaring them. If you look at the far right hand column of Table 1 (the one marked '(Score–Mean)$^2$') you will see that these have been calculated for you. The numbers in this column are added up, and then divided by the number which is one less than the number of numbers in the column. In our example, there are 10 numbers in the column, so the total is divided by one less than 10 which is (obviously!) 9 (similarly, if we had 200 numbers in the column, then the total would have been divided by 199). Why we divide by one less than the total number of numbers is complex, and need not concern us here, but it is necessary that this is done. When this calculation is complete, then we have the variance (in the case of our example, the variance is 4.944).[1]

| Table 13.1 Mean deviation, variance and standard deviation for example data | | |
|---|---|---|
| *Score* | *Score–Mean* | *(Score–Mean)$^2$* |
| 3 | 1.5 | 2.25 |
| 2 | 2.5 | 6.25 |
| 7 | 2.5 | 6.25 |
| 4 | 0.5 | 0.25 |
| 8 | 3.5 | 12.25 |
| 4 | 0.5 | 0.25 |
| 4 | 0.5 | 0.25 |
| 6 | 1.5 | 2.25 |
| 6 | 1.5 | 2.25 |
| 1 | 3.5 | 12.25 |
| mean = 4.5 | | |
| mean variance = 1.8 | | |
| variance = 4.944 | | |
| standard deviation = 2.224 | | |

1   At the risk of muddying already murky waters, it should be noted at this point that the term 'variance' is used quite loosely by some commentators. Although it means the formula just described, some commentators also use it to describe variability in general. Caution is accordingly advised.

Having calculated the variance, the next measure of variability is very easy to calculate, since it is simply the square root of the variance, and it is called the *standard deviation*. In the case of our example, the standard deviation is the square root of the variance, which is 4.944, and accordingly, the standard deviation is 2.224. In Psychology, the standard deviation is the most commonly used measure of variability. Why?

At first sight, it seems perverse to use a measure of variability which takes more time to calculate than the other methods mentioned and also seems to be calculated in a very strange way (e.g. why square the differences and then take the square root?). However, the standard deviation has a number of properties which make it very useful indeed. These refer back to the normal distribution, described above, and illustrated in Figure 3.1. Look at the figure, and place your finger on the peak of the graph. If you trace your finger along the line of the graph (either to the left or the right), you will notice that the line at first drops and then flattens out to the horizontal. Mathematically speaking, the standard deviation is the point on the graph where the curve begins to change from having a downward trend to having a horizontal trend. Statistically speaking, the standard deviation is fantastically useful, because it allows us to measure how typical a score is for a particular set of data. How and why need not concern us here, but basically, once one knows both the standard deviation and the mean, it is possible to calculate *percentiles*.

The percentile simply describes a score in terms of what percentage of the group has a score bigger than the score in question. Suppose that we find that a person has a score of 100 on a particular test. This means nothing unless we also know what everybody else does on the same test. The score, converted to a percentile, enables us to judge just this. For example, the 50th percentile denotes that 50 per cent of people have lower scores (i.e. the person is pretty average), whilst the 90th percentile denotes that 90 per cent of people have lower scores (i.e. the person is pretty exceptional). It can be readily appreciated that the percentile score is a useful ready-reckoner of how exceptional (or commonplace) a score is. The percentile is calculated using the standard deviation as the principal part of the formula.

As already stated, how percentiles are calculated in detail need not concern us here, but it is useful to remember one basic formula involving the standard deviation. Suppose that for a particular data set one knows the mean and the standard deviation. Multiply the standard deviation by 1.96. Take this number away from the mean and note down the number you get. Now add the number (i.e. 1.96 x the standard deviation) to the mean and note down this number. Between the two numbers you have noted down, 95 per cent of all the data you collect will fall. Any numbers bigger or smaller than these two extremes are accordingly fairly exceptional, because one would expect to encounter them on only 5 per cent of occasions. This is one of the reasons why most psychological journals insist that any descriptions of data include not only the mean but also the standard deviation – it enables people to determine the variability of the data being discussed, and also enables one quickly to calculate the spread of scores one is likely to find.

To recap. When we wish to describe data, we nearly always wish to make a summary of it, since there is usually too much raw data for the mind to comprehend. The commonest method of summarising data is to describe it in terms of a measure of central tendency (typically, the mean or average) and a measure of variability (typically, the standard deviation). The measure of variability enables one to see how representative the mean is of the sample of data in question. The standard deviation has the added advantage in that it not only describes the spread of figures (of which the '1.96 rule' is a useful ready-reckoner) but it also enables percentiles to be created, which enable one to judge how exceptional an individual score is. This assumes that the data are from a normal distribution. This may not always be the case, though it describes the majority of instances one is likely to encounter in normal research life.

## Statistical significance

In almost any conceivable test situation, we test only a sample of the total possible people or items available for testing. For example, if we decide to conduct an experiment on humans, we do not think it necessary to test every single human on the planet Earth. Even if we confine our studies to a relatively small group, such as patients suffering from a particular illness, then it is still highly unlikely that we would have the resources or the need to test every single person with the illness in question. Instead, we only test a sample of the population, usually because it is quicker and more convenient. However, how do we know that what we find with the sample is representative of the whole group? Or, put in more technical terms, how do we know that our study accurately reflects the *population* (i.e. all the possible items belonging to the category in question) being sampled? A lot can rest on such decisions. For example, in testing a new drug on a sample, how sure can one be that the changes in health in members of the sample will accurately reflect changes in the wider population if the drug is released onto the general market? The answer is that we determine how statistically significant the results of the test are. *Statistical significance* is the probability that a particular finding accurately represents the population being sampled. Note that it only finds the *probability* – it does not state with absolute certainty that a particular study is an accurate reflection of the population. At best the significance level can only say that it is very likely that it is. This begs the inevitable question – what level of probability is required for us to judge that a result can reasonably be considered to be an accurate reflection of the population?

Suppose that an analysis shows that a particular result has a probability of accurately reflecting the population of 1 in 100. It is highly unlikely that we would believe the study in question to be accurate. Most people would have a similar reaction if the odds were 10 in 100 or 50 in 100. However, what if the odds are shortened more? What if the odds were 90 in 100, or 95 in 100, or 98 in 100? At what point are we prepared to take a risk and say that the odds are now good enough for us to take a gamble? Traditionally in Psychology, people have taken odds of 95 in 100 or better to mean that the results are sufficiently likely to be accurate that they will accept them as bona fide. This is largely a matter of custom and practice – there is no definitive law which states that this figure of 95 per cent is the right one to choose (and indeed, other sciences have sometimes chosen different values).

When we write down these odds, we do it in a slightly perverse manner. Instead of recording the odds on the sample being an accurate reflection, we record the odds of the sample *not* being an accurate reflection. This is simply the mirror image of the figures we have been talking about. Thus, instead of stating there is a 95 in 100 chance of the study being accurate, we state there is a 5 in 100 chance of it being inaccurate (similarly, a 40 in a 100 chance of being accurate means a 60 in 100 chance of being inaccurate). This probability value is sometimes expressed as a percentage, but it is more commonly written as a decimal fraction of 1. Hence, 10 in 100 written as a fraction of 1 is 0.1; 5 in 100 is written as 0.05; 1 in 100 is written as 0.01. The crucial value here is 0.05. A result has to be *lower* than this (remember, this is the probability that the result is an *inaccurate* reflection of the population) for the result to be counted as accurate. One final piece of terminology – the 'probability of inaccuracy' (more properly called the *significance level*) is represented by the letter *p*. Experimental results often carry a summary statement such as 'the results were significant ($p<0.05$)'. Translated, this means that the chances of the result being inaccurate (p) are less than 0.05 in 1 (i.e. less than 5 per cent).

Therefore, the significance level (p) represents the probability that the results do *not* represent the population. Traditionally, psychologists have accepted that results are a fair reflection when this value of p is less than 0.05 (i.e. 5 per cent). However, this is only a statement of likelihood – it is not a definite cast-in-letters-of-bronze guarantee that this is right. On some occasions this conclusion will be wrong. In fact, we can work out how often it is likely to be wrong by looking at the value of the significance level. If there is a significance level of 0.05, this means that on 5 out of 100 occasions, the result is probably wrong. This does not sound very often, until one realises that 5 in 100 is the same ratio as 1 in 20. In other words, once every twenty times, the result will be wrong. These may not sound very favourable odds, and researchers must be aware of the dangers of making a *Type I error*. This occurs when the study supposedly finds a real result when in fact none exists. [The reverse of this is the *Type II error* which occurs when the results indicate that there is no result, when in fact one really exists.] This happens because statistical analyses always have a possibility that they are wrong. The likelihood of this happening is related to the strength of the statistical significance. We have noted that for a result to be counted as accurate, it must have a value of less than 0.05. Of course, results can go lower than this value of p, and values of p as low as 0.001 are not uncommon (a value of 0.001 means that there is a one in a thousand chance that it is inaccurate). The smaller the value of p, the more confident we can be in the accuracy of the result.

## Statistical tests

So far we have seen how to summarise a set of data and how to judge that the findings of a study accurately reflect the population being sampled. The final issue to be discussed is the types of statistical tests which are available to the psychologist. These come in three basic forms:

(1)   measures of differences in groups' scores

(2)   measures of relationships between groups' scores

and

(3)   measures of differences in proportions occupied by different groups.

All these tests have the same basic aim – to show the *significance level* of what they have analysed (i.e. the likelihood that the data represent a genuine effect which accurately represents the population the sample was drawn from). The ways in which they do this are many and varied, and for any particular experimental situation there is usually a choice of statistical tests available to analyse it. Which test is chosen often depends upon whether the data being analysed are drawn from a population with a normal distribution. There are statistical procedures available for determining if data are normally distributed (though most psychologists appear to assume that any continuous data can be classified thus: not a particularly serious crime, since most tests designed for working on normally-distributed data can cope with some statistical deviance without undue concern). Some tests can only be run on normally-distributed data, and they are generally (though not entirely accurately) called *parametric tests*. Other tests can be run on data from practically any kind of distribution, and they are called *non-parametric tests*. Generally, the parametric tests are preferred. This may sound perverse, because they are apparently much 'choosier' about the sort of data they will analyse. However, they make up for this faddiness by generally being more informative and being capable of greater depths of analysis than most of the non-parametric tests can manage.

In the following section, we will examine some of the principal types of statistical tests available to the psychologist. We will follow the sub-division outlined above, and divide the tests into sections according to whether they measure differences, relationships or proportions.

## Measuring differences

Perhaps the commonest test in the psychologist's repertoire is the *t test*. This is a test to measure if one group has larger scores than another group. It is a parametric test, and comes in two basic forms. The first – the *unrelated t test* (also known as the *unpaired t test*) – measures if two groups composed of different people have different scores on the same measure. This might be, for example, a comparison of the heights of men and women, or comparing the intelligence test scores of cricket versus football supporters. The test is called 'unrelated' because the two groups being compared are composed of different people. The *related t test* (also known as the *paired t test*) is a comparison of the scores of two groups whose members are related in a specific manner. Thus, for every member of one group there is a member of the other group who is similar in some manner which is of interest to the experimenter. One of the commonest instances is where the same people are compared before and after a particular event or treatment. Hence, the test might be used to compare the weights of the same group of people before and after dieting, or the heart rate of a group of patients before and after being given a cardiovascular drug. Where the data are not normally distributed, there are non-parametric equivalents of the t tests. These are the *Mann-Whitney U test*, which is equivalent to the unpaired t test, and the *Wilcoxin matched pairs signed ranks test* (also known as the *Wilcoxin test*), equivalent to the paired t test.

The t tests and non-parametric equivalents can only compare two groups' scores on the same measure. However, there are occasions where one wishes to compare more than two groups on more than one measure. It would be possible to do this in a piecemeal fashion by dividing the task up into pairings (e.g. if one were comparing groups A, B and C on Tests Y and Z, one could, using a t test, compare A and B on Y, A and B on Z, A and C on Y, etc). However, this would be labourious and would also, for reasons too lengthy to enter into here, greatly increase the risk of producing a Type I error. Therefore, a more sophisticated approach is required. When the data are normally distributed, the solution is to run an *analysis of variance*, or *ANOVA*. This versatile test enables one to compare the scores of two or more groups on one or more measures. Thus, one might compare three groups on one measure, four groups on two measures, two groups on eight measures, or practically any other permutation one wishes to consider (e.g. one might wish to compare four schools' results on tests of maths, English and science; or men and women on a battery of eight different measures of intelligence). The ANOVA tells us several important things. The first is that it can tell us if there is a significant difference between the scores of the different groups. Similarly, it can tell us if scores on the different tests given to the participants are the same, or whether there is a difference (e.g. showing that some tests are harder than others). A third consideration is that the ANOVA can examine if there is an *interaction* between the groups and the measures given to them. Take the schools example given above. An ANOVA might demonstrate that, overall, one school produces higher marks than the others. However, it may also demonstrate a difference in the pattern of scores. It may be, for example, that one school does relatively better at science than English or maths, a second does better at maths, whilst the third school produces roughly equal performances in all three disciplines. This difference between groups in patterns of performance is known as the interaction, and the ANOVA can identify whether this is statistically reliable.

A further, more sophisticated, procedure can also be performed, known as *post hoc testing*. Suppose that one has compared four groups on the same test and the ANOVA indicates that there is a 'group difference'. This is useful information, but it may be the case that whilst overall there is a difference between groups, some individual groups may be getting identical scores (e.g. groups C and D might be different from everybody else, but groups A and B may be performing at the same level). To measure this, a range of post hoc tests are available (these include *Dennett's, Fisher's PLSD* and many others). These compare each group with each other in a pairwise fashion (i.e. Group A is compared with Group B, Group A is compared with Group C, etc) – hence the post hoc tests are sometimes also known as *pairwise comparisons*.

This enables the researcher to pinpoint precisely where the differences lie in an overall group difference.[2]

Non-parametric tests display their shortcomings in that they cannot provide tests which are as versatile as the ANOVA (nor can they offer convincing post hoc tests) The nearest equivalents are the *Friedman-Ranks ANOVA (F-R ANOVA)*, which measures the differences between scores on three or more measures made by one group; and the *Kruskal-Wallis one way ANOVA by ranks,* which compares the scores of three or more groups on one measure only. There is not a non-parametric test which can compare more than two groups on more than one test simultaneously.

## Measuring relationships

So far we have considered tests which essentially assess whether one group has bigger scores than another. In other circumstances, we are more interested in the relationship between different data sets. One of the simplest measures of this is the *correlation*. This at its most basic measures whether when one measure changes in size, another also changes, thereby establishing a link between them. A measure which changes in size is also known as a *variable* (since its size can vary). In the case of the correlation, this measures whether the relationship between two measures or variables is positive or negative. In the case of a *positive correlation*, as one variable increases in size, so does the other variable. Likewise, if one variable decreases, so does the other. A common example of this is the height and weight of people – as height increases, so does weight, so that taller people tend to be heavier than shorter people. In a *negative correlation*, an increase in one variable is matched by a decrease in another (e.g. daytime temperature and quantity of clothing worn – the hotter it is, the fewer the clothes we wear). An important caveat to this is the old adage that 'correlation does not equal causation'. A correlation shows that two variables are related, but not whether one causes the other. We have to attribute causation by other means.

---

2  The more mathematically astute reader may ask what the difference is between this and just doing lots and lots of t tests. The answer is that there is a difference, but it would take a very long time to explain it.

Take the clothing and temperature example given above. Because there is a relationship does not mean that if we take our clothes off, the temperature will increase. We have to demonstrate by other means that the relationship in this case is one-sided and it is temperature which causes changes in the quantity of clothing worn. In other instances, the relationship may be due to a third party and the correlation may simply reflect what the variables hold in common with this third party. For example, in an often-cited case, if some strange passion drove us to measure schoolchildren's feet and give them a maths test, we would find that there is a positive correlation between foot size and test score. Does this mean that your mathematical ability is determined by the size of your feet or (more alarmingly) that being good at maths makes your feet grow? Of course not — the reason for this correlation is the influence of a third party; namely, age (the older children will have bigger feet and will also be better at maths). So the correlation must be treated with caution.

Having established that there is a positive or negative correlation, the next task is to judge the strength of the relationship. The correlation is represented by the symbol $r$, and the size of r varies between 0 and -1 for a negative correlation, and 0 and +1 for a positive correlation. If r equals 0, then there is no correlation — in other words, no relationship exists between the variables, and changes in one in no manner affect changes in the other (e.g. though this has not been checked out, it is improbable that the death rate in Bulgaria on Saturdays is affected by the number of goals scored in the English football leagues on the same day). If r equals 1 (plus or minus) then there is a perfect correlation, and an increase in one variable is met by exactly the same proportioned change in the other variable (i.e. a decrease if r is -1, and an increase if r is +1). Statistical tests run on 'real life' will typically produce correlations which lie somewhere between the extremes of no correlation and a perfect correlation, and the closer the value of r is to 1 (be it plus or minus), the stronger the relationship. Values of r are expressed as a decimal fraction (e.g. -0.23, +0.5, etc). Low values of r (typically, less than 0.2) are unlikely to be statistically significant (i.e. they indicate that the relationship would probably not be found if the experiment was run again on different samples). Most computerised statistical packages and basic statistical textbooks provide tables for working out if correlations are significant.

It is tempting to think that values of r are a direct reflection of their strength. For example, a value of r of 0.7 might tempt one to think that since a perfect positive correlation is +1, that the correlation represents 70 per cent of a perfect correlation (and similarly, that a value of r of -0.4 indicates 40 per cent of a perfect negative correlation). In fact, the correlation is a rather deceptive number. To find the percentage of a perfect correlation represented by r, one must square r and then multiply the resulting figure by 100. In the case of a correlation of 0.7, the percentage of a perfect positive correlation is 49 per cent (multiply 0.7 x 0.7 x 100 = 49). By the same token, a negative correlation of -0.4 represents 16 per cent of a perfect negative correlation. Therefore, the 'percentage of perfection' may be rather less than r at first appears to imply.

Instead of talking of 'percentage of perfection' statisticians refer to r as indicating the amount of variability in one variable which can be predicted by the variability in another, and the value of r is referred to as the *correlation coefficient*. There are many ways of measuring correlations, largely determined by the type of data which are being considered. The *Pearson correlation coefficient* measures the correlations between two variables which have normal distributions (e.g. height and weight). A non-parametric equivalent is the *Spearman correlation coefficient* (e.g. comparing the finishing orders of the same people in two separate races).

A further variant on the correlation is the *regression* equation (a parametric measure). In the correlation, one is interested in demonstrating that a relationship exists between two variables. A regression attempts not only to demonstrate a relationship, but also make a prediction of the actual value of one variable given the value of another. For example, a regression equation linking height and weight would not only attempt to demonstrate that height and weight are related, but also provide a formula for estimating a person's height given their weight (or vice versa). A common use of this is in obstetrics, where a woman's pelvic width (indicating the ease with which she may give birth) can be predicted with reasonable accuracy from her shoe size. In a 'conventional' regression equation, the relationship between two variables is examined. In a *multiple regression*, the size of one variable is predicted by two or more other variables. This often produces more accurate results. For example, in a 'conventional' regression, one might try to predict overall scholastic attainment from ability on a maths test. In a multiple regression, one might predict it using not only scores on a maths test, but also scores on an English test and science test. It is highly likely that the multiple regression would give a more accurate prediction.

## Measuring proportions

It is sometimes necessary to measure how frequently different categories are represented. This is a method which cannot compare actual scores (as in measuring differences) and falls in the domain of non-parametric tests. The only test of measuring proportions which is encountered in common usage in Psychology is the *chi squared test*. This is used where items or people may belong to one and only one of several categories – are the people or items equally likely to be in any one of the categories, or is membership of some categories higher than others?

The most basic form of this measure is the *chi squared goodness of fit test*, which measures membership differences between one set of categories. For example, suppose that one is running an ice cream stall which offers five different flavours of ice cream. Do all the flavours sell equally well? In other words, if a person comes to the stall is it equally likely that he or she will pick any one of the flavours, or are some chosen more often than others? In a more complex form the chi squared can also measure whether 2 or more groups fall into 2 or more categories with equal likelihood. For example, in the ice cream problem, suppose we consider whether men and women have different preferences for the flavours – we are now not only measuring the frequency with which the different ice cream flavours are chosen, but also whether the pattern of distribution is different for men and women. There are 2 important caveats to the chi squared analysis. The first concerns its calculation. Essentially, the test involves calculating an estimate of the membership size of each category if allocation of membership was random (these are known as the *expected values*). This is compared with the actual membership figures, and if the discrepancy is large enough, then, it is argued, the figures indicate something other than chance at work (i.e. there is a bona fide difference). In calculating the expected values, if the values are less than 5, then the test should not be run. The second caveat is that when the test is run on 2 groups and 2 categories (e.g. men and women choosing between strawberry and chocolate flavour ice cream), 0.5 should be deducted from the calculated value of chi squared. This is known as *Yate's correction*.

Statistics can appear a daunting subject when it is first approached. There are numerous new terms to learn, and its kinship to mathematics tends to deter students who did not enjoy maths at school. However, statistics is an essential tool for many areas of Psychology. At heart, it is asking no more than we should ask of an experiment – do these results apply to more than just the sample of people or things we tested? We cannot tell this just by looking at the results of an experiment – we need an objective proof, and statistics is the best thing we have for the job.

FURTHER READING

Textbooks on statistics vary in their level of readability and method of approach. It is accordingly difficult to recommend a text which will suit everyone. However, amongst those texts aimed specifically at psychologists are two which are frequently recommended by many UK courses: Greene and D'Oliveira (1982) and Coolican (1994). Stuart-Hamilton (1996) offers dictionary definitions of the key statistical terms likely to be encountered.

CHAPTER 14

# Some Concluding Thoughts

*What follows is a deliberately contentious essay to stimulate thoughts about the topics covered in the previous chapters. There are no easy answers, but the reader is invited to contemplate ways in which the problems raised might be addressed.*

This book has attempted to introduce some of the key concepts and studies which constitute what might be termed 'prototypical psychology', or more facetiously, some of 'Psychology's greatest hits'. It can be readily appreciated that Psychology fulfils the promises of Chapter 1 that is a diverse subject. William James's definition of Psychology as 'the science of mental life' can be seen to be a remarkably fair summary. However, although what Psychology *studies* can be neatly wrapped up in a few words, trying to summarise its *findings* is an entirely different matter. To what extent do we have a unified model of mental life, rather than a collection of fragments? From the cross-referencing between chapters, it is clear that there are some overlaps of interest between areas of study. For example, it is apparent that the study of psycholinguistics has an obvious affinity with, inter alia, developmental psychology and even comparative psychology. However, a universal theme or set of laws does not govern all Psychology.

This is best explained by example. In Physics, for example, there are many disparate areas of study. However, all the observations, theories, hypotheses and models created in these different specialisms all ultimately draw upon a few basic premises such as Newton's laws of motion. [1]If one considers the topics covered in this book it becomes rapidly apparent that although all examine one aspect or other of mental life, they are otherwise as alike as chalk and cheese. For example, Social Psychology is very much concerned with the interaction between individual people, largely using social communication

1    This is similar to, but nonetheless different from, the argument raised in Chapter 1.

317

as a measure. Biopsychology, on the other hand, is grounded in physiological theory, and principally examines the interaction between specific parts of brain and body, often at a biochemical level. Again, memory studies are largely concerned with finding models of functioning common to all of us, but in direct contrast, much of individual differences research deals with *differences* between individuals.

Whether a set of 'universal rules' can ever be found remains a moot point. The form that the rules might take is also intriguing. A common method currently in use is the *spatial metaphor*, in which the different processes of a mental act are conceived as separate processing units (not unlike a schematic illustration of a computer programme). However, this is an analogical description rather than a reducible set of statements.

In finding a common thread, a starting point would be that the different disciplines of Psychology would all have to be capable of being reduced to the same basic set of laws. However, reducing psychological topics yields a mass of conflicting findings. For example, reducing a social psychology experiment to its core principles will reveal a set of expectations or assumptions about rational behaviour in a social setting. On the other hand, a biopsychology experiment is grounded in assumptions about physical bodily processes. It is not possible to equate the findings of the two types of study – and that is just two of many diverse approaches. Part of the reason for this is that Psychology has freely adapted methods from a host of different disciplines: social psychology has been heavily influenced by sociology, biopsychology by physiology, cognition by computer science, etc, to which psychologists have added their own models and methods. Finding a common core is like hoping that a single root language exists behind Japanese, English and Finnish.

Adding to the problem is that humans are inherently unpredictable. To illustrate this, let us take an example of an often-used method of study – assessing the ability of a person to remember lists of numbers. The example is chosen because it produces easily quantifiable results. However, memory and cognitive research is not being singled out for criticism – any other psychological experiment might have served.

We might run the study as follows. We sit a person in a quiet room and read lists of numbers to him or her. We start with short lists (e.g. of two or three numbers) and over several trials we increase the length of the list until we find the longest list which he or she can repeat back reliably without errors. This is counted as being that person's memory span for numbers. We repeat the process with lots of other people, until we have built up a picture of the typical performance of a group of people on this experiment. We are now in a position to declare the length of list which an average person can remember. Or are we?

The above experiment raises more questions than may at first appear. Below are listed the first few which came into the author's head. There are no doubt many more which the interested reader can uncover:

(1) What if the average score is not a whole number? For example, suppose that we find that the average list length recalled by a person is 6.781 numbers. Clearly, no individual person will recall six numbers and then only remember 0.781 of the next one. So group performance does not necessarily agree with the performance of any one individual.

(2) What do we know about the people used in the experiment? Were they a representative sample of the population as a whole? For example, if one had tested members of a conference for very clever mathematicians, would you expect their performance to be identical to 'ordinary' members of the public?

(3) How was the longest list which the volunteer 'can repeat back reliably without errors' actually decided? Was it the length which he or she *always* got right, without ever making an error, or was it a length which he or she got right on a certain percentage of occasions. If so, how many — ninety, eighty, seventy? If a person got a list right on ninety per cent of occasions, then on ten per cent he or she, by definition, got it wrong. What constitutes an acceptable margin of error in this measurement?

(4) The test was done in a quiet room. However, is this a realistic measure of skill? Everyday life rarely takes place in quiet, exam-like conditions.

The same experience or worse is usually the case for most people when reading, writing or otherwise trying to do 'brain work'. So why should we assume that pure, quiet conditions, without distraction, are a fair reflection of 'real life'?

(5) Following on from the previous point, why should we want to look at memory for number lists in any case? How often in everyday life has one needed to remember a list of numbers in one's head? Barring trying to remember a telephone number, it is doubtful if it is a regular experience. So why assume that testing it is a meaningful activity?

As stated above, there are many other criticisms which could be made of our hypothetical (but in fact often-performed) experiment. However, what should be readily appreciated from the above is that humans do not give an identical performance in all situations. First, there are considerable differences between individuals (i.e. some will remember more than others); there are considerable differences in the same individual's performance on different occasions (e.g. memory performance in a noisy versus a quiet room); there are even fluctuations in performance by the same person in the same situation (i.e. he or she will not always remember exactly the same length of list); and, to further complicate matters, there will be an interaction between all of these (e.g. some people will consistently remember more than others and their pattern of response will vary in different ways across different situations).

This means that even if we could build a model for accounting for all situations, there would still be the problem of individual variability to account for. It may be fairly pointed out that there is of course variability in measurement in any science. Chemists or physicists, for example, will give their measurements and include a margin of error. However, these margins of error often are simply an indication of a limit of their measuring instruments. Within psychology, measuring instruments are often limited by the limits of human ability to report information verbally (e.g. speak a set of numbers) but also they are limited because humans may also vary between situations.

So why do psychologists apparently persist in running studies which are obviously too simplistic and have little apparent bearing on 'real life'? In fairness, it must be first stated that psychologists are fully aware of these criticisms. However, against any considerations of 'realism' and 'representativeness' must be placed the weightier issues of objectivity and confounding variables.

In measuring behaviour, we must be sure that we are truly measuring what we claim to be measuring and not accidentally picking up any stray effects from other variables. For example, suppose we are interested in the effect of temperature in the workplace on productivity, and so we measure the change in productivity after increasing the temperature of his or her office, but at the same time we increase the person's salary. If we find that productivity increases after these changes have taken place, it would be hard to attribute it to the temperature change because it occurred at the same time as other changes likely to affect productivity. Again, in our memory example, suppose that whilst the person is memorising the lists, we play typical household noises through loudspeakers. One might expect this to have an effect on the person's performance, and so one could not say that one was measuring a 'pure' memory, since the ability to memorise is compromised by distractions.

Therefore, the psychologist is put into a Morton's Fork[2] – whatever he or she does is going to displease someone. If we isolate a basic form of behaviour and test it in isolation, then we can build up a fairly accurate picture of that behaviour. Such is the case with memory for numbers, which have now been assessed in just about every permutation possible, up to and including ability to memorise whilst submerged beneath the water in diving gear. The problem is that for our knowledge to be of much practical relevance, such information has got to integrated into 'real life' situations. However, as soon as we do this, so many confounding variables enter into the mixture that it is very difficult, if not impossible to identify the original skill. Go for realism and one loses the accuracy, go for accuracy and one loses the realism. Unfortunately, there is no available answer to this conundrum – Psychology must make its way as best it can without becoming unrealistic or hopelessly over-general.

---

2    After Bishop Morton, one of Henry VII's ministers, who devised 'damned if you do, damned if you don't' paradoxes several hundred years before Joseph Heller coined the phrase 'Catch 22', which means the same thing.

# References

Abramson, L.Y., Metalsky, G.I. and Alloy, L.B. (1989) 'Hopelessness depression: A theory-based subtype of depression.' *Psychological Review, 96*, 358–72.

Ainsworth, M. and Bell, S. (1970) 'Attachment, separation and exploration: Illustrated by the behaviour of one-year-olds in a strange situation.' *Child Development, 41*, 49–67.

Allport, G.M. (1958) *The Nature of Prejudice.* New York: Doubleday.

American Psychiatric Association (1994) *Diagnostic and Statistical Manual of Mental Disorders,* 4th edition. Washington: American Psychiatric Association.

Andersson, M. (1982) Female choice selects for extreme tail length in a widowbird *Nature, 299,* 818–20.

Argyle, M. (1983) *The Psychology of Interpersonal Behaviour.* London: Penguin Books.

Asch, S.E. (1946) 'Forming impressions of personality.' *Journal of Abnormal and Social Psychology, 41,* 258–90.

Asch, S.E. (1951) 'Effects of group pressure upon the modification and distortion of judgement.' In H. Guetzkow (ed) *Groups, Leadership and Men.* Pittsburgh: Carnegie.

Asperger, H. (1944) 'Die 'Autistischen Psychopathen im Kindesalter.' *Archiv fur Psychiatrie und Nervenkrankheiten, 117,* 76–136.

Atkinson, R.C. and Shiffrin, R.M. (1968) 'Human memory: A proposed system and its control processes.' In: K.W. Spence and J.T. Spence (eds), *The Psychology of Learning and Motivation, Volume 2,* London: Academic Press.

Atkinson, R.L., Atkinson, R.C., Smith, E.E., Bem, D.J. and Hilgard, E.R. (1990) *Introduction to Psychology,* 10th edition. Orlando: Harcourt Brace Jovanovich.

Atkinson, R.L., Atkinson, R.C., Smith, E.E., Bem, D.J. and Nolen-Hoeksema (1996) *Hilgard's Introduction to Psychology,* 12th edition. Orlando: Harcourt Brace Jovanovich.

Baddeley, A.D. (1995) *Memory,* 2nd edition. London: Lawrence Erlbaum.

Baddeley, A.D. and Hitch, G. (1974) 'Working memory.' In G.H. Bower (ed) *The Psychology of Learning and Motivation,* Vol. 8, London: Academic Press.

Baillargeon, R., Spelke, E. and Wasserman, S. (1985) 'Object permanence in five-month-old infants.' *Cognition, 20,* 191–208.

Bandura, A. (1989) 'Social cognitive theory.' *Annals of Child Development, 6,* 1–60.

Bandura, A., Ross, D. and Ross, S. (1963) 'Imitation of film-mediated aggressive models.' *Journal of Abnormal and Social Psychology, 66,* 3–11.

Baron, R. and Byrne, D. (1991) *Social Psychology.* New York: Allyn and Bacon.

Bartlett, F.C. (1932) *Remembering.* Cambridge: Cambridge University Press.

Beck, A.T. (1976) *Cognitive therapy and the emotional disorders.* New York: International Universities Press.

Beebe-Center, J.G. (1949) 'Standards for use of the Gust Scale.' *Journal of Psychology, 28,* 411–419.

Bem, S.L. (1974) 'Androgyny vs. the tight little lives of fluffy women and chesty men.' *Psychology Today,* September, 58–62.

Bergeman, C.S., Chipuer, H.M., Plomin, R. *et al.* (1993) 'Genetic and environmental effects on openness to experience, agreeableness, and conscientiousness: An adoption/twin study.' *Journal of Personality, 61,* 159–179.

Bergin, A.E. (1971) 'The evaluation of therapeutic outcomes.' In A.E. Bergin and S.L. Garfield (eds) *Handbook of Psychotherapy and Behaviour Change: An Empirical Analysis.* New York: Wiley.

Berko, J. and Brown, R. (1960) 'Psycholinguistic research methods.' In P.H. Mussen (ed) *Handbook of Research Methods in Child Development.* New York: Wiley 517–57.

Berkowitz, L. (1974) 'Some determinants of impulsive aggression: The role of mediated associations with reinforcements of aggression.' *Psychological Review, 81,* 165–76.

Berkowitz, L. and LePage, A. (1967) 'Weapons as aggression-eliciting stimuli.' *Journal of Personality and Social Psychology, 13,* 200–6.

Bernardin, H.J. and Cooke, D.R. (1993) 'Validity of an honesty test in predicting theft among convenience store employees.' *Academy of Management Journal, 36,* 1097–1108.

Best, J.B. (1995) *Cognitive Psychology,* 4th edition. Minneapolis: West Publishing.

Bouchard, T.J., Lykken, D.T., McGue, M., Segal, N.L. and Tellegen, A. (1990) 'Sources of human psychological differences: The Minnesota study of twins reared apart.' *Science, 250,* 223–250.

Bowlby, J. (1944) 'Forty-four juvenile theives: Their characters and home life.' *International Journal of Psycho-Analysis, 21,* 154–78.

Bowlby, J. (1969) *Attachment and Loss, Vol 1.* London: Hogarth Press.

Bowlby, J. (1973) *Attachment and Loss, Vol 2.* London: Hogarth Press.

Bowlby, J. (1980) *Attachment and Loss, Vol 3.* London: Hogarth Press.

Breland, K. and Breland, M. (1966) *Animal Behavior.* New York: Macmillan.

Bradley, L. (1984) *Assessing Reading Difficulties: A Diagnostic and Remedial Approach.* Basingstoke: Macmillan Education.

Bradley, L. and Bryant, P. (1983) 'Categorizing sounds and learning to read: A causal connexion.' *Nature, 301,* 419–21.

Brewer, W.F. and Treyens, J.C. (1981) 'Role of schemata in memory for places.' *Cognitive Psychology, 13,* 207–230.

Broadbent, D.E. (1958) *Perception and Communication.* Oxford: Pergammon Press.

Bruce, V. and Green, P. (1985) *Visual Perception: Physiology, Psychology and Ecology.* London: Lawrence Erlbaum.

Bryant, P. and Bradley, L. (1985) *Children's Reading Problems. Oxford: Blackwell.*

Bryson, B. (1990) *Mother Tongue: The English Language.* London: Penguin Books.

Burman, E. (1994) *Deconstructing Developmental Psychology.* London: Routledge.

Burt, C (1966) 'The genetic determination of differences in intelligence: A study of monozygotic twins reared together and apart.' *British Journal of Psychology, 57,* 151.

Bushman, B.J. (1984) 'Perceived symbols of authority and their perceived influence on compliance.' *Journal of Applied Social Psychology, 14,* 501–8.

Buss, D.M., Haselton, M.G., Shackelford, T.K., Bleske, A.L. and Wakefield, J.C. (1998) 'Adaptations, exaptations and spandrels.' *American Psychologist, 53,* 533–48.

Butterworth, G. and Harris, M. (1994) *Principles of Developmental Psychology.* London: Lawrence Erlbaum.

Buunk, B.P. (1996) 'Affiliation, attraction and close relationships.' In M. Hewstone, W. Stroebe and G.M. Stephenson (eds) *Introduction to Social Psychology.* 2nd edition. Oxford: Blackwells 345–73.

Buunk, B.P. and VanYperen (1991) 'Referential comparisons, relational comparisons and exchange orientation: their relation to marital satisfaction.' *Personality and Social Psychology Bulletin, 17,* 710–8.

Carey, J. (1992) *The Intellectuals and the Masses.* London: Faber.

Carlson, N.R. (1986) *The Physiology of Behavior.* 3rd edition. Boston: Allyn and Bacon.

Cattell, R. (1965) *The Scientific Analysis of Personality.* London: Penguin Books.

Cherry, E.C. (1953) 'Some experiments on the recognition of speech with one and two ears.' *Journal of the Acoustical Society of America, 25,* 975–979.

Chomsky, N. (1965) *Aspects of the Theory of Syntax.* Cambridge: MIT Press.

Cialdini, R.B., Vincent, J.E., Lewis, S.K. *et al.* (1975) 'A reciprocal concessions procedure for inducing compliance. The door-in-the-face technique.' *Journal of Personality and Social Psychology, 21*, 206–15.

Cohen, G. (1989) *Memory in the Real World.* Hove: Lawrence Erlbaum.

Coolican, H. (1994) *Research Methods and Statistics in Psychology.* London: Hodder and Stoughton.

Coon, D. (1995) *Introduction to Psychology: Exploration and Application,* 6th edition. St. Paul, MN: West Publishing.

Corso, J.F. (1981). *Aging sensory systems and perception.* New York: Praeger.

Corso, J.F. (1987). 'Sensory-perceptual processes and aging.' *Annual Review of Gerontology and Geriatrics, 7.* New York: Springer.

Costa, P.T. and McCrae, R.R. (1988) *The NEO Personality Inventory Manual.* Odessa: Psychological Assessment Resources.

Crick, F. and Mitchison, G. (1983) 'The function of dream sleep.' *Nature, 304,* 111–14.

Crider, A.B., Goethals, G.R., Kavanaugh, R.D. and Solomon, P.R. (1989) *Psychology,* 3rd edition. New York: Harper Collins.

Crystal, D. (1996) *The Cambridge Encyclopedia of Language,* 2nd edition. Cambridge: Cambridge University Press.

Cunningham, M.R., Wong, D. and Barbee, A.P. (1994) 'Self-presentation dynamics on overt integrity tests: Experimental studies of the Reid Report.' *Journal of Applied Psychology, 79,* 643–658.

Darley, J.M. and Latan,, B. (1968) 'Bystander intervention in emergencies: Diffusion of responsibility.' *Journal of Personality and Social Psychology, 8,* 377–83.

Darwin, C. (1859) *The Origin of Species by Means of Natural Selection.* London: John Murray.

Davies, N.B. (1978) 'Territorial defence in the speckled wood butterfly: The resident always wins.' *Animal Behavior, 26,* 138–47.

Davison, G.C. and Neale, J.M. (1996) *Abnormal Psychology,* 6th edition. revised New York: John Wiley.

Dawkins, M.S. (1980) *Animal Suffering. The Science of Animal Welfare.* London: Chapman and Hall.

Dawkins, M.S. (1986) *Unravelling Animal Behaviour.* Marlow: Longman.

Dawkins, R. (1982) *The Extended Phenotype.* London: Freeman.

Deutsch, J.A. and Deutsch, D. (1963) 'Attention: Some theoretical considerations.' *Psychological Review, 70,* 80–90.

DeValois, R.L. and Jacobs, G.H. (1984) 'Neural mechanisms of color vision.' In I. Darian-Smith (ed) *Handbook of Physiology.* Bethseda: American Psychological Society.

Diamond, M.C., Scheibel, A.B. and Elson, L.M. (1984) *The Human Brain Coloring Book.* New York: Barnes and Noble.

Dutton, D.G. and Aron, A.P. (1974) 'Some evidence for heightened sexual attraction under conditions of high anxiety.' *Journal of Personality and Social Psychology, 30,* 510–7.

Dworetzky, J.P. (1994) *Psychology,* 5th edition. St Paul, MN: West Publishing.

Dworetsky, J. P. (1996) *Introduction to Child Development,* 6th edition. St Paul, MN: West Publishing.

Dywan, J. and Bowers, K.S. (1983) 'The use of hypnosis to enhance recall.' *Science, 222,* 184–5.

Elliott, D.J. (1975) *Buckingham: The Loyal and Ancient Borough.* Chichester: Phillimore.

Ellis, A.W. (1993) *Reading, Writing and Dyslexia: A Cognitive Analysis.* 2nd edition. Hove: Lawrence Erlbaum.

Ellis, A.W. and Beattie, G. (1986) *The Psychology of Language and Communication* London: Weidenfeld and Nicholson.

Ericsson, K.A. and Chase, W.G. (1982) 'Exceptional memory.' *American Scientist, 70,* 607–615.

Eysenck, H.J. (1952) 'The effects of psychotherapy: An evaluation.' *Journal of Consulting Psychology, 16,* 319–24.

Eysenck, M.W. (1996) 'Avoiding the tombstones.' *The Psychologist, 9,* 559.

Eysenck, M.W. and Keane, M.T. (1995) *Cognitive Psychology: A Student's Handbook*. Hove: Psychology Press.

Falloon, I., Boyd, J.L., McGill, C.W., *et al.* (1985) 'Family management in the prevention of morbidity in schizophrenia.' *Archives of General Psychiatry, 42*, 887–96.

Fantz, R. (1961) 'The origin of form perception.' *Science, 204*, 66–72.

Festinger, L., Schachter, S. and Back, K. (1950) *Social Pressures in Informal Groups*. New York: Harper.

Freedman, J.L. and Fraser, S.C. (1966) 'Compliance without pressure: The foot-in-the-door technique.' *Journal of Personality and Social Psychology, 4*, 195–202.

Fremouw, W.J., Perezel, W.J. and Ellis, T.E. (1990) *Suicide Risk*. Elmsford: Pergamon.

Frith, U. (1991) 'Asperger and his syndrome.' In U. Frith (ed) *Autism and Asperger Syndrome*. Cambridge: Cambridge University Press.

Gardner, H. (1983) *Frames of Mind: The Theory of Multiple Intelligence*. New York: Basic Books.

Gibson, E.J. and Walk, R.D. (1960) 'The 'visual cliff'.' *Scientific American, 202*, 64–71.

Gilligan, C. (1982) *In a Different Voice*. Cambridge, MA: Harvard University Press.

Goldberg, L.R. (1990) 'An alternative 'description of personality': The big-five factor structure.' *Journal of Personality and Social Psychology, 59*, 1216–1229.

Gottesman, I. (1991) *Schizophrenia Genesis*. New York: Freeman.

Gould. S.J. (1981) *The Mismeasure of Man*. London: Penguin Books.

Gould, S.J. (1991) 'Exaptation: A crucial tool for evolutionary psychology.' *Journal of Social Issues, 47*, 43–65.

Gould, S.J. (1997) 'The exaptive excellence of spandrels as a term and prototype.' *Proceedings of the National Academy of Sciences, 94*, 10750–5.

Graesser, A.C. and Nakamura, G.V. (1982) 'The impact of schema on comprehension and memory.' In G.H. Bower (ed) *The Psychology of Learning and Motivation: Advances in Research and Theory*. London: Academic Press.

Green, H. (1964) *I Never Promised You a Rose Garden*. New York: Holt, Rinehart and Winston.

Greene, J. and D'Oliveira, M. (1982) *Learning to Use Statistical Tests in Psychology*. Milton Keynes: Open University Press.

Gregory, R.L. (1966) *Eye and Brain: The Psychology of Seeing*. New York: McGraw-Hill.

Guastello, S.J. and Rieke, M.L. (1991) 'A review and critique of honesty test research.' *Behavioral Sciences and the Law, 9*, 501–523.

Gudjonsson, G. (1992) *The Psychology of Interrogations, Confessions and Testimony*. Chichester: John Wiley.

Hailman, J.P. (1967) 'The ontogeny of an instinct.' *Behaviour Supplement, 15*, 1–196.

Hamilton, W.D. (1964) 'The genetical evolution of social behaviour.' *Journal of Theoretical Biology, 7*, 1–52.

Harlow, H.F. and Harlow, M.K. (1969) 'Effects of various mother–infant relationships on rhesus monkey behaviours.' In B.M. Foss (ed) *Determinants of Infant Behaviour, Volume 4., London: Methuen*.

Harlow, H.K. and Zimmerman, R.R. (1959) 'Affectional responses in the infant monkey.' *Science, 130*, 421–432.

Harrison, G., Owens, D., Holden, A. *et al.* (1988) 'A prospective study of severe mental disorder in Afro-Caribbean patients.' *Psychological Medicine, 18*, 643–56.

Hayes, N. (1994) *Principles of Comparative Psychology*. Hove: Lawrence Erlbaum.

Herrnstein, R.J. and Murray, C. (1994) *The Bell Curve: Intelligence and Class Structure in American Life*. New York: Free Press.

Hewstone, M., Stroebe, W. and Stephenson, G.M. (eds) (1996) *Introduction to Social Psychology*, 2nd edition. Oxford: Blackwell.

Holmes, J. (1993) *John Bowlby and Attachment Theory*. London: Routledge.

Hospers, J. (1990) *An Introduction to Philosophical Analysis*, 3rd edition. London: Routledge.

Howe, M. (1997) *IQ in Question.* London: Sage.

Hubel, D.H. and Wiesel, T.N. (1959) 'Receptive fieldings of single neurons in the cat's cortex.' *Journal of Physiology, 160,* 106–154.

Huffman, K., Vernoy, M. and Vernoy, J. (1994) *Psychology in Action,* 3rd edition. New York: John Wiley.

Hughes, M., cited Donaldson, M. (1978) *Children's Minds.* Glasgow: Fontana.

James, C. (1980) *Unreliable Memoirs.* London: Picador.

James, W. (1890) *The Principles of Psychology.* London: Macmillan.

James, W. (1892) *Psychology: A Briefer Course.* London: Macmillan.

Janis, I.L. (1982) *Groupthink,* 2nd edition. Boston: Houghton Mifflin.

John, O.P. (1990) 'The 'Big Five' factor taxonomy: Dimensions of personality in natural language and questionnaires.' In: L.A. Pervin (ed) (1993) *Handbook of Personality: Theory and Research.* New York: Guilford Press.

Johnston, W.A. and Heinz, S.P. (1979) 'Depth of non-target processing in an attention task.' *Journal of Experimental Psychology, 5,* 168–175.

Kamin, L (1974) *The Science and Politics of I.Q.* London: Penguin Books.

Kanner, L. (1943) 'Autistic disturbances of affective contact.' *Nervous Child, 2,* 217–250.

Kendall, R.E. (1975) *The Role of Diagnosis in Psychiatry.* Oxford: Blackwell Scientific Publications.

Kentle, R.L. (1995) 'Contributions to the history of psychology: XCX. Some early precursors of five personality factors.' *Psychological Reports, 77,* 83–88.

Kleinke, C.L., Meeker, F.B., and Staneski, R.A. (1986) 'Preference for opening lines.' *Sex Roles, 15,* 585–600.

Klerman, G.L. (1988) 'Depression and related disorders of mood (affective disorders).' In A.M. Nicholi (ed) *New Harvard Guide to Psychiatry.* Cambridge, MA: Harvard University Press.

Kline, P. (1993) *The Handbook of Psychological Testing.* London: Routledge.

Kohlberg, L. (1976) 'Moral stages and moralization: The cognitive-developmental approach.' In T. Lickong (ed) *Moral Development and Behavior.* New York: Holt, Rinehart and Winston.

Kolb, B. and Whishaw, I.Q. (1990) *Fundamentals of Human Neuropsychology,* 3rd edition. New York: Freeman.

Krebs, J.R. and Davies, N.B. (1987) *An Introduction to Behavioural Ecology,* 2nd edition. Oxford: Blackwell.

Kuffler, S.W. (1953) 'Discharge patterns and functional organisation of the mammalian retina.' *Journal of Neurophysiology, 16,* 37–68.

Laing, R. D. (1959) *The Divided Self: An Existential Study in Sanity and Madness.* London: Tavistock Publications.

Land, E. H. (1977) 'The retinex theory of color.' *Scientific American, 237,* 108–128.

Levinger, G. (1980) 'Towards the analysis of close relationships.' *Journal of Experimental Social Psychology, 16,* 510–44.

Linder, R. (1965) 'Diagnosis: prescription or description? A case study in the psychology of diagnosis.' *Perceptual and Motor Skills, 20,* 1081–1092.

Lindsay, P.H. and Norman, D.A. (1972) *Human Information Processing: An Introduction to Psychology.* New York: Academic Press.

Lindsay, S.J.E. and Powell, G.E. (1994) *Handbook of Clinical Adult Psychology.* London: Routledge.

Loftus, E. (1979) *Eyewitness Testimony.* London: Harvard University Press.

Logue, A.W. (1991) *The Psychology of Eating and Drinking,* 2nd edition. New York: Freeman.

Lorenz, K. (1950) 'The comparative method in studying innate behaviour patterns.' *Symposium of the Society of Experimental Biology, 4,* 221–68.

Lorenz, K. (1958) 'The evolution of behavior.' *Scientific American, 199,* 67–78.

Lorenz, K. (1966) *On Aggression.* New York: Harcourt Brace Jovanovich.

Lyons, M.J., True, W.R., Eisen, S.A. *et al.* (1995) 'Differential heritability of adult and juvenile antisocial traits.' *Archives of General Psychology, 52,* 906–915.

Mackintosh, N.J. (1983) *Conditioning and Associative Learning.* Oxford: Oxford University Press.

Mackintosh, N.J. (ed) (1995) *Cyril Burt: Fraud or Framed?* Oxford: Oxford University Press.

MacLeod, A.K., Williams, J.M.G. and Linehan, M.M. (1992) 'New developments in the understanding and treatment of suicidal behaviour.' *Behavioural Psychotherapy, 20,* 193–218.

Main, M. and Solomon, J. (1986) 'Discovery of an insecure-disorganized/disoriented attachment pattern: Procedures, findings and implications for the classification of behaviour.' In: T.B. Brazleton and M. Yogman (eds) *Affective Development in Infancy, 95–124.* Norwood, NJ: Ablex.

Manguel, A. (1996) *A History of Reading.* Bath: HarperCollins.

Maslow, A.H. (1954) *Motivation and Personality.* New York: Harper and Row.

Maylor, E.A. (1990) 'Age and prospective memory.' *Quarterly Journal of Experimental Psychology, 42A,* 471–493.

Maynard-Smith, J. (1972) *On Evolution.* Edinburgh: Edinburgh University Press.

Maynard-Smith, J. and Ridpath, M.G. (1972) 'Wife sharing in the Tasmanian native hen *Tribonyx mortierrii*: A case of kin selection?' *American Naturalist, 106,* 447–52.

McCrae, R.R. and Costa, P.T. (1990) *Personality in Adulthood.* New York: Guilford Press.

McFarland, D. (1987) *The Oxford Companion to Animal Behaviour.* Oxford: Oxford University Press.

Milgram, S. (1965) 'Some conditions of obedience and disobedience to authority.' *Human Relations, 18,* 57–76.

Milgram, S. (1974) *Obedience to Authority.* New York: Harper and Row.

Miller, G.A. (1956) 'The magic number seven, plus or minus two: Some limits on our capacity for processing information.' *Psychological Review, 63,* 81–93.

Monte, C.F. (1987) *Beneath the Mask: An Introduction to Theories of Personality,* 3rd edition. New York: Holt, Rinehart and Winston.

Moreland, R.L. and Zajonc, R.B. (1982) 'Exposure effects in person perception.' *Journal of Applied Social Psychology, 19,* 395–415.

Mummendey, A. (1996) 'Aggressive behaviour.' In M. Hewstone, W. Stroebe and G.M. Stephenson (eds) *Introduction to Social Psychology,* 2nd edition. Oxford: Blackwells.

Murray, H.A. (1938) *Explorations in Personality.* Oxford: Oxford University Press.

Neisser, U. (1976) *Cognition and Reality.* San Francisco: Freeman.

Odegaard, O. (1932) 'Emigration and insanity.' *Acta Psychiatrica Scandanavica, Supplement 4.*

Olds, J. and Milner, P. (1954) 'Positive reinforcement produced by classical stimulation of the septal area and other regions of the rat brain.' *Journal of Comparative and Physiological Psychology, 47,* 419–27.

Packard, V. (1981) *The Hidden Persuaders.* London: Penguin Books.

Parker, G.A. (1970) 'The reproductive behaviour and the nature of sexual selection in Scatophaga stercoraria L. (Diptera: Scatophagidae). II The fertilization rate and the spatial and temporal relationships of each sex around the site of mating and oviposition.' *Journal of Animal Ecology, 39,* 205–28.

Patch, M.E. (1986) 'The role of source legitimacy in sequential request strategies of compliance.' *Personality and Social Psychology, 12,* 199–205.

Pearce, J.M. (1987) *An Introduction to Animal Cognition.* Hove: Lawrence Erlbaum.

Perrin, S. and Spencer, C. (1981) 'The Asch effect – a child of its time.' *British Psychological Society Bulletin, 33,* 405–6.

Pervin, L.A. (1993) *Personality: Theory and Research.* Chichester: John Wiley.

Plath, S. (1963) *The Bell Jar.* London: Faber and Faber.

Prechtl, H.F.R. (1953) 'Zur physiologie der angeborenen auslosenden Mechanismen I: Quantitative untersuchungen uber die sperrbewegung junger singvogel.' *Behaviour, 1,* 32–50.

Radford, J. and Holdstock, L. (1996) 'The growth of psychology.' *The Psychologist, 9,* 548–550.

Robin, A. and MacDonald, D. (1975) *Lessons of Leucotomy.* London: Henry Kimpton.

Rogers, C. (1961) *On Becoming a Person.* New York: Houghton Mifflin.

Rosch, E. (1973) 'On the internal structure of perceptual and semantic categories.' In T.E. Moore (ed) *Cognitive Development and the Acquisition of Language.* New York: Academic Press.

Rose, J.E., Brugge, J.F., Anderson, D.J. and Hind, J.E. (1967) 'Phase-locked response to lower frequency tones in single auditory nerve fibers of the squirrel monkey.' *Journal of Neurophysiology, 390,* 769–793.

Rosenhan, D.L. (1973) 'On being sane in insane places.' *Science, 179,* 250–8.

Ross, A.O. (1992) *Personality: Theories and Processes.* New York: HarperCollins.

Roth, I (ed) (1990) *Intreduction to Psychology, Volume 2.* Hove: Erlbaum in association with Open University.

Rutter, M. (1981) *Maternal Deprivation Reassessed,* 2nd edition. London: Penguin.

Samuel, J. and Bryant, P. (1984) 'Asking only one question in the conservation experiment.' *Journal of Child Psychology and Psychiatry, 25,* 315–318.

Saxe, L. (1991) 'Lying.' *American Psychologist, 46,* 409–415.

Schachter, S. and Singer, J. (1962) 'Cognitive, social and physiological determinants of the emotional state.' *Psychological Review, 69,* 379–99.

Schank, R. (1981) 'Language and memory.' In D.A. Norman (ed) *Perspectives on Cognitive Science.* London: Lawrence Erlbaum.

Schultz, D.P. and Schultz, S.E. (1987) *A History of Modern Psychology,* 4th edition. San Diego: Harcourt Brace Jovanovich.

Schultz, M. (1975) 'The semantic derogation of woman.' In: B. Thorne and E. Baisel (eds) *Language and Sex: Difference and Dominance.* Rowley: Newbury House.

Selfridge, O.G. (1959) 'Pandemonium: a paradigm for learning.' In: *Symposium on the Mechanisation of Thought Processes* London: HMSO.

Seligman, M.(1974) 'Depression and learned helplessness.' In R.J. Friedman and M.Katz (eds) *The Psychology of Depression.* Washington: Wiley.

Sherif, M., Harvey, O.J., White, B.J., Hood, W.R. and Sherif, C.W. (1961) *Intergroup Conflict and Cooperation: The Robbers Cave Experiment.* Oklahoma: Oklahoma University Press.

Sherman, P.W. (1981) 'Kinship, demography and Belding's ground squirrel nepotism.' *Behavioural Ecology and Sociobiology, 8,* 251–9.

Singer, M.T. (1979) 'Coming out of the cults.' *Psychology Today, 12,* 72–82.

Skinner, B.F. (1948) *Walden Two.* London: Penguin.

Skinner, B.F. (1971) *Beyond Freedom and Dignity.* London: Penguin.

Smith (1992) 'Longitudinal stability of personality.' *Psychological Reports, 70,* 483–498.

Solomon, R.L. (1980) 'The opponent-process theory of motivation: The costs of pleasure and the benefits of pain.' *American Psychologist, 35,* 681–712.

Sperling, G. (1960) The information available in brief visual presentations *Psychological Monographs, 74,* 1–29.

Steyer, R., Ferring, D. and Schmitt, M.J. (1992) 'States and traits in psychological assessment.' *European Journal of Psychological Assessment, 8,* 79–98.

Sternberg, R.J. (1985) *Beyond IQ: A Triarchic Theory of Human Intelligence.* New York: Cambridge University Press.

Sternberg, R.J. (1996) *Cognitive Psychology.* Fort Worth: Harcourt Brace.

Sternberg, R.J. (1998) *In Search of the Human Mind,* 2nd edition. Fort Worth: Harcourt Brace.

Sternberg, R.J., Wagner, R.K., Williams, W. M. and Horvath, J.A. (1995) 'Testing Common Sense.' *American Psychologist, 50,* 912–927.

Stevens, M (1979) 'Famous personality test. A test for measuring remote memory.' *Bulletin of the British Psychological Society, 32*, 211.

Stuart-Hamilton, I.A. (1986) 'The role of phonemic awareness in the reading style of beginning readers.' *British Journal of Educational Psychology, 56*, 271–285.

Stuart-Hamilton, I. (1994) *The Psychology of Ageing; An Introduction. London: Jessica Kingsley Publishers.*

Stuart-Hamilton, I. (1995a) *Dictionary of Developmental Psychology.* London: Jessica Kingsley Publishers.

Stuart-Hamilton, I. (1995b) *Dictionary of Cognition.* London: Jessica Kingsley Publishers.

Stuart-Hamilton, I. (1996) *Dictionary of Psychological Testing, Assessment, and Treatment.* London: Jessica Kingsley Publishers.

Stuart-Hamilton, I.A. and McDonald, L. (1996) 'Age and a possible regression to childhood thinking patterns.' *PSIGE Newsletter, 58*, 13–15.

Stuart-Hamilton, I.A., Perfect, T. and Rabbitt, P. (1988) 'Remembering who was who.' In M.M. Gruneberg, P.E. Morris and R.N. Sykes (eds) *Practical Aspects of Memory.* Volume 2.

Szasz, T. (1963) 'The myth of mental illness.' *American Psychologist, 15*, 113–118.

Tartu, U. (1995) 'A Big Five personality inventory in two non-Indo-European languages.' *European Journal of Personality, 9*, 109–124.

Teplov, B.M. (1964) 'The historical development of Pavlov's theory of typological differences in the dog.' In: J.A. Gray (ed. and trans.) *Pavlov's Typology* London: Macmillan.

Thorndike, E.L. (1911) *Animal Intelligence: Experimental Studies.* New York: Macmillan.

Thorpe, W.H. (1961) *Bird Song.* Cambridge: Cambridge University Press.

Tinbergen, N. (1951) *The Study of Instinct.* Oxford: Oxford University Press.

Tolman, E.C. (1932) *Purposive Behavior in Animals and Man.* New York: Century.

Treisman, A.M. (1964) 'Verbal cues, language, and meaning in selective attention.' *American Journal of Psychology, 77*, 206–219.

Treisman, A.M. and Geffen, G. (1967) 'Selective attention: Perception or response?' *Quarterly Journal of Experimental Psychology, 19*, 1–18.

Treisman, A.M. and Riley, J.G.A. (1969) 'Is selective attention selective perception or selective response: a further test.' *Journal of Experimental Psychology, 79*, 27–34.

Tulving, E. (1972) 'Episodic and semantic memory.' In: E. Tulving and W. Donaldson (eds) *Organisation of Memory* New York: Academic Press.

Turner, J.S. and Helms, D.B. (1995) *Lifespan Development,* 5th edition. Fort Worth: Harcourt Brace.

Underwood, G. (1977) 'Contextual facilitation from attended and unattended messages.' *Journal of Verbal Learning and Verbal Behavior, 16*, 99–106.

Valentine, E.R. (1992) *Conceptual Issues in Psychology.* London: Routledge.

Van der Veer, R. and Valinser, J. (1991) *Understanding Vygotsky: A Quest for Synthesis.* Oxford: Blackwells.

Von B,k,sy, G. (1960) *Experiments in Hearing.* New York: McGraw Hill.

Wald, G. and Brown, P.K. (1965) 'Human color vision and color blindness.' *Cold Spring Harbor Symposia on Quantitative Biology, 30*, 345–359.

Waters, E., Wippman, J., and Sroufe, L.A. (1979) 'Attachment, positive affect, and competence in the peer group: Two studies in construct validation.' *Child Development, 50*, 821–829.

Waugh, E. (1957) *The Ordeal of Gilbert Pinfold.* London: Chapman and Hall.

Wilding, J. (1990) 'Developmental dyslexics do not fit in boxes: Evidence from six new case studies.' *European Journal of Cognitive Psychology, 1*, 105–27.

Williams, L.M. (1992) 'Adult memories of childhood abuse: Preliminary findings from a longitudinal study.' *The Advisor, 5*, 19–20.

Woodworth, R.S. (1930) – *Psychology: A Study of Mental Life,* 8th edition. London: Methuen.

World Health Organisation (1992) *The ICD-10 Classification of Mental and Behavioural Disorders: Clinical Descriptions and Diagnostic Guidelines.* Geneva: World Health Organisation.

# Index